MORALITY AND THE LAW

Roslyn Muraskin
Professor of Criminal Justice
Long Island University

Matthew Muraskin, J.D.
Attorney in Chief
Nassau County Legal Ai

Prentice
Hall

Upper Saddle River, New Jersey

Library of Congress Cataloging-in-Publication Data

Muraskin, Roslyn.
  Morality and the law / Roslyn Muraskin, Matthew Muraskin.
    p. cm.
  Includes bibliographical references.
  ISBN 0-13-916958-X
  1. Criminal justice, Administration of--Moral and ethical aspects. I. Muraskin,
Matthew. II. Title.

HV7419 .M87 2000
174'.9364--dc21   00-044585

Publisher: Dave Garza
Senior Acquisitions Editor: Kim Davies
Managing Editor: Mary Carnis
Production Management: Cindy Miller
Production Editor: Michelle Sutton-Kerchner
Interior Design: Clarinda Production Services
Production Liaison: Adele M. Kupchik
Director of Manufacturing and Production: Bruce Johnson
Manufacturing Buyer: Ed O'Dougherty
Creative Director: Marianne Frasco
Cover Design Coordinator: Miguel Ortiz
Formatting: Minta Berry for The Clarinda Company
Electronic Art Creation: Asterisk Group, Inc.
Editorial Assistant: Lisa Schwartz
Marketing Manager: Chris Ruel
Marketing Assistant: Joe Toohey
Marketing Coordinator: Adam Kloza
Printer/Binder: R.R. Donnelley and Sons, Inc.
Copy Editor: settingPace
Proofreader: settingPace
Cover Design: Joseph Sengotta
Cover Illustration: John Pack, SIS/Images.Com
Cover Printer: Phoenix Color Corporation

10 9 8 7 6 5 4 3 2 1
ISBN 0-13-916958-X

Dedicated to our Granddaughters
Lindsay Anya
&
Nickia Alexandra
Who bring great smiles to our faces

CONTENTS

PREFACE

Ethics addresses questions of right and wrong, good and bad, virtue and vice. Ethics involves the evaluation of actions and lives, choices and characters. The orientation is toward *rational argument*—toward the production of *reasons* supportive of one's position. As argued by Dworkin (1977) when I take a moral position on an issue I involve myself in a distinctive sort of discourse. Many thinkers since the 17th century have sought to find a solid ground upon which to determine the correct system of morals. In this work the terms morals and ethics are used interchangeably.

This is a work on the role of morality in the various components of the criminal justice system. Specifically the role of defense counsel and prosecutor, the role of the police, the court, corrections, probation and parole officers, and the victims of crimes themselves as well as related issues.

Though defense counsel and the prosecutor are both bound by the Code of Professional Responsibility, they have significantly different roles and functions, and their ethical problems vary accordingly. The obligations of the defense counsel derives from the importance within the adversarial system of confidentiality between attorney and client, the defendant's presumption of innocence and burden of proof, the constitutional right to counsel, and the client's constitutional privilege against self-incrimination. On the other hand, we have the prosecutor who does not represent a private client, and is therefore, not affected by these considerations in the same manner.

As an example, the defense attorney may withhold evidence: there is nothing unethical in keeping a guilty defendant off the stand, and putting the government to its proof. However, it does not follow that the prosecutor is also privileged to withhold or suppress material evidence or that there is something essentially unfair in this double standard.

Is it ethical for a defense attorney to make a prosecution witness appear to be inaccurate or untruthful under cross-examination even when the defense attorney knows that the witness is testifying accurately and truthfully? As indicated by the late Chief Justice Earl Warren, "the defense is entitled to 'put the government to its proof' and to 'test the truth of the prosecution's case.'" Neither of these rationales justify a prosecutor obtaining a conviction by making a defense witness appear to be lying when the prosecutor knows that witnesses are testifying truthfully.

A prosecutor has enormous and unique discretion in defining the particular crime, affecting the punishment, and even in deciding whether or not to prosecute. This discretion explains the differences in prosecutorial ethics and defense counsel ethics to be discussed in this work.

We examine the role of the police and their use of police powers. The role of the police is to uphold the law. Police possess the power to use their authority, force, and discretion. They have the choice to arrest or not to arrest, to mediate or to charge, along with their choice to use deadly force. The police are held to the highest of standards and are supposed to be provided with standards of ethics that guide them in their work. Is this a good description of the police?

To what standards are correctional officers and probation and parole officers held? Here, too, there can be abuses of power and authority. The uniform is supposed to bestow the authority of rational and reasonable control and not be abused.

Important to the content of this work are the ethical obligations of victims not to seek private vengeance. It is the obligation of the prosecuting attorney to ensure that victims in pressing charges make correct choices and not seek any vengeance. In a civilized society crime victims and their families are expected to delegate revenge for criminal wrongs to a system of legal, rather than personal justice.

In the classroom, university professors like to upset their students by pointing out that there are no universally disapproved modes of conduct. Even a killing that we would consider murder is acceptable in some societies. There are those acts which once were or now are attacked as immoral. As indicated by Ryan in his chapter, "… moral education … should be a matter of exposure to the actions, the thoughts, and tales about virtuous people."

This work presents a full discussion of issues of morality/ethics and the criminal justice system, and is not a work best left for philosophers and philosophy classes to learn. This is a solid work that deals with issues that bring to light how the criminal justice systems works with some suggestions for change.

Roslyn Muraskin

Acknowledgments

We wish to thank all the contributors for their dedication to this project. This is a project that took a lot of thought and time and we believe we have an outstanding text as a result.

We also want to thank Kim Davies, editor at Prentice Hall; Lisa Schwartz, her assistant; and Cheryl Adams who is always a pleasure to work with.

Thanks to my husband, Matthew, who, as my co-editor/author, is great. As a team we continue to work pretty well together.

We wish to convey our thanks to Neil Marquardt for his patience and enthusiasm for this work. He is a great friend and wonderful to work with at Prentice Hall.

Thanks also to all our contributors for their hard work and endurance on this project. It is a work of love, and we thank all.

Continued thanks to the C.W. Post Campus of Long Island University for their continued support and enthusiasm for all my projects.

BIOGRAPHIES OF AUTHORS/EDITORS

Roslyn Muraskin is Professor of Criminal Justice at the C.W. Post Campus of Long Island University. She served in the capacity of Associate Dean of the College of Management (1990–1996) as well as Associate Dean of the School of Public Service. She currently serves as the Director of the Long Island Women's Institute and Executive Director of the Alumni Chapter both for the College of Management. Dr. Muraskin served as President of the Northeastern Association of the Academy of Criminal Justice Sciences as well as Vice-President of Region V for the Criminal Justice Educato´rs of New York State.

She is the Editor of *The Justice Professional,* a refereed journal published quarterly by Gordon and Breach Publishers, as well as the editor of the series "Women and Law" for Gordon and Breach. The first edition was titled, *Women and Justice: Development of International Policy.* Future volumes include *The African American Women and Criminal Justice, Sexual Harassment in Criminal Justice,* and *Minorities in Criminal Justice.* She is the author/editor of *It's a Crime: Women and Justice* (2d edition, 2000) for Prentice Hall, as well as the co-author/editor of *Visions for Change: Crime and Justice in the 21st Century* (2d edition, 1999) for Prentice Hall. She is the author of numerous articles in the areas of *Jails, Juvenile Justice, Women and Drugs* and *Measuring Disparity in the Criminal Justice System.* She is the recipient of the Award for Excellence from the Minorities Section of the Academy of Criminal Justice Sciences (1999), honored for her work with AIDS education by the Long Island Association for AIDS Care (1999), and was the recipient of the Fellow Award from the Northeastern Association of Criminal Justice Sciences (1999).

She received her doctorate in criminal justice from the Graduate Center at the City University of New York, and her Master's Degree at New York University Graduate School of Arts and Sciences. She received her Bachelor's Degree from Queens College. Her main research interests include those of gender disparity issues and constitutional issues. She is a frequent lecturer on issues of gender.

Matthew Muraskin, J.D., graduated from Washington Square College of New York University *cum laude* where he was also elected to Phi Beta Kappa. He holds a Master's Degree in Government from Cornell University where he was an Olmstead Fellow in Public Law. He received his law degree from New York University School of Law.

He serves as Attorney in Chief of the Nassau County Legal Aid Society. Prior to joining the Nassau County Legal Aid Society, he was Associate Appellate Counsel at the New York City Legal Aid Society. Over the years he has briefed and/or argued more than 600 cases in the various Federal and state appellate courts. Some of his more significant cases invalidated the wayward minor statute, obtained jury trials for youthful offenders, established the right of probation violators to appeal, and obtained for defense counsel the right to see presentence probation reports. He is also the lead counsel in two significant jail condition lawsuits, *Badgley v. Nassau County* and *Thompson v. Sheriff of Nassau County.* He was the recipient (1996) of the New York State Bar Association award for the delivery of defense services.

He is a Special Professor of Law at the Hofstra School of Law and serves as an adjunct Professor of Law at Touro School of Law.

BIOGRAPHIES OF CONTRIBUTORS

George Eichenberg is a former police officer and juvenile probation officer. He is currently an assistant professor of Criminal Justice at Wayne State College in Wayne, Nebraska. He holds an M.S. in Criminal Justice Management from Sam Houston State University in Huntsville, Texas and is completing his Ph.D. in Criminal Justice at Sam Houston State University. His dissertation is an empirical assessment of Black's general theory of social control. His recent publications have dealt with problem solving in law enforcement while his current research is focussed on ethical issues in social control and the management of rural law enforcement agencies.

Charles R. Goldburg is the law secretary to Court of Claims Judge, Victor M. Ort, in Nassau County, New York. He is a graduate of Swarthmore College and Fordham Law School. Before becoming a law secretary, he was an attorney with New York City Legal Aid Society and in private practice.

Richard R.E. Kania specializes in applied ethics, crime and mass media, police policy, and related criminal justice policy topics, including police use of deadly force and traffic "hot" pursuits. He also studies European criminal justice practices. He recently completed a year in Poland as a Senior Fulbright Professor with the Center for Social Studies of the Central European University in Warsaw. While there he co-edited *Post-Communist Transformations,* (IFIS Press, 1999), a book of readings on social, political, and economic evolution in the aftermath of the collapse of Soviet Communism. His doctorate was awarded by the University of Virginia in 1982. From 1982 through 1999 he was at Guilford College in Greensboro, North Carolina. He is presently the chair of the Department of Sociology, Social Work, and Criminal Justice at the University of North Carolina at Pembroke.

Raymond G. Keenan is a 1998 graduate of Touro Law Center (*summa cum laude*; editor and chief of the Law Review; Dean's Fellow). He is associated with the New York law firm of Guercio and Guercio where he concentrates in education law and labor law.

Chris G. McDonough graduated with his J.D. degree from Touro Law Center (*cum laude*). He has been practicing in the area of professional legal ethics during the past decade. He is an adjunct professor of professional responsibility at the Touro Law Center. He is an instructor for the Nassau County, New York Bar Association in the areas of continuing legal education. He is the former vice-chair for the Committee on Professional Ethics, for the Nassau County, New York Bar Association. He is the author of numerous articles on professional ethics.

Diana Brusca McDonough is a 1984 graduate of St. Johns Law Center. She is a former Assistant District Attorney for Nassau County in the Felony Trial Bureau. She is a partner in the New York law firm of Speyer and Perlberg concentrating in areas of commercial litigation.

Martin L. O'Connor, J.D., is an attorney and Associate Professor of Criminal Justice at Long Island University, C.W. Post Campus. He is also the Book Review Editor of *The Justice Professional* and a Village Justice, Mill Neck, New York. Prior to entering academe, Professor O'Connor was the Deputy Police Commissioner in charge of legal affairs for the Nassau and Suffolk County New York Police Departments. He has more than thirty years experience as a law enforcement executive. He has lectured extensively regarding Labor Law, Discrimination Law, and policing issues. He is a member of the Nassau County Bar Association, Police Executive Research Forum, the International Association of Chiefs of Police, and the American Academy of Professional Law Enforcement. Professor O'Connor has written numerous book reviews and articles including "Warrantless Searches of Mobile Vehicles," "Criminal Procedure Laws," "The Historic, Social, and Legal Forces that have Shaped the Police Response to Spouse Abuse," and "Bright Lines, Blanket Rules and the Fourth Amendment: The Supreme Court's Enthusiastic Endorsement of the Knock and Announce Rule."

Victor M. Ort is a Judge of the New York Court of Claims. He is a graduate of the American University (B.S.), Suffolk University (M.B.A.), and New England School of Law (J.D.). Before his appointment to the Court of Claims, he was chief clerk of the Nassau County Court, New York, law secretary to Supreme Court and Appellate Division Justice James F. Niehoff, and an appeals and trial attorney with the Nassau County Legal Aid Society.

Hal Pepinsky, Ph.D., J.D., teaches criminal justice at Indiana University in Bloomington. His primary research these days is in finding processes by which people, especially children, become safer from personal violence.

Harriet Pollack, Ph.D., is Professor Emerita of Constitutional Law at John Jay College of Criminal Justice of the City University of New York. For 10 years she was the Chair of the Department of Government and Public Administration at the College. She holds a Ph.D. in political science from Columbia University and has had various articles on constitutional law published in periodicals as diverse as the *Saturday Review* (when Norman Cousins was editor) and *Federal Probation*. She was a consultant to the Congressional Commission on Marijuana and Drug Abuse and is co-author of *Some Sins Are Not Crimes* and the third edition of *Criminal Justice: An Overview*. In addition, along with Alexander B. Smith, she co-authored *Civil Liberties and Civil Rights in the United States*.

Kevin F. Ryan is an Associate Professor of Justice Studies and Sociology at Norwich University, Vermont. He holds graduate degrees from Princeton University and the University of Denver. He is a member of the Colorado Bar. Much of his published work has focused on drug policy.

Alexander B. Smith, Ph.D., J.D., is Professor Emeritus of Social Psychology at John Jay College of Criminal Justice of the City University of New York. He was the first Dean of Studies and the first Chairman of the Division of Social Studies at the

College. Before coming to John Jay he was a Case Supervisor in the Probation Department of the Supreme Court of Kings County, and before that he was a practicing attorney in Yew York City. He has been a member of the New York Bar since 1931 and is a certified psychologist in New York State. Since 1963 he has been consultant to the President's Commission of Obscenity and Pornography, the Office of Juvenile Delinquency (Department of Health, Education and Welfare), and the Commission of Marijuana and Drug Abuse. He has written widely in the field of criminal justice, having co-authored 14 books and over 60 articles. His latest works are third editions of *Treating the Criminal Offender* (Plenum) and *Criminal Justice: An Overview* (West).

Rod Tabriztchi is a student at Boston College School of Law. He is a graduate of The Johns Hopkins University and State University of New York College at Old Westbury, New York.

Chapter 1

OVERVIEW

Roslyn Muraskin

Among the best known aphorisms in the field of criminal justice is the observation by Anatole France (1927, p. 91) in *The Red Lily (Le Lys Rouge)* that "the law, in its majestic equality forbids both the poor man and the rich man to sleep under bridges, to beg in the streets, and to steal bread." What is it that France meant, and how adequate is his statement as a proxy for the roster of inequities in the criminal justice system (Geis, 1988)? Michael Weisser (1979) has pointed out that Anglo-Saxon criminal codes adopted the slogan of "equal justice under law" in the wake of barbaric practices in the eighteenth century. The doctrine sought not only to eliminate brutality and arbitrariness, but also to do so without unduly jeopardizing the basic safeguards that were only just being awarded to the emerging bourgeoisie. As noted by Weisser:

> It was therefore absolutely essential to preserve the criminal justice system along class lines, although the political exigencies of the period forced liberals to demand the abolition of the more gross and obvious manifestations of class justice. [Cesare] Beccaria provided the vital synthesis by linking a decrease in the severity of punishment with the concept of individual responsibility for criminal acts. This was the essence of the dictum 'equal justice before the law.' This thesis assumed equality of treatment, but more important, an equality of social circumstances. The modern criminal justice system has thus invented a social fiction in order to disguise its legal fictions (p. 137; cf. Jenkins, 1984).

As pointed out by Eugene Ehrlich (Ehrlich, 1836, p. 238), "the more the rich and poor are dealt with according to the same legal propositions, the more the advantages of the rich are increased." Criminal justice, in this respect, is much like the fair-minded toss of a die, except that the die is heavily leaded on one side.

Disclosures of hypocrisy and moral laxity infect those in leadership positions from Washington to Wall Street. Although some would maintain that present times have witnessed an impressive revival of moral awareness, with the continuing controversies over abortion, civil disobedience, and capital punishment, all of which give evidence of the eagerness of our society to identify and argue moral issues, probably most observers would agree that there has been over the years a decline in private and public morality.

The terms *morality* and *ethics* have been used interchangeably. This is an inaccurate use of the terms, although the terms are clearly interrelated. *Ethics* is a philosophy that examines the principles of right and wrong, good and bad. *Morality* on the other hand, is a practice of these principles on a regular basis, culminating in a moral life. Morality is conduct that is related to integrity. Consequently, while most people may be technically viewed as ethical (by virtue of knowing the principles of right and wrong), only those who internalize these principles and faith and fully apply them in their clear relationships with others should be considered moral. There is no area, perhaps, in which ethical dilemmas are more prominently seen and their mishandling more forcefully placed before the public eye than the criminal justice system.

Morality, therefore, can be viewed as requiring us to examine our actions in a way that does not violate rights. This work concerns itself with "what should I do," and "how should I be." What is the correct way, the moral way for those in criminal justice is our concern. Yet, these terms will be used interchangeably.

It is the role of the criminal justice system to ensure that both justice and due process are delivered to those offenders accused of crime. The players in the criminal justice system have the obligation of promoting the fair administration of justice. Eternal vigilance is promoted as being part of the price of liberty. Acting in an ethical manner is a prerequisite to all actions taken within the criminal justice system. In the words of Justice Louis Brandeis, "To declare that in the administration of the criminal law the end justifies the means—to declare that the government may commit crimes in order to secure the conviction of a private criminal—would bring terrible retribution" (*Olmstead v. United States,* 1928).

During the process of investigating the alleged wrong doings of President Clinton, Monica Lewinsky was taken into "custody" by federal prosecutors assigned to the Independent Counsel Kenneth Starr's office. Her testimony before the Whitewater grand jury indicated that both prosecutors and federal agents took her by surprise by holding her in the Ritz-Carlton Hotel, not allowing her to communicate with anyone outside, including her attorney, while indicating that if her attorney was spoken to, she would be subject to immediate prosecution. There was also the suggestion that she might have to wear a recording device for the purposes of catching Vernon Jordan, adviser to the President, in an incriminating conversation. If this kind of tactic is standard operating procedure for prosecutors, their action is beyond the realm of what is known as proper ethical behavior. Government lawyers are lawyers who are subject to the ethical rules of conduct applicable to all members of the bar.

The prosecutors are under obligation to abide by basic rules of attorney ethics. In *Berger v. United States,* 295 U.S. 78, 88 (1935), Justice Sutherland indicated that

"[The prosecutor] is the representative not of an ordinary party to a controversy, but of a sovereignty whose obligation to govern impartially is as compelling as its obligation to govern at all; and whose interest, therefore . . . is not that [he] shall win a case, but that justice shall be done. . .. He may prosecute with earnestness and vigor—indeed, he should do so. But while he may strike hard blows, he is not at liberty to strike foul ones."

" '*Thou shall not give false witness against thy neighbor.*' In the old days, a false accusation of wrongdoing could end with the innocent accused being stoned to death. Because the Ninth Commandment is thousands of years old, one surmises that lying snitches were around before Moses" (Jack King, "Twisted Justice: Prosecution Function in America Out of Control" http://209.70.38.3/public.nsf/championarticles/99mar01?opendocument p. 9). Prosecuting attorneys have great responsibility in seeing that the alleged offender receives a fair trial. According to Northwestern University law professor Lawrence Marshall in an interview in the *Tribune*, "[W]e generally condone a great deal of misconduct when we think it serves the ultimate ends of justice. Many players in the system—judges, defense lawyers, prosecutors—know some of the stuff that happens, but nonetheless tend to turn a blind eye. There's a feeling that that is how it works, that it's legitimate to bend the truth sometimes when you are doing it with—quote, the *greater good*, end quote—in mind."

Under the canons of ethics of attorneys, you do not win at any cost. "Some prosecutors have come to believe that they are exempt from the code of legal ethics, that the rules of civilized conduct don't apply to them. We look to prosecutors to enforce the law, but who will protect us when the prosecutor becomes the lawbreaker?" (http://209.70.38.3/public.nsf/newsrelease/99mn001?open document).

Lawyers are not above the law. They cannot ignore the laws against interrogating citizens, employees of both corporations and small businesses charged with either civil or criminal offenses. Every lawyer must abide by the state licensing authorities' rules of ethics. No lawyer (prosecuting or defense) is exempt from following the requirements of ethics rules (*United States ex rel. O'Keefe v. McDonnell Douglas Corp.*, 1998 WL 1924 (8th Cir. Jan. 6, 1998)).

In the case of *Gideon v. Wainwright* 372 U.S. 335 (1963), the United States Supreme Court held that because the assistance of counsel in criminal cases is a fundamental necessity under the sixth amendment to the Constitution, attorneys must be appointed to represent "any person haled into court, who is too poor to hire a lawyer." The fact that there are continuous budget cuts in legal representation for the poor, is no excuse for attorneys acting in an unethical manner. Resources must be made available. There are no short cuts.

The American justice system is a system that seeks the truth. Witnesses in cases must be instructed to testify honestly. They cannot be induced to testify in return for some favor or monetary reward. Our system is based on fairness at every level of federal, state, and local government. Due process must be afforded to all; those who are accused of committing a crime, those who are witnesses to a crime, victims of a crime, and those found guilty must be adjudicated in a fair and lawful manner.

Though both defense counsel and the prosecutor are both bound by the code of professional responsibility, they have significantly different roles and functions and their ethical problems vary accordingly. The obligations of the defense counsel derive from the importance within the adversarial system of confidentiality between attorney and client, the defendant's presumption of innocence, the constitutional right to counsel, as well as the client's constitutional privilege against self-incrimination. On the other hand, we have the prosecutor who does not represent a private client, and is therefore, not affected by these considerations in the same manner. Though neither defense counsel nor the prosecutor may violate the cannons of ethics the prosecutor is obligated to do justice while the defense lawyer can either put on an affirmative case or merely put the government to its proof.

For example, the defense attorney may withhold evidence: there is nothing unethical in defense counsel not calling a witness adverse to the defendant and putting the government to its proof. However, it does not follow that the prosecutor is also privileged to withhold or suppress material evidence, or that there is something essentially unfair in this double standard.

Is it ethical for a defense attorney to cross-examine a prosecution witness to make him appear to be inaccurate or untruthful, even when the defense attorney knows that the witness is testifying accurately and truthfully? As indicated by the late Chief Justice of the United States, Earl Warren, "the defense is entitled to 'put the government to its proof' and to 'test the truth of the prosecution's case.'" Neither of these rationales, however, justify a prosecutor in obtaining a conviction by making a defense witness appear to be lying when the prosecutor knows that the witness is testifying truthfully.

A prosecutor has enormous and unique discretion in defining the particular crime, affecting the punishment, and even in deciding whether to prosecute or not. The prosecutor has great discretion. Herein lies some of the differences in prosecutorial and defense counsel's ethics to be discussed further in this text.

The role of the police is to uphold the law. Police possess the power to use their authority, force, and discretion. They have the choice to arrest or not to arrest, to mediate or to charge, and the decision to use deadly force. The police are held to the highest of standards and are supposed to be provided with standards of ethics that guide them in their work.

What happens to the actions of police? Who is policing the police? Police perjury is considered to be a serious problem in the criminal justice system. Police officers must be held accountable for their actions. Having a "reckless disregard for the truth," demonstrates conduct totally unethical, and totally unacceptable for and by the police.

Similarly, correctional, parole, and probation officers also need to follow a code of ethics. There can be and often are abuses of authority and/or power. The uniform is supposed to bestow the authority of rational and reasonable control. It is not to be abused. The power of a probation or parole officers' recommendation regarding release cannot be ignored. Relationships with inmates, probationers, and parolees are all included in this work. When officers become personally involved their professional judgment leaves questions with regard to their professional conduct.

It may be that not all stable societies are good, but all good societies should be stable. What are the rules for the judiciary? Are judges expected to avoid impropriety as well as its appearance? Are the social activities of judges limited under the rules of ethics? The judge is required to accord the right of every person to be heard. All matters are expected to be disposed of promptly and efficiently. It is the judge who is in control of the trial proceedings and all other proceedings in his/her courtroom. The rules dictate that at all times judges must perform their duties impartially and with diligence. This behavior is expected at all times.

Important to the content of this book are the ethical obligations of victims not to seek private vengeance. It is the obligation of the prosecuting attorney to insure that victims in pressing charges make correct choices and not seek vengeance. In a system such as ours, how are victims to be handled? In a civilized society, crime victims and their families are expected to delegate revenge for criminal wrongs to a system of legal, rather than personal, justice. The ethical arguments both for and against personal revenge are discussed in this work.

In the realm of probation and parole, an established ethical code of behavior is expected of all its workers. In effect these officers must uphold the law with dignity, strive to be objective, and further to render professional services to the justice system. The best ethical means is to serve both the client and the community. With the high number of offenders on both probation and parole, the issue of proper ethical behavior is crucial for this discussion.

What of the issue of capital punishment? Support for executions as an ethical exercise of state power can be found in the moral and religious doctrines of the leading western religions and in the acceptance and interpretation of the social contract. Executions may be found to be legally defensible within established ethical frameworks. In the academic criminal justice community of today, there exists a moral revulsion to the use of the death penalty.

The correctional system is supported by a caring ethic. Correctional officers, like all other law enforcement personnel, wear uniforms representing the authority they have in their institutions. But the authority of the uniform is not what gets anything accomplished. Personal respect and proper use of authority is what gets the job of the correctional officer done. Correctional officers, like other law enforcement officers, have their own code of ethics, to which they must adhere.

"Pending the arrival of that nirvana, it is essential that we appreciate thoroughly that the idea of 'equality under the law' is a benign, lulling facade behind which lurks a vast array of inequities, and that it is incumbent upon persons of goodwill to strip away that facade and rebuild the system so that true fairness comes to prevail to the greatest extent possible" (Geis).

Speaking about the application of ethical theories to criminal justice situations, Larry Sherman has maintained that "there are many competing frameworks that can be applied to criminal justice ethics. Some of them are widely rejected, such as the theory that might makes right. But others are widely accepted, and the means for choosing among them are unclear" (Sherman, 1982).

In any discussion of moral and ethical actions, many issues must be taken into consideration, including how far to go in order to preserve our criminal justice system without doing anything unethical. Laws are the creation of man. Laws have evolved out of a need to resolve human conflict. As such there are differences and agreements; and, the role ethics and fairness play in our criminal justice system leads to continuous debate.

REFERENCES

France, A. (1927). *The red lily*. (Winifred Stephens, Trans.). New York: Dodd, Mead.

Geis, G. (1973). Abortion and prostitution: A matter of respectability. *The Nation*, 217, 179–180.

Geis, G. (1988). On sleeping under bridges and unequal criminal justice. In R. Muraskin (Ed.), *Ethics and fairness in criminal justice*. Criminal Justice Institute, C.W. Post Campus of Long Island University.

Sherman, L.R. (1982). *Ethics in criminal justice education*. New York: The Hastings Center.

Weisser, M. (1979). *Crime and punishment in early modern Europe*. Atlantic Highlands, New Jersey: Humanities Press.

Cases:

Berger v. United States 295 U.S. 78 (1935)

Gideon v. Wainwright 372 U.S. 335 (1963)

Olmstead v. United States (1928)

United States ex. rel. O'Keefe v. McDonnell Douglas Corp. (1998) WL 1924 (8th Cir. Jan. 6, 1998)

Internet:

King, J. (1999). *Twisted justice: Prosecution function in America out of control* [On-line]. Available: 209.70.38.3/public.nsf/chapionarticles/99mar01/open document:9

http://208.70.38.3/public.nsf/newsrelease/99mn001/opendocument

Chapter 2

DOING RIGHT, BEING GOOD: THE SOCRATIC QUESTION AND THE CRIMINAL JUSTICE PRACTITIONER*

Kevin Ryan

Ethics[1] addresses questions of right and wrong, good and bad, virtue and vice. Ethics involves the effort to answer the question raised by the ancient Greek philosopher, Socrates: "How best is it to live?" Over the centuries many thinkers have sought to develop distinctive answers to this question. At both ends of this history—in ancient Greece and again today—we see thinkers asking the question "How should I be?," and their answers have drawn attention to the formation of character and to the character traits we call virtues and vices. The middle of this history—starting roughly in the Middle Ages, accelerating in the seventeenth and eighteenth centuries to a position of dominance in the nineteenth and most of the twentieth centuries—we see thinkers addressing a somewhat different question: "What should I do?". While the ancients, and their modern followers, address questions of character and the good life, much modern moral philosophy[2] has focused more on developing a set of principles that

---

*I would like to thank Brad Watson and Verbena Pastor for their comments on an earlier draft of this chapter.

[1]Though some writers draw a distinction between ethics and morality, the two terms are used interchangeably in common parlance and will be treated as equivalent for our purposes.

[2]By "modern" moral philosophy I mean moral theorizing from roughly the Enlightenment through most of the 20th century. A disproportionate amount of ethical theory has been taken up with the question "what should I do?". This disproportion is reflected in the discussion of ethical theories in this essay.

help us solve moral dilemmas.[3] Faced with the observed diversity of views on moral questions, many thinkers since the seventeenth century have sought to find a solid ground upon which to determine the correct system of morals, or to figure out the best approach to decide how to behave in certain circumstances.

These, then, are the two predominant questions of ethics. What should I do? How should I be? Thus, ethics involves the evaluation of actions and lives, choices and characters. But evaluation of this sort involves a certain orientation and calls our attention to certain sorts of considerations. The orientation is toward *rational argument*—toward the production of *reasons* supportive of one's position. As Ronald Dworkin (1977) has argued, when I take a moral position on an issue I involve myself in a distinctive sort of discourse. For one, I must produce some reasons for my view, and what counts as a reason is governed by shared criteria. Thus, for example, *prejudices*, which take into account considerations such as physical, racial, or other characteristics over which a person has no control, do not count as acceptable reasons according to our shared criteria. Nor do *emotional reactions* or *rationalizations*. The former appear to us as the very antithesis of reason, while the latter are usually seen as frauds to which we resort after-the-fact in a lame attempt to justify misbehavior. Further, taking a moral position means offering your own reasons rather than simply and solely *parroting* the views of others. Not only must I offer reasons for my position, but my position must be reasonable in another sense: I must *accept the theory my reason supposes*. That is to say, my other views and my behavior should be consistent with the moral principle or theory presupposed by the reason(s) I give. My moral position on one issue is expected to be consistent with my thinking and action on other issues. If it is not, I am suspected of special pleading to suit my own present desires.

In addition to the orientation of ethical thinking toward rational argument, a number of considerations seem to be particularly salient in ethics. We will see that the major ethical theories draw our attention to one or another of these considerations. To begin with, any *obligations* I may have are generally viewed as relevant to ethical evaluation. Some of my obligations derive from choices I have made, either by way of promises or by taking on particular roles. When I promise you something, I take on an obligation to do what I have promised. When I choose to become a police officer, I take on an obligation to perform the duties associated with that role. But not all of our obligations are products of choice. The duties of a son or daughter, or of a citizen, and many others are not usually acquired voluntarily. And even the duties linked to our professional roles are not understood and freely chosen one by one; rather, we choose the position without necessarily choosing the duties that go with it. Of course, this does not mean that we do not have the duties anymore than the absence of choice means that children have no duties toward their parents. *Rights*, a

---

[3]This is not to suggest that ancient Greek thinkers were not at all concerned with what to do in particular circumstances. Rather, it is to suggest that a subtle though important shift occurred in the emphasis of moral thinking: from a primary focus on the character of a whole life to a primary focus on decision-making procedures for situations of ethical dilemma. See Anscombe (1958) and Pincoffs (1986).

common term of ethical evaluation, can be thought of as a subset of obligations, for rights are the correlative of duties.[4] If I have a right to do something, you have a duty not to interfere. If I have a right not to be treated a particular way, you have a duty not to treat me that way. If I have a right to have something, you have a duty to provide it. Notice that obligations look backward. The reasons for action, the influences on character, to which they refer lie in the past: promises made, positions held, jobs undertaken, rights possessed from birth or gained over time.

Other important ethical considerations draw our attention to the future, to the *consequences* of our acts. The results I produce when I act, whether I have chosen to act or not, are always relevant to the ethical evaluation of my acts. To the extent that those results are harmful, whether to me or to others, then my action has one strike against it. One central feature of ethics is that it makes us think about the effects of what we do on others. The welfare of others lies at the heart of ethical evaluation.

A third set of considerations focuses our attention on *character*. These considerations pull us beyond the evaluation of isolated actions to the examination of a whole life. They ask questions about the *good life*, about virtues and vices. They explore the character traits that attract us to the company of good people and repel us from the company of bad. They look at the dispositions people have, the pattern of their desires, the underlying motivations for their way of life. These considerations take us beyond the focus on decision making in particular situations to a larger focus on the character a person develops over time, on the virtues and vices that reveal that character, and on the contents of the good life.

CHALLENGES TO ETHICS

Relativism

Ethics, then, involves the rational consideration of actions and choices, characters and lives. The goal of ethical theory is to develop general principles to help us decide what to do and how to be. There are those, however, who would argue that no such ethics is possible. Many contend, for example, that ethical principles are relative, varying from one setting to another, one group to another, one person to another. *Relativism* involves a denial of the existence of absolute and universal moral principles. This view has a long history, extending back to the first historian, Herodotus (trans. 1972)—according to whom "custom is king"—and forming the underlying implication of much of modern social science. Relativism pervades the unexamined ethical views of many of us. It seems to many of us, exposed as we have been to the incredible diversity of cultures and ways of life that humans have produced, that attempts to find universal principles are vain. Relativism, then, constitutes a major challenge to the very idea of ethics.

---

[4]Natural rights theory, as we shall see below, would see it the other way around: rights are the source of obligations. My point is merely that obligations and rights fall into the same category of ethical considerations.

A relativist believes that there are no absolute moral truths. Instead, moral truth is relative, varying from one place to the next, one era to the next, one culture to the next, even one person to the next. Why? The genesis of relativism lies in what we can call *cultural relativism*. Cultural relativism is based on the relatively undisputed observation that what is considered morally right and wrong varies from society to society. Moral *beliefs* really do vary across historical periods, across societies and cultures, even among individuals. Our own moral code, cultural relativists are quick to remind us is merely one code among many possibilities, no one of which has any universal standing.

Cultural relativism, as the mere observation of diversity of morals, is relatively uncontroversial. Cultural diversity does seem to be a fact. But is it misleading to emphasize this diversity and remain blind to the remarkable similarities across human cultures? There is much more agreement between cultures on fundamental issues than relativists would have us see. As Richard Brandt (1959) has argued, certain features of a cultural system seem to be required for the maintenance of life, such as mating, rearing and educating children, jobs and training as well as motivation structures, and security. These common requirements of a peaceful, stable society lead to much common ground in value systems. For example, virtually all societies contain a presumption in favor of truthfulness, though they may vary as to the circumstances under which that presumption can be defeated. As another example, all societies contain prohibitions against unauthorized killing. In sum, some moral rules, or types of moral rules, seem to exist in all societies because those sets of rules are necessary for society to exist.[5]

What cultural relativists may be observing is a diversity in *ethical judgments* rather than a diversity in *ethical standards*. Different human groups certainly make different judgments about what is right and wrong, good and evil, virtuous and vicious. But could it be that these groups start from the same standards, the same premises, and reach different conclusions due to different circumstances? Every society believes that uncontrolled killing of others is wrong. But the framework according to which killing is controlled may vary given different situations—economically, socially, politically—found in those societies.

Even though we may concede that diversity of ethical beliefs exists, does the diversity of *beliefs* mean that there is a diversity of *truths*? The view that it does is rooted in what Louis Pojman (1988) has called the "dependency thesis:" the claim that all moral principles derive their validity from cultural acceptance. Our moral values are rooted in socialization into specific social groups. As part of the socialization process we learn responses to certain actions and certain sorts of character traits—i.e., we develop a *moral sense* in which our judgments of good and bad are rooted. As John Mackie (1977) has described it, moral codes reflect "ways of life." We accept monogamy as right and polygamy as wrong, because our way of life is monogamous. Again, this is relatively uncontroversial. But does it ground the much stronger claim made by *ethical relativism*: that principles and judgments are *true* if they are accepted as true by the relevant culture, society, generation, group, or individual. The ethical

---

[5]Similar observations underlie, as we shall see, natural law theory.

relativist claims that universal ethical truth does not exist; for the relativist, all ethical truth is contingent, particular, dependent. As a corollary, the ethical relativist contends that it is wrong for people of one society (group, period, etc.) to condemn or interfere with the lives and moral behavior of another society (group, period, etc.). Since each group is right as long as it thinks it is, we have no business condemning them or righteously meddling in their affairs.

Ethical relativism can take two forms. *Individual relativism* asserts that moral truth varies from person to person, so that what one individual thinks is right *really is* right no matter what others might think. While some would vigorously defend the claim that moral truth differs from person to person, most relativists (probably because they accept the dependency thesis) opt for what we can call *group* (or "conventional") *relativism*: the view that all valid moral principles are justified by virtue of their acceptance by some group. The relevant group could be a society, a culture or subculture, an historical period, or any other collection of people.

One particularly common form of group relativism, and one particularly relevant to the material in this book, asserts that ethics differ from profession to profession: that what is morally right or virtuous for a lawyer may be different from what is morally right or virtuous for a non-lawyer; that the ethical truths of a police officer, a judge, a priest may differ from the ethical truth of outsiders to those professions. According to what Alan Gewirth (1986) has called the "separatist thesis," professionals, by virtue of their expertise and their consequent roles, have rights and duties unique to themselves. These rights and duties may be not only different from, but even contrary to, the rights and duties found in other segments of morality. In other words, different professions have different, separate, perhaps conflicting, rules, principles, and standards of virtue. By virtue of this separateness, the professional may act in ways that would be immoral if done by a non-professional. For example, lawyers are permitted to undermine a truthful prosecution case and vigorously cross-examine a distraught and truthful victim. Lawyers may keep certain facts secret—even facts about guilt, about the disposition of victim's bodies, etc. (Freedman, 1966)—simply because their role in the system demands rules protecting confidentiality of client communications. In the same vein, police may be permitted to lie—for example, by engaging in deceptive undercover operations—because their role in the criminal justice system requires such behavior. According to the "separatist" view of professional ethics, then, the moral truths that apply to the rest of us do not apply (at least not always) to professionals. Moral truth varies with one's role in society.

One persistent problem with group relativism—including separatist versions of professional ethics—is the indeterminacy of the relevant group. What standards can be used to determine the bounds of the group that counts for purposes of ethical truth? Is it the whole society? But if so, what about those within the society who disagree with the dominant social values? Why are they considered irrelevant to the process of determining what is right according to society? In general, most social groups are characterized to some extent by *conflict* of values; each social group, beyond the simplest and most primitive, reveals a diversity of moral views. Group relativism seems to ask us either to ignore this conflict and diversity, or to choose sides in the conflict. Again, to determine the truth about professional ethics do we look at the views of the whole profession, or only those with the power to write their views into professional codes? Do we look at the whole police force, or only the vice squad, or at some professional association? If one part of the force has a different view about accepting free coffee, shaking down drug dealers, or committing perjury to protect a fellow officer are their views right for their group?

Beyond these problems, a number of other criticisms can be offered of ethical relativism. Recall that an ethical relativist claims that principles or judgments are right if they are believed to be right by the relevant group or individual. Do we really believe this? If I really think that torturing little children is right, is it morally permissible for me to do so? What if I think that killing all members of a particular racial or ethnic group is right? What if my group thinks that? Would action on this belief be truly moral? Was slavery really morally unobjectionable in the eigthteenth century simply because many people (not everyone, of course) believed it to be? What about female circumcision or human sacrifice? Surely these actions disturb our *moral sense* (that body of intuitions that form our initial response to actions, choices, and characters).[6] Further, as many writers have pointed out, moral language (words like "right," "evil," "vice," and "good") carry universal implications. When we use them we imply (and mean) more than that the beliefs they describe are our personal attitudes; moral language does more than report what we think about our own behavior. Rather, moral language makes claims about the status of others' behavior. If I say killing is wrong, I mean it is wrong for others as well as for me—that's what *wrong* means. (Try this out on any moral claim. Watch the gyrations the relativist must go through in order to avoid the inference that her claims apply to others as well as to herself.) Finally, relativism forces its defender to claim that two inconsistent beliefs are both right at the same time—a logical contradiction. Officer Jones says accepting a free cup of coffee from a shopkeeper on his beat is morally permissible; her captain says it is wrong. The individual relativist must say both are right. But how can that be? Indeed, relativism would go further: since we are all members of different groups, which may have different standards, we could be both right and wrong at the same time according to the different standards. Such a conclusion seems, to say the least, bizarre.

Another set of objections to ethical relativism points to its pragmatic consequences. For one, such a view would make it impossible for us to claim that the customs of other societies, or the behavior or character of another person, are morally inferior to our own. How could we ever criticize others, as long as they adhered to their own standards of morality? Even then, if the actor defined hypocrisy as good, we would be disqualified from criticizing her for inconsistency. Secondly, ethical relativism of the group variety means that we decide what is right and wrong merely by consulting the standards of our own society. But few of us see our society's moral

---

[6]I employ this notion of a "moral sense" often in what follows. The basic idea is that we all, or most of us, share certain intuitions about moral matters, however differently those intuitions have been developed in our particular societies. We develop this moral sense, as we do other attitudes, through the process of socialization. But notice that our moral sense rarely involves total agreement with society's values; our moral intuitions often tell us that the way our society (or our group) does something falls short of the appropriate moral standard. For recent treatments of ideas similar to the "moral sense" see Wilson (1995) and Murdoch (1993).

code as perfect. We often find fault with the morals of our society, our group, our historical period. But relativism undermines the ground for such critique, for it entails the conclusion that our attempts to criticize group morals is misguided; it is, after all, the group itself that determines moral truth. Likewise, relativism calls into question the idea of moral progress. If relativism is true, we can no longer say we have improved morally over previous generations. Indeed, reformers would be acting immorally, because they challenge the morality of their group. Of course, their position may become right over time, but if group morals are the ultimate standard of right and wrong, by calling that standard into question the reformers violate valid rules of morality in making their critique.

These concerns about the consequences of adherence to ethical relativism do not refute relativism, but they do undercut the obviousness of its conclusions by showing us that they imply consequences that do not fit our moral intuitions. These objections may convince us that the acceptance of relativism entails too big a conflict with our moral sense.

Finally, something should be said about the ethic of tolerance often derived from ethical relativism. If moral truth really does vary, so the argument goes, we must be tolerant of the moral views and the actions of others. But is this not an *absolute* (rather than a relative) conclusion—telling us to "tolerate!" others, that any other response is morally wrong? The attempt to derive an ethic of toleration from relativist premises fails because it is internally incoherent. Among the moral views that vary from era to era, group to group, culture to culture, even individual to individual, are views about the proper response to the moral outlook, the actions, and the character of others. Toleration is but one of the possible responses, and it is by no means universally accepted. Were we to be relativist about tolerance, we would have to tolerate the intolerant and the oppressive, as long as they acted consistently with their own moral standards. The moral commitment to tolerance, however, forces us to abandon moral relativism. Many evils have been perpetrated by intolerance and interference with others' lives. But these are *evils* precisely because some moral claims (like this one) are *not* relative, or, at least, we neither talk nor act as if they were.

Egoism

Even we were to reject relativism we would still not be rid of the challenges to the very idea of ethics. Another important challenge is provided by *egoism*. As with relativism, egoism appears in two guises. *Psychological egoism* contends that people always do what pleases them or what is in their own interest. It is a theory about what people are really doing when they act, rather than a normative theory in its own right. For the psychological egoist, altruism is impossible—what appear to be altruistic acts, even if done by saintly souls who appear entirely selfless, are really done out of self-interest. Thus, the community police officer who extends a helping hand to a homeless person on his beat would be understood as doing so intentionally, or subconsciously, for his own benefit—perhaps to save himself some trouble later on, or to impress his supervisors with his community policing skills. The lawyer engaged in *pro bono* work must be seen as doing so for some personal advantage: the favorable opinion of the partners in the firm, perhaps, or the "charge" one gets when one feels morally superior to others. Even more, when I extend a helping hand to a fellow officer, an aged relative, my own child, the egoist tells me I do so primarily for the benefits (in self-esteem, returned friendship and love, etc.) that I expect to receive in return. According to the psychological egoist, there are no moral saints, if by that term we mean someone who does good because it is good, regardless of the consequences. If the psychological egoist is right, ethical behavior (if by that is meant acting at least in part out of selfless concern for others) is constitutionally impossible for creatures such as we.

But surely these interpretations of apparently altruistic acts are strained. In general, they depend upon a prior commitment to egoism that is not susceptible to falsification by contrary evidence: no matter how good someone may be, no matter how self-sacrificing her conduct, the egoist insists on seeking out selfish motives for action. But at some point this cynical sort of interpretation becomes unconvincing, not to say preposterous. Our sense of things tells us that some people are truly good, that some actions are selfless, that altruism is possible.

Psychological egoism is really a theory of human nature: it purports to describe how we actually behave and, in effect, denies the possibility of doing otherwise. *Ethical egoism*, on the other hand, is a normative theory: it tells us how we *should* behave. According to ethical egoism, the only valid moral standard is the duty to promote our personal well-being. According to the ethical egoist, one evaluates alternatives on the basis of the consequences to oneself, regardless of the consequences to others. This view can take several forms. One form is the claim that "I ought to promote myself above others at all times." Though there undoubtedly are people who believe this, they cannot publicly advocate this position because persuading others of its validity would lead those others to pursue their own interests, most likely at the expense of those of the persuasive egoist; that is, persuading others to be egoists in this sense would undermine my own interests, so I should not seek to persuade them. A second form of ethical egoism claims that "everyone ought to promote my interests above any other interests at all times." Again, while some people surely believe this (at least, many act as if they believe it), they would find it extraordinarily difficult to convince others to adopt it as their own moral guideline. "Why should the whole world act so as solely to benefit you?," one can hear them ask.

A third, and more persuasive, form of ethical egoism contends that "everyone ought to promote self above all others at all times." This position could be persuasively advocated publicly, but it too suffers from serious shortcomings. Would this view, if rigorously followed, maximally promote my interests? Probably not, because others would be looking out not for my interests but for their own—meaning that they would choose to do things that might very well harm my interests. In fact, my interests would stand a greater chance of being advanced if all others were required to follow impartial rules, compelling them on occasion to ignore their own interests and act in ways that ultimately benefit me at their cost. The point is that no rational egoist could advocate the universal adoption of this form of egoism, for that would not maximize his own interests. The best possible situation would be for me to be free to seek my own good at all times, while others would be required to follow impartial rules of morality. But notice that we are back at a formulation of egoism that would be hard to advocate publicly. Why would others go along with such a suggestion? Anyway, the genuine egoist is a rare bird indeed. Virtually everyone cares about someone else once in awhile. Most of us value the welfare of human beings, not just our own welfare, for its own sake. For example, we want our children to be happy and healthy just because we do, not because it will maximize our self-interests (unless we enter the tortured world of psychological egoism).

In sum, the challenge egoism poses for the attempt to develop a valid morality fails, just as did the challenge of relativism. Both views have crept into the implicit thinking of many of us. But when made explicit, both views prove unconvincing because they are too inconsistent with a wide range of our other moral intuitions we espouse.

WHAT SHOULD I DO?

Many of the most prominent ethical theories seek to answer the question "what should I do?". They seek to provide principles by which we can choose the morally correct action in any given moral situation. That is to say, they focus on situations of moral dilemma, circumstances in which I am faced with two or more alternative actions and must decide which one is the right thing to do. For this reason, we can refer to these theories as *choice theories*. Choice theories can take two general forms, based on the sort of ethical consideration they emphasize. *Consequentialist theories* assume that what is right and wrong can only be determined by examining the likely consequences of the available alternatives. For consequentialists, nothing is inherently right or wrong; rather, the moral status of an action depends upon the foreseeable consequences it produces. *Non-consequentialist theories,* on the other hand, assume that what is right and wrong is so regardless of the consequences; right and wrong is determined by reference to reasons other than the consequences of one's actions, and that means that some choices can be inherently wrong despite their positive results.

Consequentialist Theory: Utilitarianism

The primary form of ethical consequentialism is *utilitarianism*. According to Jeremy Bentham (orig. pub. 1789), a principle supporter of utilitarianism, one ought always to choose that alternative that maximizes pleasure or minimizes pain for all persons affected by the action—what Bentham called the "principle of utility." That is, one should seek to achieve the best overall consequences for everyone concerned—or in Bentham's phrase, "the greatest happiness of the greatest number." The principle of utility, therefore, requires strict impartiality: the consequences to oneself do not weigh more than the consequences to anyone else. Utilitarians argue that other moral considerations, such as duty, rights, and justice are subordinated to (indeed, their content is determined by) the principle of utility (i.e., the tendency of an act to produce pleasure or pain)[7]. I have an obligation to maximize pleasure and minimize

---

[7]Bentham was what is called a *hedonist*—i.e., he believed the primary value was happiness. It should be noted that many contemporary utilitarians have rejected hedonism, and emphasize the consequences associated with values other than happiness.

pain; people have the rights that are determined to be most beneficial to everyone concerned; what is just *is* that state of affairs in which the greatest utility is achieved; and, of course, as circumstances change, foreseeable consequences can change, and so do our duties, rights, and the requirements of justice.

One should note that utilitarianism essentially requires a person to do a cost-benefit analysis of alternative choices (Bentham spoke of it as a "calculus"). An act is permissible if and only if its net utility is at least as great as that of any alternative act the agent could perform in the situation. The decision process is straightforward. First, determine the available alternatives. Then, for each alternative, evaluate the pleasures and pains to everyone affected. This is done by adding up all the happiness caused by the action, adding up all the unhappiness, and subtracting the unhappiness from the happiness to determine the net utility. Once one has determined the net utility of each alternative, one chooses the alternative with the greatest net utility—the one that comes out on top when you compare the bottom lines. Indeed, utilitarians contend that *one has a moral obligation to choose the best alternative.* Any other choice is immoral. The process seems simple, but is actually quite complicated if done correctly. Utilitarians insist that we not privilege the effects an action will have on us or on those we care about. So, we must look at the pains and pleasures anticipated for *all* persons our action will affect, and we must not give extra weight to the pains and pleasures experienced by ourselves or those close to us. In addition, we must look at *all* the available alternatives. We must resist the temptation to consider only the alternative that strikes us first (perhaps because it is the path we would most like to follow).

So far we have been describing a variety of utilitarianism known as *act utilitarianism.* Act utilitarians evaluate each separate action, and opt for those actions with the greatest balance of pleasure over pain. Act utilitarianism implies an absolutism of principle—one should always act according to the principle of utility—but not of rules. What one should do is determined by the circumstances and the reasonably foreseeable consequences, not by any preexisting assessment of what is inherently right and wrong. No action, no rule, is absolutely right or wrong in itself. All rules are revisable in light of the principle of utility. Thus, for example, the utilitarian judge would strongly resist the implementation of sentencing guidelines because such rules short-circuit the process of considering the consequences of alternative dispositions for each particular defendant in each particular set of circumstances. Likewise, an act utilitarian police officer would contend that her choices on the beat should not be governed by broad policies and rules; instead, she should have strong discretion (Dworkin, 1977, 32, 33), allowing her to evaluate each situation as it arises and choose the alternative action that produces the greatest net utility. Act utilitarians resist the temptation to establish rules to govern their actions: they point out that observance of general rules (such as "you ought to tell the truth") does not always promote the general good. Rules have no independent force: in all circumstances we should do whatever maximizes utility, even if that means violating rules.

A number of criticisms have been offered of act utilitarianism and we can do no more than briefly survey them here. For one, many have observed that factors other than consequences are important to ethical evaluation. For example, act utilitarianism, given the right set of circumstances, would require us to punish an innocent person—say, in order to stop rioting or lynchings. But doing so, say the critics, is *unjust*: it is simply unfair to punish someone for a crime he did not commit, regardless of the consequences of doing so. Could a society of sadomasochists force an unwilling person to participate in their activities if the members derive great enough pleasure from it (greater pleasure than they would from a more willing participant)? We want to say "no," because doing so violates the *rights* of the unwilling victim. Or again, act utilitarianism would tell us that the activities of voyeurs, who derive great pleasure from watching their unsuspecting targets, might well produce a greater net utility than any other alternative employment of the voyeur's time, and so would be morally permissible (indeed, it would be morally required). Again we balk at this conclusion because such an analysis seems not to take into account the privacy rights of the innocent victim. Our moral sense tells us that other *obligations* may outweigh a set of positive consequences. If I promise to pick up my children after school, that promise, we think, should carry weight even if I must give up a present alternative that would produce greater net utility.

As an answer to these objections, some have proposed what is known as *rule utilitarianism*. According to this view, an act is permissible if and only if it is not prohibited by the best set of rules—that set that has the greatest overall utility when compared with all other possible sets. In other words, rule utilitarians propose the adoption of a moral code, determined by evaluating the net utility of alternative sets of moral rules. Moral acts are those that are not prohibited by the ideal moral code. Rule utilitarians argue that, on balance, a set of rules that prohibited punishing the innocent, violating privacy rights, or breaking promises (except, perhaps, under certain specified circumstances) would produce greater overall utility than a set of rules that would allow these activities. Hence, actions such as the voyeur's, which run counter to the best set of moral rules, must be deemed immoral. Some sort of rule utilitarianism lies behind the formulation and promulgation of departmental policies and professional ethical codes.

But act utilitarian critics have been swift to accuse rule utilitarians of superstitious rule worship. The problem, they contend, is that following moral codes (no matter how beneficial overall) can sometimes force us to choose an act with low net utility. While the rules of the ideal moral code may allow for limited exceptions, they cannot allow for an exception every time utility could be maximized by violating the rule, for then there would really be no rules at all.

Further, rule utilitarianism does not surmount other possible objections to utilitarian reasoning. For one, some critics have pointed out that utilitarianism demands too much. It obliterates the distinction between morally obligatory actions and *supererogatory acts* (acts above and beyond what is required); for if there is an alternative act that goes above and beyond, it is that alternative that truly maximizes utility, and so it would be that alternative that is morally *required* for the utilitarian. For example, utilitarianism may require us to make heroic self-sacrifices, such as giving up virtually all of our resources to help the poor and needy around the world. The best expenditure of a police department's budget may be to aid starving children around the globe, rather than to police suburban neighborhoods. Utilitarianism seems to require that the department choose the former option, however. Once again, we are faced with a conclusion that violates our moral sense. We would like to maintain the distinction between heroic or saintly acts and what is morally required; we would like to think that some acts go beyond what we are obligated to do, and are to be praised for just that reason.

Another troubling objection to utilitarianism follows from the observation that the utilitarian standard would often require us to give up the projects and commitments in life about which we care most (the health of our families, the prospects of our children, our own professional and personal development, the welfare of our local community). Can it really be morally right to sacrifice these projects and commitments to the welfare of unknown others? Is it likely that anyone will do so? Is it not too much to expect each person to make the happiness of all others a matter of personal responsibility? Even when we are unselfish or altruistic, it is usually "self-referential altruism"—that is, concern for those others who have some special relation to us. Even wider affections tend to be limited to causes, nations, religions with which we have personal ties, rather than to all humans. Adoption of a rigorous utilitarian principle would force us to give up core parts of ourselves and our ties to those people and things that make life worth living: close affections, private pursuits, and many kinds of competition.

Non-Consequentialist Theories

Whereas virtually all consequentialist theories are variations on the utilitarian idea, non-consequentialist theories can take a variety of forms. We shall examine two major sorts of non-consequentialist theory: *naturalist theory*, including natural law and natural rights theories, and *deontological theory* as developed by Immanuel Kant.

NATURALIST THEORIES

From the beginning, one underlying assumption of philosophy has been the belief that nature can be understood by reason, that humans have the power to grasp the workings of the natural world. The goal of philosophy was to discover the underlying rational order of things, and, according to the ancient Greeks, that meant finding not only the physical laws but also the values and purposes that pervade the universe: to these thinkers values are *part* of nature. The Stoics, for example, contended that the proper rules of morality are built right into the structure of nature in the same way that physical laws are: just as there are natural physical laws, so there are natural moral laws. The Stoics held that one ought to follow nature rather than custom and convention, and the dictates of nature can be discovered by human reason. What reason teaches, they contended, is that things are as they ought to be when they are serving their natural purposes. Moral rules can be derived, then, by observing the purposes of nature, and these rules—the *natural law*—are universal, applicable to all humans everywhere, simply because nature is the same everywhere.

Perhaps the most influential exponent of natural law theory was St. Thomas Aquinas, who lived in the thirteenth century. Aquinas (trans. 1988) observed that the fundamental principle of morality was to do good and avoid evil. But how do we discover the content of good and evil? Aquinas contended that the moral law was rooted in human nature, specifically in those natural inclinations all humans share. Whatever promotes the fulfillment of human nature is good and should be done; whatever detracts from the fulfillment of human nature is evil and should be avoided. Humans, he argued, have numerous natural inclinations. Some of these we share with all substances, such as the desire to preserve our own being. From this it follows that whatever preserves life or wards off threats to it is part of the natural law. Other inclinations we share with all animals, such as the drive to procreate and to rear our offspring. From this it follows that whatever aims toward these goals is good.[8] A third set of inclinations we share are specifically human, such as our drive to know, to exercise our reason, to form relationships with others in society, and to form friendships. From these inclinations it follows that we should shun ignorance, avoid giving offense to others, value our friends, and so forth.

Aquinas' theory is *teleological*—that is, right conduct is determined by its goal or purpose rather than its consequences. This means that the prohibitions and prescriptions of natural law are absolute; they are not dependent upon the foreseeable results of action in specific situations. Not that consequences are totally irrelevant: moral decision-making requires us to consider the probable results of our actions; otherwise, we would be unable to tell whether or not we are fulfilling the demands of the natural law. Prudence must be our guide: sometimes what appears on its face to be the morally correct action in the long run produces consequences that destroy society, undermine friendship, create obstacles to human prosperity, and so forth. But consequences cannot drive our decision, for none of the values specified by natural inclinations may be directly violated. Nor can basic values be traded off against one another: no one of these values is any more, or any less, important than another. Because the theory is teleological, intention is the key to moral evaluation. The intention of an action can be determined by what the person acting wills, either as a means to a further end or as an end in itself. Thus, an external view of an action will often fail to distinguish the key moral fact—the intention of the actor—and therefore will often fail to distinguish morally distinct actions. One implication of this view is that an action might be praiseworthy (e.g., visiting a friend in the hospital), but the person performing it is not to be commended because she does it with the wrong intention (e.g., in order to get the friend to loan her money, rather than out of true concern about his health).

The absolute nature of these moral rules, however, creates a problem for the person trying to decide what to do in morally difficult circumstances. Sometimes we are faced with a situation in which *both* options are evil, at least on first glance, because they violate the dictates of the natural law. I may be placed in a situation in which I must take a life to protect one, for example. How do we decide what to do? Natural law theory offers two principles to help us in these dilemmas. According to the *principle of forfeiture*, a person who threatens the life of an innocent person forfeits his or her own right to life. This principle can be used to justify self-defense,

---

[8]Aquinas' thought exercised a powerful influence on the doctrines of the Roman Catholic Church. This second natural law, that we should avoid those activities that prevent the fulfillment of the natural inclination to procreate, underlies the Catholic doctrine that the use of contraception is immoral.

shooting a fleeing dangerous felon, fighting a war, and even capital punishment. According to the *doctrine of double effect*, in certain circumstances one may rightly perform an action that has, besides the effect desired, a second effect that could not rightly be willed as a means or end itself. That is to say, if in order to achieve a morally proper purpose I inadvertently cause a result that, if intended, would have been immoral, I am morally innocent of that second effect. There are four conditions that must be met for this excusing doctrine to apply. First, the act, considered in itself and apart from its consequences, must at least be morally permissible. Second, the bad effect must be unavoidable if the good effect is to be achieved; that is, there must be no alternative course that could achieve the good effect without producing the bad effect. Third, the bad effect must not be the means of producing the good effect, but only a side effect. Thus, for example, terrorist acts, no matter how good the ends they seek to achieve, are immoral because they involve a violation of the basic rules of natural law. But if in seeking to defend my child from an attack I inadvertently injure an innocent bystander, I have done nothing morally wrong. Fourth, the two effects must be proportional, so that the bad effect does not vastly outweigh the good effect.

Thus, according to natural law theory, an act is morally permissible if it is in accord with the basic values derived from human inclinations or if it is excused by either the principle of forfeiture or the doctrine of double effect. Further, any act that is morally permissible, and to which there are no morally permissible alternatives, is morally required.

Critics of natural law theory have pointed out a number of difficulties. First, many have seen a problem with the attempt to derive a conclusion about values from observations about nature. These critics disagree with the fundamental assumption of natural law theory that moral values are written into the nature of things. Instead, they contend that conclusions about what we "ought" to do cannot be derived from data about what "is."[9] The theory has also been challenged on the grounds that its selection of natural features, particularly features of human nature, is unjustifiably partial and narrow. Equally salient aspects of human nature include our tendency toward malevolence, our selfishness, our desire for pleasure, and so forth. A moral theory based on these other aspects of human nature would look vastly different than does natural law theory. What justification is there for highlighting only certain features of human nature and treating only those as sources of moral rules? In addition, many have called into question the presupposition of natural law theory that nature is purposeful—that features of nature, such as human action, have a specific purpose toward which they must tend if they are to be moral (e.g., the claim that natures purpose of sexual activity is procreation). But if nature is not purposeful in this sense, its texture cannot have moral implications.

In the seventeenth and eighteenth centuries a different form of naturalistic theory came to prominence in political and ethical thought: *natural rights theory*. According to this view, humans are endowed by nature with certain "rights." These rights belong to humans simply because they are human; they are inherent in the

---

[9]The classic version of this argument is found in Hume (org. pub. 1978).

human condition, existing prior to society, prior to government, prior to law. Some rights that we possess—*conventional rights*—derive from agreements or conventions, such as contracts, organizational charters, and so forth. But not all rights are conventional; not all rights are subject to change through agreement. Some of our rights—*natural rights*—derive from our very nature. Not only do these rights precede government and law, but the very purpose of these human institutions is to protect our natural rights. Indeed, government, according to writers such as John Locke (1960), is only justified if it is the product of an agreement among the people of a society to protect their rights—what these thinkers called the *social contract*. Hence, the notion of natural rights was closely linked to the idea of limited government.

But what exactly is a "right?" Rights have been described as "valid claims" against others (Feinberg, 1973, 65–66), or as "entitlements" that act as "trumps" in moral discussion (Dworkin, 1977, xi). If I have a right to free speech, I have a morally valid claim that you should not interfere with my speaking. If you want to pass a law preventing me from speaking I can counter with the assertion of my entitlement to speak freely, and that assertion defeats any argument, at least any consequentialist argument, you can make in favor of your law. Thus, rights theorists insist that mere benefit to the community is not sufficient to override my rights. Hence, my rights set up boundaries around me over which no one is permitted to cross, even if doing so is indisputably for the good of the community. To return to an example we used above, the right to privacy possessed by the voyeur's victim means that the voyeur is morally obligated to refrain from crossing the boundary established by that right. The voyeur acts immorally because his victim is entitled to be free from his peeping; the victim has a valid claim against the voyeur no matter how happy the voyeur may be, no matter how cost-free his activity is to the victim.

Of course, conceiving of rights as trumps leaves open the possibility that someone else will play a higher trump card—that they will assert a weightier right. One issue that preoccupies rights theorists is just this issue of how to handle conflicts of rights. Inevitably there will be situations in which someone's rights must be violated in order to honor someone else's rights. Thus, for example, in order to protect my right to be free from undeserved harm, I may need to restrain your liberty. But it is not clear which principles govern such tradeoffs, and rights theorists often disagree about how exactly we are to resolve these dilemmas.

Many writers in the natural rights tradition distinguish between two sorts of rights. *Negative rights* are claims to others' omissions or forebearances—they give you a right that others *not do* something. Negative rights can be active or passive. *Active rights* are rights to act or not act as one chooses. For example, I may have a right to say what I want (a right to free speech) or go where I will. *Passive rights* are rights not to be done to by others in certain ways. For example, I may have a right to be let alone, a right to enjoy my property, a right to keep my affairs secret, a right to keep my reputation undamaged, a right to keep my body unharmed.

The second sort of rights are *positive rights*, claims that other persons act in particular ways. My positive rights give me an entitlement to others' actions; they require others to *do* something. For example, Article 23 of the United Nations Declaration of Human Rights provides in part that "everyone has the right to . . . just and favourable conditions of work and to protection against unemployment." This provision gives persons a positive right to a certain work environment, and requires others (particularly governments) to insure that this environment is delivered.

According to rights theory, morality requires us to examine the rights implications of our actions, and choose always to act in a way that does not violate rights or, in situations of conflict of rights, violates rights the least. Rights theory has had an enormous impact on our way of conceiving of morality. To some extent all of us speak of rights, and use rights claims as trumps in moral argument (or at least as considerations of great weight). Nevertheless, rights theory has a number of weaknesses. For one, there is very little agreement about what rights we actually have. We live in a world characterized by an explosion of rights claims. Thomas Jefferson's three negative rights—life, liberty, and the pursuit of happiness (by which he meant "property")—have been supplemented by a host of new positive rights in the Universal Declaration of Human Rights, many of them controversial. New groups claim new rights on an almost daily basis. But how can we decide exactly which rights we possess by nature?

Indeed, despite the assertion by Jefferson and others that some rights are self-evident, many have argued that no convincing case can be made for the view that humans have *natural* (as opposed to conventional) rights. Jeremy Bentham (orig. pub. 1816), for example, described rights as "nonsense upon stilts," and Karl Marx (orig. pub. 1844) pointed out that rights language works very effectively to shield the greedy actions of capitalists from moral scrutiny. How do we *know* that humans have rights by nature? Certainly, prior to the seventeenth century very few people imagined the existence of natural rights. In fact, rights language did not even exist prior to the late Middle Ages. Does this not suggest that "rights talk" is only *our way* of speaking, rather than a recognition of the way things really are? If there are such rights attaching to humans *qua* humans, why did no one recognize this fact until the late Middle Ages?

Further, the claim that humans, by nature, have certain rights carries with it an assumption that all persons are equal in some respect that gives them "worth." That is, in order to say all humans have rights, I must point to something all the relevant parties have in common to which the rights attach. What this means is perhaps easier to see in relation to conventional rights. Everyone who has a right to drive a car meets certain basic requirements (e.g., a certain age, a certain ability to see, few previous traffic violations, and so forth). That is, all those with this right are equal with respect to these basic features. Surely a claim to possess a natural right must be subject to the same sort of linkage with natural features. Otherwise we could not distinguish between those who have the right and those—amoebas, trees, unhatched chicken eggs—that do not. But what are these natural characteristics upon which rights are based? In what ways are all humans equal? Not only is this a difficult question to answer, but also whatever characteristics you choose to ground rights claims work to include and exclude certain beings as holders of rights. For example, some have argued that it is the human capacity for "rationality" that underlies equal human rights. But this capacity may actually exclude certain humans, such as babies, some of the very aged, and the mentally challenged, who are simply not rational in the same sense you and I are. Others have pointed to the human liability to pain and suffering as the basis for rights claims. But this liability would seem to expand the category of rights holders to include most members of the animal kingdom. I suspect that most of us, however, would be reluctant to extend to animals the same rights that we claim for ourselves.

DEONTOLOGICAL THEORY

Deontology derives from the Greek words for duty and science; hence, deontology refers to the science of duty. In modern ethical debates, deontological theory holds that morally right actions are those done because we have a duty to do them. Our duties, in turn, are determined by reference to something other than the consequences of the action. Undoubtedly the most influential deontological theory is that of Immanuel Kant. According to Kant (orig. pub. 1785), an act must be done from a sense of obligation in order to have moral worth. Just doing the right thing is not enough; it must be done *because* it is one's duty to do it. Further, an action's moral value depends upon the *maxim* from which it is performed, rather than to its success in realizing some desired end or purpose. A maxim is a succinct formulation of a fundamental rule or principle. Every act we take can be described as reflecting some maxim, even if we do not have the maxim in mind when we perform the act. For example, when I skip class I may not stop and think which rule I am following in doing so, but my act can be described as reflecting the rule that I may skip class whenever it is convenient to do so. According to Kant, we determine the moral worth of an action by considering the maxim it reflects, not the consequences it produces.

Based on these principles, Kant developed the notion of the "categorical imperative." An imperative is an order or command; it must be obeyed—I have a duty to do what it prescribes. Many imperatives are hypothetical or practical: they take the form "If I want to obtain end X, then I *must* do Y." Such imperatives are not absolute, however, because they are subject to changes in my ends or purposes. If I want to lighten my caseload, I must arrange for quick guilty pleas by my clients. But once I no longer want to lighten my caseload (if, for instance, my caseload has grown smaller), I no longer need to arrange pleas so quickly. A *categorical imperative*, on the other hand, permits no exceptions because it is not based on some goal I have; I must obey it regardless of any ends or purposes I have. Thus, we have an absolute duty to obey categorical imperatives.

According to Kant, there is only one categorical imperative. Nevertheless, he expressed this fundamental duty in several different ways, each designed to emphasize a different aspect of our obligation. We will focus on two of these formulations. According to the first, a person should act only according to that maxim that at the same time she would will to become universal law. This complicated formulation means that you should choose to act in a way reflective of a maxim you would (if you had the power) make into a law that everyone was required to obey. The categorical imperative, then, provides us with a procedure for determining what is right and wrong. It tells us to ask what we might call the "categorical imperative question": would I want everybody to be required to do what I am doing now?

Kant used "promising" as an example. Suppose I have promised to do something for you, say, to work your shift so you can attend a family birthday party. Now, however, another friend has offered me a ticket to the baseball game, and I would really like to go. What should I do? Should I break my promise to you? The categorical imperative tells me first to determine what maxim I would be following in breaking my promise—something like "I can break a promise if I feel like it." Then I should ask myself if I would like that maxim to be turned into a universal law that everyone was required to obey. Consider the consequences of such a law: if everyone was required to break promises whenever they felt like it, promises would mean nothing; the whole institution of promising would break down and human society would be deprived of the benefits of that institution. Therefore, I should not break my promise.

A different formulation of the categorical imperative requires me to act so that I treat humanity, whether in my person or in that of another, always as an end and never solely as a means. Again, though the language is complex, the idea is straightforward. Humans, by virtue of their reason, exist as ends-in-themselves—that is, humans have absolute worth and deserve our respect. Any action that does not treat a human being with respect, but rather uses that person as a tool to help achieve my ends, is wrong. If I involve someone in a scheme of action to which he could not in principle consent, then I am using him as a mere means (much the same way I use a lawnmower as a means to achieve the end of a well-groomed lawn).

Thus, for example, using a prostitute is wrong according to Kant because in doing so I am treating another person solely as a means to obtain sexual gratification. Equally, slavery is wrong because that institution involves the use of other people solely as means to achieve other ends; it involves treating people as the equivalent of lawnmowers. It should be noted that this formulation does not forbid using another as a means, so long as at the same time you treat them with respect, as having worth simply because they are human. So, while a police officer uses a citizen as a means when he tries to get information from the citizen in order to capture a fugitive, no moral wrong has been committed as long as the citizen is treated with respect, with a recognition that citizens have their own purposes aside from their utility in helping the police.

A number of problems can be discerned with Kant's theory. First, it is not always easy to figure out the maxim of my action. In fact, any action can be said to reflect a number of maxims, some broad, some narrow. For example, in breaking my promise to work for you, the maxim could be narrowed so that it refers to the specific facts of the situation—I can break promises to work for someone only when a friend offers me tickets to a baseball game. Turning that maxim into universal law might make people more careful during baseball season, but it would hardly undermine the social institution of promising. Kant himself always drew *very general maxims* from his examples. But doing so almost guarantees that universalization will be quite rare: if the maxim simply speaks of killing, or breaking promises, or stealing, then of course you would not want them to be required of everybody. But the more you factor in the specific circumstances, the less objectionable the maxim. And our moral sense tells us that sometimes the circumstances *are* important to the ethical evaluation of an action.

A second, related, objection focuses on the absolutism of the rules Kant derives from the application of the categorical imperative: do not kill, do not break promises, never lie, and so forth. Are moral rules really this absolute? Is it not the case that sometimes foreseeable consequences alter the moral status of an action? For example, lying may be wrong in many situations, but what if the local Nazi commandant is at the door asking you if you are hiding Jews in your attic (and you are). You know the commandant will believe you, whatever you tell him. Must you really tell him the truth? Kant would seem to say "yes;" our moral sense, I think, would tell us "no."

Third, sometimes Kant's categorical imperative simply does not help us resolve difficult moral dilemmas. Assume a SWAT commander faces a choice between two alternative ways to nab a terrorist who has taken a dozen hostages. One way involves turning over to the terrorist a fellow officer hated by the terrorist; the terrorist has already announced that he will torture and kill this officer. A second way involves refusing to turn over the officer; the terrorist has already announced that he will kill all the hostages if the officer is not turned over. There are no other alternatives. How should the SWAT commander decide? In this situation it seems that *both* available alternatives involve treating someone as a mere means: either he uses the hostages as a means (and only as a means because their prospects and purposes are not being taken into account) to protect the fellow officer and to dramatize a point about not giving in to the demands of terrorists; or he uses the officer as a means (and only as a means because his prospects and purposes are not being taken into account) to protect the hostages. Kant's categorical imperative simply fails to help us in this situation.

RETURN TO THE SOCRATIC QUESTION: THE ETHICS OF VIRTUE

You should note that the Socratic question—"how best is it to live?"—is much broader and more general than the question raised by modern ethicists. Socrates' question is about a manner of life; it focuses our attention on a whole life rather than a particular moment in that life. It asks us to consider how to be, rather than what to do. It asks for the conditions of the *good life* for human beings as such. And it asks not only about me—how should I live?—but also about others, indeed about everyone— how should everyone live? It pushes us to examine questions of *character* and the virtues and vices that reveal character.[10]

Many of the earliest writers on ethics addressed these questions. Thinkers such as Plato and Aristotle saw ethics not as a matter of solving personal dilemmas, of deciding how to behave in particular situations, but as a matter of developing a good character. As we have seen, modern theories of ethics have concentrated much more on solving ethical dilemmas, on providing principles useful for deciding what to do in particular situations. Recently, however, a number of thinkers have begun to return to the Socratic question. In part this is due to dissatisfaction with the results of the modern assumption that the subject matter of ethics is moral problems and their solutions. These thinkers contend that the modern inclination toward choice moral-

---

[10]Popular discussion today often uses the word "character" as a positive trait ("he has character"). But the implication of such a usage is that some people can *lack character*. Virtue ethics teaches that we all have a character: some of us have a character that, on balance, is good; others, on balance, have a bad character. None of us, at least no adult, is devoid of character.

ity has led to the neglect of important questions of character. Ethics, they tell us, should not simply be a matter of figuring out how to act in dilemmas; it should also address what we should be like during the rest of our lives. After all, they argue, moments of ethical dilemma are really quite rare, and how we act in those situations is likely to be heavily influenced by the virtues and vices that characterize our lives. These thinkers have produced a renaissance of *virtue ethics*.

What is a virtue? Aristotle (trans. 1987) defined it as a disposition to act in a certain way. Virtues do not, however, occur naturally; people are not born with virtues or vices. Rather, virtue is bred by proper training and by exercise—virtues are *habits*. Other writers have built on Aristotle's notion by describing virtues and vices as qualities we refer to in seeking out or avoiding the company of others. The Greek word for virtue, *arete*, also means *excellence*. Virtues provide standards of excellence: the virtuous person is one who meets certain standards of excellence.

From where do these standards come? How do we know what counts as a virtue? Aristotle believed that universal reason revealed virtues to us. Modern writers, less comfortable with assertions about universal reason, offer alternative approaches. Alasdair MacIntyre (1984), for instance, has linked virtues to what he calls "practices." A *practice* is a cooperative arrangement in pursuit of goods internal to the arrangement. We speak of the "practice" of medicine or of law; but equally policing can be a practice as can other collective endeavors, such as politics or baseball. Every practice has certain goods associated with it. Some of these goods are *internal* to the practice; that is, they are at the heart of what the practice is about. Thus, for example, the practice of medicine seeks the goal of health; the practice of law strives for justice; the practice of policing attempts to achieve public safety. Other goods are *external* to the practice; that is, they are not directly related to the goals of the practice. Thus, lawyers, doctors, baseball players may earn significant amounts of money; police officers gain respect; politicians get to associate with the wealthy and live in fine houses. But these goods are external to the practices with which they are associated; they come, as it were, as side effects of the practice. Virtues are those traits that permit one to achieve the internal goods of a practice. The virtues of the good doctor are those traits that conduce to health; the virtues of the good lawyer are those traits that lead to justice; the virtues of the good police officer are those traits that promote public safety.

Further, argues MacIntyre, the standards of excellence of a practice are partially definitive of that form of activity. Thus, for example, the standards set by the good pitcher in baseball partially define what pitching is—it is these standards that are used wherever baseball is played to judge good and bad performances, successful and less successful careers, and so forth. The more one's throwing diverges from the standards of excellence in pitching, the less the activity qualifies as baseball. The same is true of the standards of excellent medical practice, legal practice, and policing. The standards of excellence of any practice are rooted in history and tradition: the standards develop over time and are exemplified in the history of the practice. Very often a practice will contain a body of stories that depict the virtues and vices associated with that practice: stories of good doctors, good lawyers, good police officers, good judges, good pitchers. The virtues of a practice can be drawn from these stories, and are often taught using these stories.

One implication of virtue ethics is that the virtues of a good person and the virtues of a good practitioner are unlikely to conflict. The latter virtues may be more detailed, more directed to the specifics of a particular practice, but they are always consistent with our sense of the virtues of a good person in general. The stories that tell us about the good police officer almost always depict someone who is also a good person, a person of good character, a person whose virtues go beyond what is required for the practice of police work. The good judge, we find when we think about it, sounds like a good person; she possesses the same virtues—justice, moderation, honor—and lacks the same vices as do the moral models we would like to become ourselves. Consequently, for virtue ethics the separatist thesis of professional ethics makes no sense: the ethics of the good practitioner and of the good person are the same; good practitioners are *good persons in practice.*

What, then, are the virtues of the good person? Aristotle discussed such traits as bravery, temperance, generosity, magnificence, magnanimity, mildness, friendliness, truthfulness, wit, and justice.[11] Other writers have produced different, usually longer, lists. But in all cases the underlying idea is the same: virtues are those characteristics that we esteem; vices are characteristics we disdain. According to Aristotle, a virtue is a *mean* between two extremes. Thus, bravery is a moderate form of the same inclination that produces the extremes of foolhardiness and cowardice. While the exact content of bravery in any given situation depends upon the circumstances, in all cases the brave action is the one that the brave person is naturally disposed to perform. Sometimes it may be the brave thing to place oneself in the line of fire; other times bravery may require retreat. Keep in mind, however, that a virtue is a disposition, a habit. We cannot be said to be brave simply because we have performed a single brave action. We possess the virtue of bravery if we always incline toward the brave action, if our life reflects a bravery others only manage on rare occasions.

In the discussion of utilitarianism above, we pointed out that utilitarians seem to lose the distinction between morally obligatory acts and superogatory acts—that theory seems to require us always to behave in an ideal fashion, to be entirely selfless, to sacrifice ourselves willingly for the benefit of others. Virtue ethics approaches the distinction between the moral minimum and the superogatory in a more satisfying way. From an external point of view (the viewpoint of the outsider looking in on virtue ethics in practice), virtues are dispositions to act in ways that exceed the baseline requirements of morality. Unless someone has a duty to act courageously (police officers, firefighters, and lifeguards have such a duty), we normally do not condemn the person who does not do the courageous thing—the bystander who does not leap into the flames to save people he does not know, or the

---

[11]While there has been a good deal of popular attention to "virtue" and "character" in recent years, it should be noted that Aristotle's list of virtues includes a number of traits, more expansive and positive traits such as generosity, magnanimity, wit, and justice, that are seldom mentioned in popular discussions.

civilian who does not try to stop an armed robbery by tackling the robbers. At the same time, we praise those who *do* act in these ways: we consider them heroes, people who have gone above and beyond the call of duty. From this point of view, then, virtues are *moral ideals* that lead us beyond what is morally required.

Virtue ethics takes heroism and saintliness seriously. A hero is someone who goes beyond the moral minimum, who exercises notable virtues in difficult circumstances. All too often today we call people heroes who simply do their duty. But for virtue ethics there is nothing heroic about doing one's duty—*that* is required. Thus, the officer who is shot in the line of duty is not a hero, unless she was performing actions and exercising virtues that exceed what was required by her contract as an officer. Saints, likewise, exceed the moral minimum; they go beyond what is obligatory to perform actions that reflect exceptional virtue.[12]

From an external point of view, virtue theory does not compel us to condemn those who lack specific virtues, or who fail to act the way the virtuous person would in a particular situation. Virtue ethics maintain the distinction between the *saint* and the *hero* and the rest of us who are not bad, but not moral models either. From an internal point of view, however, virtue ethics seems to merge moral ideals and the moral minimum. When I assess my own character and find it flawed, lacking important virtues but possessing troubling vices, I *do* engage in moral condemnation. I evaluate myself negatively for failing to be virtuous. If I reject choice morality as my ethical guide, and emphasize good character and its virtues, moral ideals have become my moral baseline. To the extent that I am not a saint, I have failed.

What are the limitations of virtue ethics? The primary weakness of this approach relates to its fundamental difference from modern ethical theories: virtue ethics offers little guidance in situations of ethical dilemma. According to virtue theory, right action in a particular situation is what a good person would do. But such an answer is unsatisfactory for it tells me little about how I, striving to be virtuous but not there yet, should act. For purposes of moral education, if nothing else, virtue theory needs to supply clearer guidance about how to make ethical decisions in situations where the right thing to do is ambiguous. Writers in this tradition would have us focus on moral models; moral education, they contend, should be a matter of exposure to the actions, the thoughts, and tales about virtuous people. But still, unless those models have faced *my* situation, their reaction in other situations may not help much. Similarly, virtue ethics offers little guidance in resolving moral conflicts in which two virtues seem to point in different directions. Can one virtue be traded off with another one? And if so, what principles govern the tradeoff? Can a virtuous police officer engage in deception in order to capture a dangerous criminal? We want to say yes, but it is not clear how virtue ethics helps support our inclination.

---

[12]Curiously, while our use of the word hero reflects a "flattened" moral universe in which heroism is too often equated with simply "being in the wrong place at the wrong time" (usually out of duty), we are extremely reluctant to employ the word "saint" to describe others. Perhaps this hesitation indicates a discomfort with the religious connotations of the word.

CONCLUSION

Virtue ethics, then, suffers from the same sort of incompleteness that characterized the other major ethical theories: it captures only part of the ethical universe (albeit the larger part). Virtue ethics correctly brings us back to the Socratic question, pushing us to broaden the scope of ethical thinking from a single act to a whole life. The question "how best is it to live?" lies at the heart of ethics. But the good life not only requires the development of good habits, of a good character, it also requires us to be equipped with habitual ways to resolve moral dilemmas. Virtue ethics correctly points out that most of the time we do not face difficult ethical quandaries, and that a preoccupation with techniques for solving those quandaries is misguided. But that does not mean we do not have need, on occasion, for such techniques. Sometimes we *do* need to decide how to act in certain circumstances; indeed, the desire to make a morally correct choice reflects the virtue of our character. How do we make these choices? Our character will influence that decision, but other considerations seem relevant to making a correct choice. It is here that the true value of modern ethical thought can be found. In deciding what to do, we must refer to obligations and consequences, as well as virtues.

So both of our questions—"What should I do?" and "How should I be?"—are critical to the ethical enterprise. The good life—the life that is best to live—involves habits *and* correct choices. To focus only on the latter, as do many modern treatments of professional ethics, is to foreshorten the realm of ethics; such a focus offers only a narrow and crabbed ethics that does not address our lives as a whole. Those concerned with criminal justice ethics cannot ignore questions of character, of virtue and vice, of the goodness of a whole life. The good criminal justice practitioner is a *good person* as well as a good decision maker in difficult circumstances.

REFERENCES

Anscombe, G.E.M. (1958). Modern moral philosophy. *Philosophy, 33,* 1–19.

Aquinas, Saint T. (1988). *St. Thomas Aquinas on politics and ethics* (P. E. Sigmund, Ed. & Trans.). New York: Norton.

Aristotle. (1987). *Nicomachean ethics* (T. Irwin, Trans.). Indianapolis: Hackett.

Bentham, J. (1982; orig. pub. 1789). *An introduction to the principles of morals and legislation* (J. H. Burns & H. L. A. Hart, Eds.). London: Methuen.

Bentham, J. (1987; orig. pub. 1816). Anarchical fallacies. In J. Waldron (Ed.), *Nonsense upon stilts: Bentham, Burke and Marx on the rights of man.* London: Methuen.

Brandt, R. B. (1959). *Ethical theory.* Englewood Cliffs, NJ: Prentice-Hall.

Dworkin, R. (1977). *Taking rights seriously.* Cambridge, MA: Harvard University Press.

Feinberg, J. (1973). *Social philosophy.* Englewood Cliffs, NJ: Prentice-Hall.

Freedman, M. H. (1966). Professional responsibility of the criminal defense lawyer: The three hardest questions. *Michigan Law Review,* 64, 1469–1484.

Gewirth, A. (1986). Professional ethics: The separatist thesis. *Ethics, 96,* 282–300.

Herodotus. (1972). *The histories* (A. Selincourt & A. R. Burn, Trans.). Harmonsworth, UK: Penguin.

Hume, D. (1978; orig. pub. 1739–1740). *A treatise of human nature* (P. H. Nidditch, Ed.). Oxford: Oxford University Press.

Kant, I. (1959; orig. pub. 1785). *Foundations of the metaphysics of morals* (L. W. Beck, Trans.). Indianapolis: Bobbs-Merrill.

Locke, J. (1960; orig. pub. 1690). *Two treatises of government* (P. Laslett, Ed.). Cambridge: Cambridge University Press.

MacIntyre, A. (1984). *After virtue* (2d ed.). Notre Dame, IN: University of Notre Dame Press.

Mackie, J. L. (1977). *Ethics: Inventing right and wrong.* Harmonsworth, UK: Penguin.

Marx, K. (1987; orig. pub. 1844). On the Jewish question. In J. Waldron (Ed.), *Nonsense upon stilts: Bentham, Burke and Marx on the rights of man.* London: Methuen.

Murdoch, I. (1993). *Metaphysics as a guide to morals.* London: Penguin.

Pincoffs, E.G. (1986). *Quandries and virtues: Against reductivism in ethics.* Lawrence, KS: University of Kansas Press.

Pojman, L. P. (1988). A critique of ethical relativism. In L. P. Pojman (Ed.), *Ethical theory: Classical and contemporary readings.* Belmont, CA: Wadsworth, 24–32.

Wilson, J. Q. (1995). *The moral sense.* New York: Free Press.

Chapter 3

DEVIANCE AS CRIME, SIN, OR POOR TASTE

Alexander B. Smith
Harriet Pollack

Not all stable societies are "good" societies, but surely all "good" societies are stable. Throughout human history, philosophers have tried to define the nature of the good society but while there have been as many definitions as there have been philosophers, one element of any good society has to be stability—stability, which maximizes predictability in life, and minimizes disruption and misfortune. Without stability the unforeseen is just around the corner. The degree of stability in society rests on the degree of consensus from its members on its laws and mores. Such consensus is not easy to build and never in human history has every person agreed on the correctness of every mode of conduct, but when *most* people in a group agree, then social arrangements can be said to be reasonably stable. (Enforce consensus, as in a police state, is actually inherently unstable over long periods of time.) The smaller the group, the easier it is to reach consensus. The appropriate way of behaving is easier to establish in a hamlet than in a metropolis, but even in hamlets, or for that matter even in nuclear families, there almost inevitably is dissent. When that dissent is carried over into behavior that is unacceptable, we call such conduct deviant. What is deviance? When does it become so dangerous that it threatens the society, large or small, in which it arises? When should that society take action? When should deviance be tolerated? Is deviance ever beneficial?

Superficially, it is very easy to define deviance. A deviant person is one who does something we would not do. He is an outsider, one who is outside the consensus of what constitutes proper conduct. The problem is that from someone's point of view we are all outsiders in one respect or another. Discussions of deviance, therefore, really turn on searches for universals, for modes of conduct that all human societies consider unacceptable. Such unacceptability is frequently defined as immorality, and sometimes, in extreme cases, as crime. In the classroom, anthropology professors like to upset their students by pointing out that there are no such universally disapproved modes of conduct. Even a killing that we would consider murder is acceptable in some societies: infanticide was common in Sparta as was deliberate starvation of old people by Eskimos. In actuality, however, assaultive acts against the person or someone else's property, such as murder, assault, rape, and robbery, are considered taboo in almost all human societies, and people who perform such acts are clearly deviant, and usually criminal. These acts, however, constitute only a tiny fraction of all the modes of conduct that our own and other societies have from time to time labeled as wrong.

If today we were to ask a middle-class, middle-aged, white American man what kinds of acts (outside of assaultive crime) he considered deviant, he might respond as follows:

Being a homosexual; reading dirty books or seeing pornographic movies; going to prostitutes; engaging in sex outside of marriage; having illegitimate children (especially if the children wind up on welfare).

Using drugs, not prescription drugs or over-the-counter items like Alka Seltzer or Geritol or vitamin E, but heroin, LSD, and pep pills.

Drinking too much; eating enough to make you fat; smoking cigarettes (maybe); smoking marijuana (positively).

Not taking care of your obligations; being lazy or shiftless; losing more money than you can afford at gambling; swearing and using bad language publicly.

If we accept this list as typical, it is as interesting for the conduct it omits as for that which it includes. Many acts which once were or now are attacked as highly immoral are not even mentioned: for example, contraception, abortion, and sexual and racial discrimination. Our Everyman also seems unconcerned about profiteering, sharp dealing, tax evasion, consumer fraud, and other kinds of white-collar crime. To be sure, if questioned specifically about these unmentioned acts, he would disapprove of all of them (except probably contraception), but the term deviant conduct would not bring them immediately to mind.

The reason for our Everyman's perceiving deviance selectively lies in our description of Everyman: middle-class, middle-aged, male and white. From where he stands, some acts affect his world adversely, others have little effect, and some are simply irrelevant. He doesn't care especially about racial or sexual discrimination because he is neither black nor female. He believes in sexual regularity because he is a family man and his world is stabilized by the nuclear families of his friends and neighbors. Furthermore, illegitimacy (as he sees it) is a direct and undeserved burden on taxpayers like him because of its effect on the welfare rolls. On the other hand contraception doesn't seem wrong to him since his middle-class status probably depends on his success in limiting the size of his family. Even abortion has much to be said for it, since anyone can get into trouble even in the best of families, and anyway maybe abortion will keep some of those babies off welfare. He doesn't worry too much about tax evasion because he is not aware of the activities of large-scale tax evaders, such as giant corporations and wealthy individuals whose accountants and tax lawyers have created tax shelters for them; and small scale tax evasion is probably a fairly common and socially acceptable activity in his milieu. Sharp dealings (such as exploitative landlord-tenant or seller-consumer transactions) are not unheard of as a middle-class way of making a living; and in any case, most middle-class persons are able to cope with dishonest landlords or tradesmen. On the other hand, persons who take or sell drugs are enormously threatening, both because drug use frequently leads to assaultive or dangerous criminal conduct and because drug addicts threaten the stability of the social system by their aberrant attitudes toward work and other social obligations. In fact, if there is one thread that runs though the fabric of Everyman's scheme of desirable social conduct, it is the desire to maintain stability, to preserve the status quo. As a member of the middle class, he has made it, and he recognizes that life is as good for him as it is ever likely to be. He doesn't want to lose what he has. Change is threatening and makes him very uncomfortable.

The laundry list of unacceptable conduct varies with the age and status of the person compiling it. Inner city blacks, for example, might list racial discrimination and not list gambling at all. Marijuana smoking might be quite acceptable to middle-class university students, but tax evasions, sharp dealing and profiteering would be high on their list of forbidden conduct. In the Bible Belt of the Deep South, blasphemy, secularism, and atheism are still heinous offenses, yet relatively free use of firearms, moonshining, and blatant racial discrimination are regarded with considerable tolerance.

Obviously, deviance is to some extent in the eye of the beholder, but only to some extent. All classes and status groups reject violent assaultive crime. They differ, however, in respect to other types of unacceptable conduct, some of which in our system are illegal, some of which are immoral, and some of which are merely displays of poor taste. In considering these widely varying perceptions of what constitutes deviant conduct, we must ask not who is right and who is wrong but what kinds of conduct society can tolerate and still exist as a viable society and what kinds it cannot accept. Part of the answer to this basic question must lie in one's perception of a desirable society. For purposes of this discussion we are assuming an ideal closely akin to the traditional Jeffersonian model: an open society predicated on a belief in equality of opportunity and equality before the law, with a reasonable level of material comfort and economic security for all. In such a society, what kinds of behavior are necessarily out of bounds? In this connection, we propose to discuss three categories of conduct: crime, sin, and actions that are in poor taste.

DEVIANCE: CRIME

Clearly, heading the list are murder, rape, arson, assault, robbery, burglary, and larceny, acts which are totally unacceptable and which can be condoned, if at all, only under very special circumstances. We label these acts *crimes*, meaning that their violation of the public order is so severe that they must be handled punitively and coercively by the police, courts, and prisons. Even those who commit them agree that this type of conduct is wrong. A housebreaker does not want his own house to be burglarized and, except in Robin Hood legends, robbers do not argue that what they do is legitimate. Revolutionaries, however, who do rob, assault and kill, consider this conduct legitimate precisely because it destabilizes society, but this type of conduct is taboo if social stability is the goal. The control of such conduct, indeed, is one of the central problems faced throughout history by philosophers who have attempted to construct model societies. Whatever their point of view and whatever type of Utopia they have created, they all agree at least that this type of act must be forbidden. While Hobbes and Locke, for example, differed radically in their perceptions of the fundamental nature of man and in their prescriptions for social control of human conduct, they agreed that the principal difficulty in human society is controlling violent assault by one individual against another.

However, assaultive conduct is only one category of crime. So-called "white-collar" crime, while nonviolent, is basically an attack on legitimate property arrangements in society. Acts such as tax fraud, stock manipulations, commercial bribery, misrepresentation in advertising and salesmanship, short weighting and misgrading of commodities, embezzlement, etc., are all methods of obtaining money or other property illegitimately. Since the function of an economic system is to prescribe how one may properly obtain property, white-collar criminals are subversive of accepted economic relationships. As such, like their more violent criminal counterparts, they are a threat to a viable society and it is reasonable that their acts be included in the penal codes, although the social stigma (and usually the penalties) for these crimes is far less than for violent crimes.

Basically our law is ambivalent. Property crimes are crimes, but they are not really heinous if they are not violent or potentially violent. Far less ambivalence in regard to so-called economic crimes was exhibited in the Soviet Union during the Stalinist period, when some offenses of this type, such as currency manipulation, were punishable by death sentences whereas certain kinds of homicide were treated relatively leniently. This probably reflected the orientation of the legal system toward preservation of the Soviet economic and social order rather than, as in this country, protection of individual rights. From this point of view, the inconsistency of the American system, which punishes personal crimes more severely than property crimes, is understandable.

Whatever our ambivalence, however, it is clear that nonviolent crimes of property must be handled punitively, at least to the extent necessary to maintain the legitimacy of both our property arrangements and our system of law. The latent admiration of Americans for robber baron types may never disappear from the culture. Nevertheless, if business dealings are to be conducted in an orderly way and if prohibitions on assaultive crimes are to be taken seriously, there must be reasonable enforcement of the law relating to white collar offenses. Stock fraud and manipulation of the stock market seriously affect a good part of the population, especially since investing in the stock market is widespread and many workers' pensions are invested in stocks.

Our penal law, thus, contains prohibitions against both assaultive crimes against persons and property and nonassaultive crimes against property. Assaultive crimes offend our notions of the natural justice; nonassaultive property crimes undermine the economic arrangements that are basic to the stability of society. In the past however, the penal codes frequently contained punishment for a number of modes of conduct that were included because of a parochial cultural determination that they were immoral: swearing, drinking, gambling, homosexuality, doing business on Sunday, prostitution, contraception, abortion, etc. At the time these prohibitions were enacted, the particular legislative majority which enacted them doubtless felt they were preventing subversion of the legitimate social system. We still have many "morals" laws on the books, though fewer than in earlier times, but many of these regulations are both inconsistent and incomplete. Prostitutes are punished but not their customers; heroin is forbidden but not amphetamines; it is permissible to bet on a race but not on a football game, etc. With the exception of laws relating to certain drugs—heroin, cocaine, LSD and marijuana—most morals laws seem to be withering away.

DEVIANCE: SIN

Some modes of conduct that our middle class Everyman thinks are deviant are *not* regulated by law. Many of these modes of conduct were originally thought of as sin and were *religiously* prohibited. Our use of secular law to regulate them is a relic of the time when the authority of the state was used to enforce the rules of an established church. That era is past, but we can see our cultural heritage most clearly, perhaps, in the laws we inherited from the Puritan theocracy in New England. We had, in the past, laws against blasphemy, obscenity, contraception, Sabbath breaking, extramarital sexual relations, lewdness, homosexuality, gambling, and drunkenness. We have also inherited a distrust of self-indulgence and hedonism: even a rich man is expected to be constructively, if not gainfully, employed.

This heritage reflects a culture in which religion once was dominant. As our culture has changed, as religion has waned in importance, as our economic system has developed, as scientific discoveries have occurred, and as improved communications and the development of the mass media have reduced both social and cultural isolation, our feelings about what constitutes sin that is punishable by law, have undergone a marked change. Some behavior once regarded as sinful has become virtually acceptable today, for example, blasphemy; some, like heroin use, is still taboo. About other forms of conduct such as gambling, drinking, homosexuality, and abortion, we have ambivalent feelings. Some of this conduct is still subject to criminal sanction; some is not. If we remove the religious component, the criterion for whether the conduct in question should be forbidden should rest on whether *there is any demonstrable, objectively measurable social harm resulting from it.* To determine this, we must separately consider and evaluate each mode of conduct. In a totally rational world we would expect to find a correlation between the prohibition of conduct and its objective harmfulness. But this is not a totally rational world and the correlation frequently does not exist.

Of all the modes of conduct in this culturally determined category, drinking is probably the most harmful and also one of the most widely accepted. Alcohol is involved in at least half of all fatal automobile accidents, a majority of private airplane crashes, thousands of industrial accidents, millions of lost person-days annually, etc. We have in this country approximately 12,000,000 alcoholics who are unable to support their families, do their jobs, or function normally in the community. Alcohol use is involved in 55 percent of the arrests made by the police. From a medical point of view, furthermore, even moderate drinking puts a strain on the liver and complicates many maladies. Yet alcohol consumption is widely accepted today in the United States, where nondrinkers constitute only a small minority of the population. Historically, the temperance movement waxed and waned in strength for over a century before it culminated in the "noble experiment" of Prohibition in 1920. However, within a few years after enactment of the Eighteenth Amendment, it became apparent that Prohibition was a disaster and, since the repeal in 1933, the temperance movement appears to be all but moribund. Thus, drinking has been handled both coercively and noncoercively. Contrary to what was predicted, not only has our current noncoercive approach had fewer adverse effects in the form of enforcement difficulties and police corruption, but public attitudes toward excessive drinking are changing. Consider the campaign of groups like MADD (Mothers Against Drunk Driving), increased enforcement of the DWI rules, and the emphasis on designated drivers who forego drinking to act as a chauffeur for those who do. There has also been a substantial drop in the consumption of hard liquor in favor of beer and wine.

Even more permissive than our attitudes toward drinking are our feelings about cigarette smoking and overeating. The medical evidence against both smoking and obesity is overwhelming but to forbid them by law would be ludicrous, a civil liberty horror. Even attempts to regulate cigarette advertising have met with great resistance. Again, however, the noncoercive approach to eliminate cigarette smoking has resulted in a substantial drop in smoking among adults. Obesity, however, is an unsolved problem, probably because its physiological causes are not well understood scientifically.

The use of drugs, however, is still both illegal and socially taboo, at least publicly. In contrast to drinking, smoking, and overeating, however, there is relatively little medical evidence of physiological harm from reasonable heroin consumption. That many heroin or marijuana users exhibit undesirable psychological symptoms is undoubtedly true. It is not clear, however, whether these symptoms are a result of drug use or whether both drug use and behavioral dysfunction result from a prior existing pathological, psychological, or sociological condition. Most of the other adverse sociological effects of drug use, such as crime and prostitution, result from our present coercive handling of the drug problem rather than from drug use *per se*. Yet few modes of conduct are looked upon with more social disapproval than heroin use and only recently has a similar attitude toward marijuana been softening. Moreover, in certain respects our method of handling drug use has been precisely opposite from our handling of alcohol: alcohol, formerly handled punitively, is now handled nonpunitively; opiates and marijuana, formerly handled nonpunitively, are now handled punitively. Neither punitive handling nor extreme social disapproval has resulted in a decline (or even a stabilization) of the number of marijuana and heroin users in the United States. In 1972, there were thought to be in the United States about 300,000 addicts of whom 150,000 were in New York City. Twenty-five years later the estimates had almost doubled: 500,000 addicts in the United States, with 250,000 in New York City.

In contrast to our attitudes toward alcohol and drug use, which have fluctuated between acceptance and rejection, our attitude toward deviant sexual conduct has become consistently more permissive. During the eighteenth and nineteenth centuries in this country, man-woman relationships reflected a society that placed high value on premarital chastity and monogamy. Divorce was frowned upon, and premarital dalliance (except possibly for young men who were sowing their 'wild oats') was strictly taboo. Prostitution, at least from the middle-class point of view, was considered degrading and abhorrent, and the fallen woman became a stock figure in literature. In the same period, homosexuality was considered so dreadful that there was no public discussion of the subject, and except for some very guarded indirect references, no literary mention of the problem. Today we are permissive in regard to premarital sex, we permit divorce, we have ambivalent attitudes toward prostitution, and we are slowly coming to a grudging acceptance of homosexual conduct. Some of these attitudinal changes have been reflected in changes in either the criminal law or its application; others have not. Nevertheless, few people would dispute the proposition that our attitudes toward sexual conduct have changed substantially even if the conduct in question has not. To understand this phenomenon one must appreciate that the older rules for sexual conduct were drawn up in a society which had vastly different needs: until the twentieth century the need was for more population rather than less; venereal disease was an uncontrollable plague; and production of goods and services was directly dependent on the family in a way that no longer exists. Medical knowledge and technology have turned the older rationale for monogamous units upside down. One hundred years ago, a couple might have to produce ten or twelve children to be certain that five or six would survive them; today the parents of two can reasonably expect to raise both to adulthood. Formerly children represented a source of income and social security for one's old age; today children are economic liabilities at least until they reach adulthood, and sometimes even longer. In the face of these substantial changes, it is understandable that many of the older rules of sexual conduct are anachronistic. This is not to say that our commitment to monogamous union (so called 'family values') as the basis of family structure has diminished. Nor does it mean that actual sexual practices (as opposed to the accepted social standard for what those practices should be) have changed very much. What it means is that deviation from these sexual norms is accepted more readily and less fearfully than before. We are not so hysterically defensive about our rules of sexual conduct because we no longer regard deviations from them as subversive of the entire social order. We no longer need a strict sexual code to provide for population maintenance or growth, industrial or agricultural production, or prophylaxis against rampant venereal disease. We adhere to our family structure, and hence our sexual code, not so much to meet societal needs as to fulfill our own: the achievement of personal happiness and an optimal setting in which to raise children. Under these circumstances the desire of some individuals to find personal happiness through premarital sex, homosexuality, prostitution, etc., becomes less terrifying and is, if not acceptable, at least understandable.

Gambling, however, is a mode of conduct which probably has come closest of all to shedding the stigma of immorality inherited from the past. American attitudes toward gambling have always been ambivalent. Even in Puritan times we find mention of gaming and lotteries at the same time churches were exhorting against such worldly pleasures. Gradually, however, our attitudes have softened, probably because of the general relaxation of the personal standards of behavior and possibly because of the possibilities of relief for the hard-pressed taxpayer through state-sponsored lotteries. In any case, at the present time, not only have many states legalized gambling, but increasingly the criminal justice system is refusing to use its resources to enforce antigambling laws. The police protest openly at the futility of picking up small-time gamblers that are prosecuted and handled by the courts perfunctorily and with minimal penalties. The change in public opinion, the negative attitudes of police and prosecutors toward gambling law enforcement, and general awareness that *illegal* gambling is a major source of income for organized crime have combined to hasten the repeal of most gambling statutes. There is virtually no effective interest group in the United States today, that advocates the retention of gambling laws. Apparently, legislative repeal where it is still needed, is retarded only by public apathy and the fear of criticism by zealots.

DEVIANCE: POOR TASTE

In contrast to acts which are crimes or sins, are actions that are matters of taste and which, even when disapproved, are rarely regulated by law. Manners and style fall within this category. Pants on women were once an object of scandal; girls' bobbed hair in the 1920s was viewed as dubiously as boy's long hair in the 1960s. In Puritan New England, it was a misdemeanor for a man and a woman to kiss in public even if they were married; today, we think nothing of more overt expressions of affection although we become increasingly offended as the conduct becomes more explicitly sexual. Adults smile benignly at little Boy Scouts and Girl Scouts in their uniforms, but glare at black-jacketed Hell's Angels and similarly dressed members of black and Hispanic youth gangs. French men may kiss each other heartily; American men may not. It is all right to wear a cross or a mezuzah, but a swastika armband, a hooded sheet, and a clenched fist salute are perceived with considerable hostility and, under certain circumstances, are forbidden by the authorities.

To the visitor from Mars, all of this can be very confusing. Why, for example, is it alright for an adult to appear in public wearing a skimpy bathing suit but not okay to appear in his underwear? To us, however, it is not confusing at all, although few people when pressed could rationalize all the idiosyncrasies of manners and style that go to make up taste. It is clear that to a great extent these modes of conduct are cultural accidents. Pants are no more ordained by nature for men than skirts are for women, and in some tribal societies men do wear skirts and women pants. There is nothing in the shape of a cross that necessarily suggests Christianity and nothing in the shape of the swastika that necessarily equals fascism. As a method of greeting, handshaking is neither more nor less rational than a kiss on the cheek or a deep curtsy. But while the conduct in question may be irrational, the inferences drawn from it may be highly rational. The wearing of the swastika by American fascists is a reliable indicator of a belief in racial inequality, a totalitarian system of government, etc. A man who appears in public in a woman's dress probably is sexually deviant. What we object to in these modes of conduct, therefore, is that they suggest or anticipate other actions to which we take exception. They are in a sense symbolic conduct, symbolic of some type of overt action to which there is or may be a rational objection. Thus, the objection to the swastika is an objection to fascism; and the more we object to fascism as a mode of conduct, the more we will object to the swastika. Many modes of dress are objectionable because they appear to anticipate undesirable sexual conduct: short shorts and thong bikinis on women, long hair and feminine looking clothing on men. Interpersonal conduct, modes of greeting, and communication with other people are evaluated by our interpretation of the hidden messages those modes send out. When attempts are made to change matters of manner and style, there is frequently vigorous objection simply because such changes are viewed as precedent to a change in more serious forms of nonsymbolic conduct. Opposition fades away when the symbolic conduct loses its symbolism. In Victorian times a woman who showed her ankles was freely considered 'fast,' aggressively inviting promiscuous conduct. When enough women wore short skirts without the occurrence of the undesirable sexual conduct that had been anticipated, short skirts became acceptable. The first men wearing long hair in the current style were considered to be homosexually inclined. When the majority of adolescent youths and young men adopted the fashion, long hair as a symbol of homosexuality faded.

Thus the problem in regard to matters of taste is to recognize, first of all, that they are cultural accidents and may be intrinsically quite irrational. We must also recognize, however, that such conduct is symbolic conduct and may be the surface manifestation of far more meaningful attitudes and actions. In regulating such matters of taste, then, we must know when the surface conduct is truly symbolic and when it has lost its symbolism. If the symbolism is extant and the conduct to which it refers is truly harmful, it is possible that even symbolic action may need to be regulated socially.

CONCLUSION

To sum up, deviant conduct is ubiquitous in a society such as ours. While deviance lies, to some extent, in the eye of the beholder, certain forms of conduct that are objectively and measurably harmful to the community or that violate rational institutionalized expectations are always deviant. The roots of deviance lie in sociological and psychological pressures generated within the individual by a complex set of social and biological forces, some of which may be very great. Since, however, the very notion of a free society is based on the responsibility of each individual for his own conduct, the responsibility for the control of deviant conduct lies with both the individual and the community at large. Physically coercive punishment must be used as a last resort and for the protection of the community, for it has almost no rehabilitative effect and serves only to keep the offender away from the community. The criminal process, therefore, should be reserved almost exclusively for persons who commit violent crimes or who are otherwise seriously disruptive of the peace and good order of the community. For others who are less seriously disruptive but still disturbed and disturbing, semi-coercive strategies like probation may be appropriate. Education and counseling may help. But in regard to those whose conduct harms no one but themselves, *we should let them alone*, recognizing that to some extent we are all deviants.

Chapter 4

ETHICAL CONCERNS OF A CRIMINAL DEFENSE ATTORNEY

Matthew Muraskin

One distinction, though not always crucial, that marks the practice of law as a profession is the existence of an external code of conduct, the violation of which can lead to the imposition of sanctions upon the offending lawyer. Patterned after the Code of Professional Responsibility of the American Bar Association every jurisdiction, both state and federal, has adopted some version of this Code.

While the public may perceive these codes to be the ethical norms that lawyers must adhere to, an analysis suggests that while they deal with ethical considerations they are also concerned with protecting the business of lawyers in the same fashion as any association of tradesmen. Thus, lawyers are required to be zealous advocates for their clients regardless of the amount of money paid and at the same time are enjoined not to split fees with non-lawyers. (New York Code of Professional Responsibility, 6/30/99 §1200.17). Originally the codes governed the direct conduct of lawyers and dealt with non-lawyering actions only to the extent that it bore on the individual's fitness to practice law.

Lawyers, therefore, must protect the confidences and secrets of their clients (American Bar Association Opinion 155, 1936) because such conduct relates to their fitness to engage in their profession. Recently some codes have been amended to include prohibitions on acts which would not seem to generally impact on the practice of law. And, some jurisdictions have even adopted precatory codes of civility. With regard to mandatory provisions, a lawyer can now be sanctioned for sexually harassing a client (*Matter of Bernstein*, 1997) though in context of sexual intimacy the American Bar Association's model code does not appear to specifically bar sexual relationships between lawyer and client. Strong, however, reports at least an emerging opinion that disavows such sexual relationships (Strong, 1995 301) and New York, for one, has added to its ethics code a bar to sexual intimacy between attorney and client in domestic relations cases and a general bar to requiring sex as a condition of employment or the use of coercive or intimidating means in entering sexual relations with a client. (New York Code of Professional Responsibility, 6/30/99 §1200.29-a).

Strong concludes his analysis by noting that both lawyer and client are placed in vulnerable positions vis a vis the exercise of professional judgment if the relationship is clouded by sexual intimacy. In most instances, therefore, it would be improper for an appointed criminal defense lawyer to be sexually involved with a client.

Though the argument can be made that defense attorneys should not become sexually involved with their clients, the same can be said for any profession. On this basis the relationship could be deemed ethical or not on the specifics of the individual matter as governed by the existing Codes of Responsibility without the addition of a specific ethical norm prohibiting sexual contact (Strong 1995, footnote 15).

Though the practice of law is, de facto, split into many specialties, the same code of professional responsibility applies to all attorneys whether they limit their work to corporate tax matters or the defense of individuals charged with violations of the criminal law. Indeed, though their work would appear to be antagonistic both prosecutors and criminal defense lawyers are governed by the same code of ethical conduct.

Within the criminal justice system the roles of the defense lawyer and the prosecutor are patent. Beyond the obvious, however, these adversaries have a concomitant obligation, imposed upon them by their codes of professional responsibility to protect the process.

In addition to codes of professional ethics lawyers are bound by the various statutes and regulations that govern the conduct of all members of the criminal justice system. Therefore, a lawyer is barred from knowingly using perjured testimony during a case by virtue of both the penal law and the code of professional responsibility. Thus, the violation of any law involving moral turpitude would be grounds for discipline under the various codes (American Bar Association Model Code of Professional Responsibility, 1980, DR1-102).

In measuring proper conduct for a lawyer the codes go far beyond prohibiting acts which themselves violate the law and deal with the entire gamut of his or her relationships with the client, the court, and others because lawyers see themselves as "guardian of the law" playing ". . .a vital role in the preservation of society" and therefore have an obligation to maintain the highest standard of ethical conduct (Preamble, American Bar Association Model Code of Professional Responsibility, 1980).

Outside of governmental funding of a public defender, assigned counsel, or a legal aid society, a criminal defense lawyer's relationship with a client is established with a private agreement between the two or others for the lawyer to represent the individual. In establishing this lawyer-client relationship the lawyer is ethically bound to ensure that he or she is capable of handling the matter (American Bar Association Code of Professional Responsibility Cannon 6, 1980) and that the fee for services to be rendered is a reasonable one (New York State Code of Professional Responsibility, 6/30/99 §1200.11; American Bar Association Model Code of Professional Responsibility, 1980, DR 2-106).

In order to ensure that a lawyer is competent to take on a particular case many jurisdictions have imposed continuing legal education requirements. With regard to counsel assigned by the court to represent indigent persons in criminal cases, some localities have also imposed a system of peer review and fulfillment of objective criteria before a lawyer can be admitted to various panels used to select attorneys for assignment (assigned counsel plan, Nassau County, New York). In the final analysis, however, a lawyer's capacity to handle a case is the private determination of that attorney, because, while claims of incompetent counsel are often made, the standard applied is so high that few are able to sustain their burden. Generally speaking a lawyer's actions will be held incompetent if the representation amounts to or is akin to a sham and a mockery (*Strickland v. Washington*, 1984).

In making an incompetency determination courts tend to conclude that the lawyer's actions were part of a thoughtout strategy rather than a manifestation of incompetence. Thus, where a defendant raised numerous instances of his counsel's inadequacy including such items as failing to assert a claim of actual innocence as well as the quality of his efforts to suppress a confession, the New York Court of Appeals, in an often cited case, held these were tactical decisions involving a difficult and innovative defense (*People v. Baldi*, 1982).

With regard to the fee, even if it is paid by someone other than the client, the lawyer's loyalty and concern must be to the client and not to the person paying the fee. (American Bar Association Model Code of Professional Responsibility, 1980, DR 5-107B). In the 1997 Boston Nanny case an au pair was charged with intentionally killing the baby she was hired to care for. The lawyers hired to defend her were selected, however, not by the defendant or her family but by the au pair agency that placed her with the family of the deceased baby. The attorney's ethical dilemma was patent. If the defendant were convicted of some form of negligent homicide, the agency that hired him might be liable to the parents of the baby for failing to exercise due care in selecting, training, and placing the defendant. An acquittal or conviction of an intentional homicide would eliminate the agency's liability for any act of the defendant. Therefore, when the defense lawyer argued against a lesser charge of manslaughter (a crime involving negligence) being submitted by the court to the jury the ethical question arose as to whether he made the application based upon his analysis of the case or out of some loyalty to the company paying his fee.

Though the record is silent on this matter one would presume the attorney recognized the dilemma and made full disclosure to his client so that she could be aware of the problem and make an informed decision as to whether to continue with that lawyer.

In selecting a lawyer, many prospective clients feel their attorney would work harder for them if the fee was conditioned upon the result; similar to the contingent fee arrangement in a negligence case. An argument can be made in support of this point as well for the proposition that it allows greater access to counsel for people with limited means. The ethical dilemma, however, as to whether the lawyer is working in the best interest of his client or merely doing what is necessary to protect his fee has been taken away from counsel. The determination has been made that a contingent fee in a criminal case is forbidden because of policy concerns of "corrupting justice" and practically on the grounds that a criminal case does not produce a *res* from which the fee can be paid (American Bar Association Model Code of Professional Responsibility, 1980, DR 2-106(c) and Ethical Consideration EC2-20). It should be noted, however, that although a lawyer can be disciplined for taking a criminal case on a contingency, a conviction of a defendant would not be subject to a *per se* reversal unless actual prejudice can be demonstrated (*People v. Winkler*, 1998).

The question arises, however, as to whether this is truly a matter of morality or a policy decision that is lawyer generated. See, for example, Restatement of Contracts, 542(2) NYS Bar Opinion 412 (1975). Contingent fee arrangements between lawyer and client in negligence cases are not subject to prohibition by the Codes of Professional Responsibility. Distinguishing between criminal (and domestic relations) matters on the availability of a *res* to pay the fee may be too fine, for the *res* usually exists only because a third party—an insurance company—is available to pay a judgment. As for the policy argument there does not appear to be empirical support that contingent fees in criminal cases are detrimental to either lawyers or the public.

For the most part criminal defense lawyers have not chafed under the prohibition regardless of whether such acceptance is ethically wrong because the very nature of the work makes it more than unlikely that a lawyer would accept a case on a contingency. (MacKinnon, 1964).

In agreeing to take on a case a lawyer must also be concerned with the problem of multiple defendants. The United States Supreme Court has held that absent a searching inquiry on the part of a trial judge to make sure the several defendants are aware of the situation a lawyer should not take on the task of representing more than one defendant charged with the same crime. (*Glasser v. United States*, 1941); see also American Bar Association Model Code of Professional Responsibility, 1980, DR 5-105). The reasons for this rule are fairly straightforward. A lawyer has an obligation to furnish her singular loyalty to her client and that obligation is not lessened by the fact that she may have multiple clients in the same case. The problem then is what to do if the interests of each client are antagonistic to the other. In a drug case each of two clients could claim that the other was the seller that entrapped him or her into buying the prohibited substance. In such a circumstance the lawyer has an obligation to be loyal to each client but in fact can be loyal to neither. The better course would be to avoid the issue and not take on the problem of multiple defendants at all (American Bar Association Code of Professional Responsibility, Ethical Consideration EC5-15, 1980). A similar scenario arises when a lawyer's client in one matter turns out to be an informant to the prosecution on other cases in which the attorney is counsel. Again, the lawyer is bound to use information known about one client to defend her other one but at the same time she is forbidden to do so.

Since the ethical dilemma of dual loyalty cannot be resolved, the lawyer should withdraw. The obligation to withdraw may even go to both cases as the attorney's loyalty does not terminate at the end of her representation.

In dealing with ethics and morality *vis a vis* Codes of Lawyers professional responsibility it sometimes appears that the two are not necessarily defined the same way as in Chapter 1, In preparing his or her case a defense lawyer is free to attempt to speak with anyone whom he or she thinks will be of assistance in the case. This includes the complaining witness and any other person who plans to testify for the prosecution. The only bar is that the individuals need not speak and cannot be compelled to do so. While the prosecution may tell a witness that he or she does not have to talk to the defense lawyer, the prosecutor may not prohibit the encounter. Despite the apparent freedom to speak with anyone the defense lawyer wishes to, the Codes of Professional Responsibility generally forbid the lawyer to speak with a co-defendant or other person who is presently represented by counsel in the same matter (American Bar Association Model Code of Professional Responsibility, 1980, DR 7-104). New York, however, in June 1999, modified its rules to allow a lawyer to cause his client to communicate with a represented person provided the lawyer gives notice to his adversary. (New York State Code of Professional Responsibility, 6/30/99 § 1200.35(b)).

In discussing matters in terms of right and wrong this rule seems grounded in protecting a lawyer's turf rather than in some moral principal. In practical terms a lawyer representing a person charged with robbery cannot speak with the co-defendant without the permission of the co-defendant's lawyer even if the co-defendant wants to exonerate his client and state that he was not involved. A troublesome aspect of the rule is that its violation does not lead to a suppression of the statement obtained. Thus, if the lawyer for the robbery co-defendant gets a statement from the other defendant exonerating his client and inculpating himself, the lawyer may be subject to a grievance proceeding or a possible suit for damages. The prohibition, however, does not extend to a defendant acting on his or her own to get a statement from a co-defendant. A lawyer, therefore, can use a statement obtained by his client from the co-defendant without any fear of being sanctioned so long as he or she was not party to its solicitation. This area becomes murky because a defendant who obtains an exonerating statement from the co-defendant more often than not gets the statement by intimidating the co-defendant and then gets separately charged with that offense.

A defense lawyer, as is the case with all lawyers, is charged with keeping the secrets and confidences of his client. (American Bar Association Model Code of Professional Responsibility, 1980, Cannon 4). This is more commonly known as the lawyer-client privilege. Clergymen, physicians, and certain other health care providers are also covered by a "privilege," though, unlike lawyers, theirs is statutory only. Privilege granted to attorneys is grounded in the right to counsel and therefore has a constitutional dimension. The lawyer's privilege is not absolute and in reality belongs to the client and not the attorney.

Under the terms of the lawyer-client privilege, a lawyer may not reveal present or past acts confided to him by the client as part of their professional relationship. If in the course of the representation a client confesses to murder and tells the lawyer where he buried the victim, the attorney is duty bound to reveal neither the murder nor the whereabouts of the body. However, if the client advises his lawyer that he plans to rob a bank sometime in the future, the privilege does not attach and the lawyer is in the same legal and moral predicament as any other person in deciding whether to report the possible future crime, though there is a 1965 ethics opinion by the American Bar Association (Opinion 314) which states the attorney must disclose that confidence if the facts that the lawyer has, indicate, beyond a reasonable doubt, that the client will be committing a crime.

The lawyer-client privilege is really not an issue of ethics or morality. Rather, it is a lawyer generated rule designed to promote candor between a client and his counsel.

The argument runs that a lawyer can do his or her job only if the client is 100% truthful and candid. But, unless a client was assured of the confidential nature of the discussion, few would be either completely truthful or candid.

While the rule itself is grounded in neither ethics nor morality its application may greatly impact upon the public sense of right and wrong. In the example given above, a lawyer who learns from his client that he killed a person and buried the body in some isolated locale must, on pain of being sanctioned keep that matter secret regardless of the torment to the grieving family worrying about the location and status of their missing relative. A lawyer who learns from his client that he rather than another is guilty of some crime or misdeed must keep that revelation to himself even if that other is wrongly imprisoned for a crime he did not commit.

Since the privilege belongs to the client, not the lawyer, the client may waive it. If the client waives the privilege, the lawyer can no longer assert it on the client's behalf. In the murder case mentioned before if the client tells the police he killed the particular individual and left a note with his lawyer stating where the body was buried, the lawyer could not resist turning over the note to the police on the grounds that it was a privileged communication between himself and his client.

Whatever problems there may be with regard to a lawyer's client no such issue exists *vis a vis* a witness; and it is both illegal and immoral for a lawyer to knowingly use perjured testimony or otherwise suborn perjury. This, however, does not answer the question of witness preparation. On occasion, a witness may be asked on cross examination if he or she has spoken to counsel prior to the giving of testimony. Rather than saying yes, some witnesses feel there is something wrong with having gone over the testimony in advance and equivocate in their response and sometimes even falsely deny the preparation. There is, however, nothing wrong with preparing a person to give testimony and few lawyers would put a witness on the stand without first knowing what that individual is going to testify to. The larger issue is whether the lawyer prepared the witness or put words in his or her mouth. It is perfectly proper for a defense lawyer to refresh a witness' memory if he or she cannot remember the occurrence and then to focus the individual's attention on the salient points that are important to the case.

In a bank robbery case where the issue is the identification of the defendant, a witness with faulty memory could be refreshed by reference to prior statements about the case made by him or her or others. Indeed, even visual aids with regard to the scene could be shown to refresh the recollection of what happened and then the witness could be focused on the all important issue of whether he or she saw the defendant commit the crime and test the ability to make an identification by reference to the surroundings such as lighting, face coverings, and disguises and even the time necessary to make an identification. The crucial ethical distinction is to prepare without putting words in the witness' mouth. Indeed, many lawyers make the witness aware that he may be asked if there was discussion prior to the testimony and to say "yes" if so asked and then to respond, if asked what he or she was told to say, as is the case, "I was told to tell the truth".

While prosecutors may not use perjured testimony at all, defense lawyers who practice under the same restrictions have the additional problem of what to do when the client intends to take the witness stand and commit perjury.

The present debate over anticipated perjury probably began with Monroe Freedman's lecture to the Criminal Law Institute in 1966 when he advised defense lawyers to present their client's anticipated perjured testimony in the same way as any other (McCarthy and Brook, 1995, p. 164). Opposition was immediate and widespread and included former Chief Justice Warren Burger (Burger, 1996, p. 11).

The issue arises because of the convergence of several different ethical norms. A criminal defense lawyer must, as any lawyer, be loyal to his client (American Bar Association Model Code of Professional Responsibility, 1980, Cannon 7) and preserve his confidence (American Bar Association Model Code of Professional Responsibility, 1980, Cannon 4) as part of his "...overarching duty to advocate the defendant's cause" (*Strickland v. Washington*, 1984). However, as an officer of the court, the attorney has the obligation not to allow or assist in fraudulent or criminal acts (American Bar Association Model Code of Professional Responsibility, Ethical Consideration 7-5, 1980). While a criminal defendant may have a right to testify, the Supreme Court has held that right does not extend to testifying falsely. (*Nix v. Whiteside*, 1986).

Though anticipated client perjury is often discussed by academics, no clear answer as to what a lawyer should do has as yet emerged (McCarthy & Brook, 1995, p. 164).

Freedman notes that the American Bar Association Model Rules of Professional Conduct 3.3 appear to require defense attorneys to reveal anticipated client perjury to the court but the wording of the rule then undercuts the position by holding the lawyer must maintain confidentiality unless he "knows" the client is committing perjury. But as the standard for determining "knowing" is so high, it is only in the rarest of cases that a lawyer will have to come to grips with the issue (Freedman, 1995, p. 141).

Despite academic preoccupation with the perjury issue, practicing defense attorneys rarely face the dilemma. (McCarthy & Brooks, 1995, p. 148). Anecdotal evidence from the 48 lawyers at the Nassau County New York Legal Aid Society as well as members of the bar in the Nassau & Suffolk County area indicate the problem of anticipated client perjury is a nonissue because the few clients who plan to commit perjury do not take their lawyers into their confidence either in advance or after the fact.

In dealing with the opposite issue of past perjury most jurisdictions require the lawyer to reveal the fraud to the tribunal or effected person provided the information "clearly" establishes the fact and the information is not protected as a confidence or secret (New York Code of Professional Responsibility, 6/30/99, §1200.33(b)). As with anticipated perjury the codes of professional conduct provide no really clear guide as to what the lawyer should do so that the lawyer, though subject to possible sanctions for his acts, must make his decision on the basis of his own ethical norms.

Another concern of the criminal lawyer is what to do if she believes the witness she is about to cross-examine has testified to the truth.

For the prosecutor the answer is relatively easy. If the witness has testified to an ultimate fact bearing on the innocence of the defendant the lawyer may have to re-think the reason for the prosecution (New York Code of Professional Responsibility, 6/30/99, §1200.34).

While the general public might think this places a defense counsel in an ethical quandary most lawyers would not. First, the lawyer has to question whether he or she really "knows" the witness is telling the truth. As was seen with anticipated perjury the standard for determining what is "known" is very high. It may be, therefore, that the lawyer's "knowledge" of the truth is really not unequivocal. Second, and probably more important, is that in a criminal case the defendant is presumed innocent, with the burden of proof being with the prosecution to establish guilt beyond a reasonable doubt. Defense counsel as part of his ". . .overarching duty to advocate his client's case" puts the prosecution to its proof by testing the veracity and accuracy of a witness without regard to his own belief.

In the same vein most lawyers face no ethical dilemma in representing individuals whom they believe to be guilty. First, the same principles mentioned in client perjury and cross-examination of truthful witnesses apply. Second, in cases where the lawyer has the option of turning down a matter, she is enjoined to put aside her personal feelings and not refuse the representation because of hostility in the community or the unpopularity of the cause. (American Bar Association Code of Professional Responsibility, Ethical Considerations EC 2-27, 1980).

In simplistic terms, a person charged with a criminal offense is entitled to the assistance of counsel and an attorney who undertakes the representation is just doing her job. More often than not, an individual who questions the lawyer's ethics in representing a person whom she believes to be guilty fails to appreciate the distinction between litigant and lawyer; and that whatever taint attaches to the accused does not rub off on the attorney. Indeed, when a lawyer is appointed to represent an individual who is unable to retain counsel because of indigency or other reasons, she should not seek to avoid the representation unless there are compelling reasons which do not include the ". . .repugnance of the subject matter" or the lawyer's belief that the client is guilty. (American Bar Association Code of Professional Responsibility, Ethical Considerations 2-29, 1980).

In essence, a criminal defense lawyer in the practice of his or her profession is faced with the same ethical problems as would anyone else engaged in other activities. In addition, a lawyer is faced with particular ethical dilemmas imposed by the strictures of the profession. In resolving the ethical dilemmas the codes of conduct promulgated by the bar are not always the clear-cut guides that they would seem to be. In the final analysis, the defense lawyer must conduct himself or herself in an ethical manner based upon principles of morality already learned over his or her lifetime.

REFERENCES

American Bar Association. (1980). *Model Code of Professional Responsibility*. Chicago, IL: Author.

Burger, Warren. (1966). Standards of conduct for prosecution and defense personnel: A judge's viewpoint 5. *American Law Quarterly 11*.

Disciplinary Rules of the Code of Professional Responsibility Amending New York State Code of Responsibility, effective 6/30/99.

Freedman, Monroe H. (1995). But only if you "know." In Rodney J. Uphoff (Ed.). *Ethical problems facing the criminal defense lawyer*, Chicago, IL: American Bar Association.

MacKinnon, Fredrick B. (1964). *Contingent fees for legal services*, Chicago, IL: Albine Publishing, 52.

McCarthy, Terrence & Brook, Carol A. (1995). Anticipated client perjury truth or dare comes to court. In Rodney J. Uphoff (Ed.). *Ethical problems facing the criminal defense lawyer*, Chicago, IL: American Bar Association.

New York State Code of Professional Responsibility. (1992). *McKinney's Consolidated Laws of New York 1992*, St. Paul, MN: West.

Cases & Opinions

American Bar Association, Opinion 151, 314.

Glasser v. United States, 315 US60.

Matter of Bernstein, 237 AD2d 89 (2 Dept. NY 1997).

Nix v. Whiteside, 475 U.S. 157.

People v. Baldi, 54 NY2d 137 (1982).

People v. Winkler, 71 NY2d 592 (1998).

Strickland v. Washington, 466 US668, (1984).

Chapter 5

THE ETHICAL OBLIGATIONS OF THE CRIMINAL PROSECUTOR

Chris McDonough
Diana Brusca McDonough
Raymond G. Keenan

Prosecution is a legal proceeding, maintained in accordance with the law, and includes every phase of the undertaking from inception to conclusion. The term *prosecution* is used in law to describe both civil and criminal proceedings. However, when most people hear the word prosecution, they think of a criminal proceeding rather than civil. It is the criminal prosecution, and the prosecutor himself that this chapter will examine.

In a criminal case, prosecution is pursued by several different officials, depending on the nature of the charge. For example, local District Attorneys ordinarily prosecute most defendants charged with violating state law. At times, the state's Attorney General will prosecute certain violations of state law. If the defendant violated a federal law, the United States Attorney will prosecute the case.

The Federal Constitution imposes an obligation to provide the criminal defendant with certain rights during criminal prosecutions, whether under federal or state law. The job of assuring that criminal defendants receive their just constitutional protections falls mainly to the courts and the criminal defense attorney. Yet, the criminal prosecutor is also charged with duties and obligations running to the criminal defendant.

As we will explore in this chapter, a criminal prosecutor constantly engages in a balancing act between conflicting obligations. On the one hand, he must strongly advocate for his client, the citizenry of the community from which he is appointed or elected. On the other hand, he must also act to protect the criminal defendant's constitutional rights and fairly participate in the search for justice as well.

How did the criminal prosecutor come to be encumbered by these seemingly conflicting obligations? To answer this question, we must look at the Constitution of the United States and its impact on criminal prosecutions, examine the unique dual role fulfilled by the criminal prosecutor, and explore where and why the duties of a prosecutor differ from that of other legal advocates.

United States Constitution

The Bill of Rights, which is the first ten Amendments to the United States Constitution, provides certain protections for individual liberties. The particular provision of the Bill of Rights pertaining to a fair trial of a criminal defendant are applicable to the States under the due process clause of the Fourteenth Amendment. Due process may be thought of as "fairness." Whenever the government seeks to take away a protected liberty or right, it must provide the effected individual with an opportunity to contest the action, it must follow its own previously established rules for taking the action, and it must refrain from acting beyond the scope of its authority. The due process clause of the Fifth Amendment obligates the Federal government to provide the same due process protection in a federal prosecution. Both due process clauses mandate that a criminal defendant be afforded a fair trial. They do not, however, dictate *how* the government is to provide a fair trial.

Specifically, police may not engage in unreasonable searches and seizures (the Fourth Amendment); the defendant may not be forced to incriminate himself or be tried more than once on the same charge (the Fifth Amendment); a criminal defendant has the right to counsel, the right to a speedy public trial by an impartial jury, the right to confront witnesses who testify against him, and the right to compel witnesses to testify on his behalf (the Sixth Amendment); and the States may not engage in cruel and unusual punishment (the Eighth Amendment).

State Court Interpretation of Federal Due Process Standards

Criminal defendants are guaranteed a level of due process at least as protective as that provided in the Bill of Rights. States may provide only the guaranteed minimum level of protection or they may grant equal or greater protection to the criminal defendant than required by the Bill of Rights by enacting their own laws. They may not, however, structure or interpret their laws to offer less than the minimum level of protection required by the U.S. Constitution.

The duty to insure due process to each and every criminal defendant rests with the various participants in the criminal justice system: the police, the courts, corrections personnel, and others—including the criminal prosecutor. The due process obligations and ethical responsibilities of these other entities are discussed elsewhere in this book. In this chapter we will isolate and examine the obligations of the criminal prosecutor only. To do so we must also understand what he does and why.

THE POWER OF A CRIMINAL PROSECUTOR

Prosecution is the process through which criminal accusations are made against individuals and resolved. Essentially, the prosecutor is responsible for bringing an accused person before the court and to justice. The prosecutor alone has the power to initiate judicial action in a criminal case. Because of the great amount of power and discretion granted to him, the criminal prosecutor may be considered the most powerful player within the criminal justice system.

The power and discretion granted to him are the main reasons that the duties and obligations of the prosecutor differ in many respects from all other lawyers. This power and discretion has resulted in closer scrutiny and higher standards than those imposed on other legal advocates.

The prosecutor has the power to decide who is to be charged, or even if charges will be brought at all. He determines what crimes an accused is to be charged with, essentially setting the entire prosecution in motion and determining its course and scope.[1] By comparison, a judge may have the power to dismiss a charge under limited circumstances, or find a defendant guilty after trial, but he cannot control the decision to bring charges. That decision is the prosecutor's alone.

Because there is little actual control over the prosecutor's decision-making and exercise of discretion with regard to charging a suspect, it is easy to imagine that an unethical prosecutor would present a very great danger to society and the individuals who come within his control. Any individual suffers when charged with criminal conduct. However, an innocent person wrongly enmeshed in the criminal justice system, or a person charged with more serious crimes than her actual criminal conduct warrants, suffers undeservedly.

The founders of the United States considered it preferable to protect the innocent at any cost, even if it meant that the guilty must sometimes go free. This preference provides the rationale for the high evidentiary burdens put on prosecutors and police. To better understand the inherent danger associated with the prosecutor's boundless discretion, consider the effect of an arrest on an innocent person:

Bill, a forty year old welder and father of two young children goes out for a walk. He happens to be in the area of "Joe's Gas and Go" when it is robbed by two armed masked men, Ed and Mike. During the robbery, Joe is shot and seriously wounded.

---

[1] On serious (felony) charges, a prosecutor's decision to prosecute and which crimes he charges an accused with, will be reviewed by a Grand Jury. A Grand Jury will determine if the charges initially brought will stand as charged. However, the Grand Jury system is often perceived as less than effective because of the influence a prosecutor can have over the Grand Jury because he acts as its counsel. As skeptically stated by New York's former Chief Judge Sol Wachtler, and often quoted, a Grand Jury would indict a ham sandwich. See *People v. Carter*, 77 NY 2d 95, 107, Titone, J. dissenting (1990).

As he leaves the store, Ed takes a pack of Marlboro cigarettes off the counter. Before collapsing into unconsciousness, from which he never recovers, Joe calls 911. He informs the operator of the robbery and shooting, gives a description of the two men who committed the crime, and tells of the cigarettes which were taken.

Joe's general description of Ed also fits Bill, who is wearing the same color jacket and also has a tattoo on his left arm. A police officer, responding to the call, sees Bill in the area and stops him. The officer notes that Bill is holding a pack of Marlboro cigarettes and has a tattoo on his arm. Bill is unable to account for his actions to the officer's satisfaction and is brought in for questioning.

Despite his failure to provide any support for his claim that he was not involved, Bill is released by the police after questioning. However, the investigating detective learns from the FBI that as a young man, Bill had been twice arrested and convicted for burglary, a fact Bill failed to reveal during questioning due to embarrassment and fear. The detective communicates this information to the prosecutor. Based on the strength of the victim's description, his proximity to the crime scene and the pack of cigarettes, a decision is made to arrest Bill.

Three days after the robbery, the police arrest Bill at his home. He is handcuffed in front of his wife and children and taken to a police precinct for processing. Because the paperwork is not completed until late evening, and because of the seriousness of the crime, Bill is detained in the precinct until he can be brought to court the following morning. Bill is fingerprinted and strip-searched. His clothing and personal effects are taken from him. He is given an orange jumpsuit to wear before he is placed in the holding cell. The cell is small and crowded with others awaiting arraignment. It contains nothing but cots and a sink/toilet. The following morning Bill is transported in handcuffs to the courthouse, where he is placed into another holding cell until his case can be called in the arraignment courtroom.

At arraignment the only issue before the court is bail. Bill will probably be denied the right to contest the fact of his arrest at that time and will either enter a plea of guilty or not guilty to the charges. In a case involving charges as serious as those facing Bill, bail will either be denied or set very high. This means Bill is taken into custody by the local Sheriff and held in a local jail with others awaiting criminal process until either his bail is paid or until his next court date.

Whether released on bail or held in jail, Bill must now find a lawyer to represent him. He will have to pay a steep retainer for a competent criminal practitioner to defend him on these serious charges. He will also have to make multiple appearances in court, suffer a loss of earnings, and reveal the fact of his arrest to his employer.

As you can see, even if ultimately exonerated, the wrongfully accused has suffered personal humiliation, monetary expense, irreparable damage to his reputation and possibly to his career. His familial relationships may also have been damaged.

The potential for abuse and serious harm to those improperly accused is the reason that the power of the criminal prosecutor has been tempered by constitutional case law which restricts and penalizes improper activities of prosecutors. For example, a criminal prosecutor may not single out individuals for prosecution when others who engage in similar conduct have not been charged (selective prosecution). He must turn over to the accused exculpatory information in his possession, which is information that tends to show that the accused is not guilty of the crime charged. The prosecutor may not bring a prosecution in retaliation for other conduct. He may not charge someone twice for the same criminal conduct (double jeopardy) and he cannot make improper comments before a jury. If the prosecutor substantially violates any of the above standards, the charges will ordinarily be dismissed by the court.

While there are many constitutional controls over prosecutorial conduct once a charge is formalized, few standards exist to control the initial decision to prosecute and with which crimes to charge the defendant. The only true accountability flows from the ballot box when the prosecutor runs for election. This often results in a prosecutor striving for a reputation as a strict enforcer of the laws with a high conviction record, rather than that of a prosecutor who is concerned with the rights of criminal defendants.

The Role of The Criminal Prosecutor

Most persons unfamiliar with the criminal justice system have a specific image of a prosecutor that is influenced in large measure by television and the movies. This public perception of a prosecutor is commonly that of a crusading courtroom cowboy who will do whatever it takes to put the bad guy in jail. This common view is far from accurate. The real-life performance of the criminal prosecutor is narrowly restricted by constitutional law and ethical obligations. These restrictions demand that the prosecutor play a very different role; a role more like that of a tightrope walker than a cowboy.

Multiple Roles of the Prosecutor

The position of criminal prosecutor is more complex than that of most attorneys because of the conflicting duties he owes. The job of the criminal prosecutor can be divided into three distinct phases: the pre-trial stage, which includes the investigation, arrest, decision to prosecute, charging and arraignment; the trial stage, the finding of guilt or innocence, either by trial or plea negotiation; and the post-trial phase including sentencing, appeals, and parole.

While we examine the specific tasks performed by the criminal prosecutor, keep in mind the special role he plays and the obligations placed upon him are not applicable to other lawyers.

Investigation, Arrest, Charging and Arraignment

The Criminal Investigation

The prosecutor is considered the chief law enforcement officer in most jurisdictions and is regularly involved in criminal cases before an arrest is even made. The police may have the assistance of the prosecutor in the investigation stage prior to making a decision to arrest, a decision that will be made by the prosecutor in many serious cases.

The prosecutor is normally involved in applying to the court for search warrants or wiretaps required by the police. He may be consulted regarding a proposed police sting to determine its lawfulness and avoid an entrapment defense. He usually is consulted prior to an arrest warrant being issued. In major crimes, the prosecutor may be called to a crime scene to examine evidence in its undisturbed setting. He will help the police interpret the evidence and may assist in developing an investigatory plan designed to assure that the offender does not escape eventual justice due to police error which, if it violates a suspect's constitutional rights, may result in suppression of physical evidence or incriminating statements. A prosecutor may also be involved in the training of police officers.

The Arrest

Once an arrest is made, the criminal prosecutor must evaluate the arrest of the subject to determine if the arrest was proper and if prosecution is warranted (if he was involved in the decision to arrest as that decision was being made, this evaluation becomes unnecessary). You may wonder why the prosecutor simply cannot accept that his partners in law enforcement, the police, have made a valid arrest and let the defense attorneys worry about proving that the arrest was inappropriate. Indeed, requiring the prosecutor to examine the propriety of an arrest by the police seems to be putting the prosecutor on the defense team. This obligation appears to conflict with his duty to prosecute the 'bad guys' arrested by the police.

In fact, that is precisely what the prosecutor must do to comply with his obligation to practice law ethically. The rules governing attorney conduct state that a criminal prosecutor should not institute criminal charges when he knows or should know that the charge is not supported by probable cause to believe that the subject to be charged actually committed the crime.[2]

Think back to the circumstances of Bill's arrest. Joe provided a description of the robber that matched Bill, he was in the general area of the robbery, he had a tattoo, and he had a pack of Marlboro. Was there probable cause to believe that Bill was one of the robbers? At the time of the arrest, it was reasonable to believe that Bill was involved in the robbery. It is permissible to bring criminal charges with less evidence than is necessary to sustain a conviction, yet indictment requires more than just a mere hunch of criminality.

The Decision to Prosecute

The decision to formally charge a person for a criminal act has serious implications for the person so charged. As we saw with Bill, the decision to prosecute may have devastating societal and economic impact upon the arrested subject, who is referred to as the criminal defendant after being charged. The decision to charge is usually

---

[2]American Bar Association Model Rules of Professional Conduct, Rule 3.8; American Bar Association Model Code of Professional Responsibility, DR 7-103(A).

within the sole discretion of the prosecutor. It is here that the prosecutor has the ultimate decision-making authority, and also where the potential for abuse is greatest.

One exception to the above concerns a Grand Jury investigation.[3] In this case, the prosecutor will assist the Grand Jury in its investigation of allegations of criminality, through the coordination and presentation of witnesses, obtaining of subpoenas, and directing of police investigations. Only when a Grand Jury is empaneled to investigate a crime is the decision to prosecute not reserved for the criminal prosecutor. However, the prosecutor acts as a liaison to the Grand Jury, is the one who empanels it, and instructs it as to the law prior to any charges being brought or arrests made. While the Grand Jury alone makes the decision to prosecute and what charges to bring, it is effectively led to its decision by the prosecutor. Once they decide to indict a criminal subject and formal charges are brought, the criminal prosecutor then assumes his normal role, as if his office had brought charges after an investigation and arrest by the police.

The first, and often the most stunning impact of an arrest, is the possibility of immediate loss of liberty. Upon being arrested, the accused is usually taken into police custody and brought before the court so the court can set bail or take other steps to ensure that the defendant does not flee the jurisdiction and returns to court as required. In less serious cases, the police are permitted to issue the defendant a document that sets a court date to appear for formal charging. However, in more serious cases the police will detain the subject until he can be brought before the court to make a bail decision.

The Arraignment

The initial court appearance of an accused is at the arraignment. The purpose is to formally charge the defendant and set bail. It is at this stage that the charging document, an indictment handed down by a Grand Jury or a charging instrument drawn by the prosecutor, is presented to the defendant. In many courts, the charges are read aloud before the defendant is asked to plead to the charges. The defendant at this stage can plead guilty, plead not guilty, or stand mute.

After the plea, the judge sets bail. The court will usually ask the criminal prosecutor for a bail recommendation. The prosecutor will make his recommendation to the court on bail status based on: the defendant's roots in the local community, both economic and familial; whether there is a record of past criminal conduct and whether the defendant previously appeared in court as required; the severity of the potential punishment should the defendant be found guilty and the likelihood that the defendant might flee to avoid that punishment; and other factors that would indicate whether the defendant will return and attend court as required. He will urge that the defendant be held without bail, be released upon the deposit of a specific

---

[3]An investigatory Grand Jury differs from a Grand Jury which reviews a prosecutor's charges as discussed at footnote 1. Here the Grand Jury undertakes the task of bringing charges on serious police arrests as opposed to the more common Grand Jury empaneled to review the charges presented by the prosecutor.

sum of money (cash or bond) to secure his return (bail), or be released without bail pending the next court date.

It is unlikely that our innocent defendant Bill would receive a favorable bail recommendation from the prosecutor. In his favor, Bill is gainfully employed and has a family to support. This will make it less likely that Bill would flee the jurisdiction. On the other hand, Bill has a prior criminal record (albeit over twenty years old) and the punishment he faces if convicted is severe, and may include the death penalty. These factors argue against setting bail at all or setting the bail extremely high. In murder cases, as Bill's prosecution would be because of Joe's death, bail is ordinarily not available.

DETERMINING GUILT OR INNOCENCE

The second stage of the prosecutor's involvement is to marshal the evidence, engage in plea negotiation with the defendant, and either arrive at an acceptable plea arrangement or try the case before the court and a jury, if requested.[4]

The Evidence

The criminal prosecutor must prepare his case like any other lawyer. To the prosecutor, this usually involves collecting and examining the evidence provided by the police. However, the prosecutor has special additional obligations regarding evidence that other lawyers do not have.

The first consideration when examining evidence is a practical one: is there sufficient evidence to get a conviction? In criminal cases the prosecutor must prove his case "beyond a reasonable doubt." This is an exacting burden of proof that requires that the prosecutor prove the case to a high degree of certainty. Should the trier of fact, either judge or jury, have a reasonable doubt as to the guilt of the defendant at the close of trial, they must acquit.

If the evidence is not certain to convince a trier of fact that the defendant is guilty, the prosecutor must decide at this point if the case merits dedicating scarce resources to it; resources that might be better spent on more provable cases. Other factors to be considered in making the decision whether to proceed with the prosecution are the victim's cooperation and his attitude toward the crime, the cost of conviction compared with the severity of the crime committed, the possibility of excessive and undue harm to the offender by the prosecution, the offender's cooperation with the prosecutor in convicting other more desirable criminal actors, and the possibility that the offender will make restitution to the victim.

There is one more factor criminal prosecutors will in all likelihood consider when deciding whether there is sufficient evidence to move a case to trial—the

---

[4]In most states the right to trial by jury can be waived, except in a capital case. When a jury trial is waived, the judge decides factual issues ordinarily reserved for the jury in addition to deciding legal matters. Thus, the judge becomes the "trier of fact."

prosecutor's conviction rate. Prosecutors want to maintain a high conviction-to-loss ratio. A high conviction rate allows the prosecutor to plea bargain more effectively because defendants are less likely to take their chances against the prosecutor at trial. This, in turn, enables the prosecutor to conserve his resources and limit trial case backlogs. A high conviction rate, which includes the number of cases resolved in plea negotiations, also helps the prosecutor in getting re-elected.

Would the district attorney prosecute Bill without being absolutely certain that he was the culprit? He probably would prosecute despite the fact that the evidence used to justify Bill's arrest would ordinarily be insufficient to obtain a conviction because a jury is not likely to find "beyond a reasonable doubt" that Bill committed the crimes. Bill's acquittal would also negatively affect the prosecutor's conviction rate, another drawback.

However, when serious crimes are involved, such as armed robbery or murder, the district attorney will be more willing to dedicate resources to a less favorable case for several reasons. He may succeed in removing the defendant from society during the trial, thereby increasing public safety. Other evidence may become available before or during the trial that tends to inculpate the defendant. The defendant may decide to enter a plea bargain rather than face the uncertainty of a jury verdict. In sum, it may be advantageous to prosecute even though it is unlikely that a conviction can be obtained.

Exculpatory Evidence

One of the most important obligations of a criminal prosecutor to a defendant concerns exculpatory evidence; evidence that demonstrates, or tends to demonstrate, the defendant's innocence or that mitigates his conduct. If such evidence is within the prosecutor's control, he must turn it over to the defendant before trial even if this will aid in a defense victory. In *Brady v. Maryland* the United States Supreme Court held that suppression of exculpatory material by prosecutors is a violation of the due process rights of criminal defendants. The penalty for such violations is the setting aside of any conviction that may result. The Supreme Court held that, in order to avoid an unfair trial of the defendant, prosecutors have a generalized duty to disclose exculpatory evidence upon request of the defense. This duty affects evidence in the prosecutor's possession as well as evidence possessed by the police which was not turned over to the prosecutor.

Plea Negotiations

Once a defendant is charged, but prior to trial, the prosecutor will engage in negotiations with the defense, in an attempt to arrive at a reduced plea agreement or "plea bargain." The goal of such negotiations is to try to arrive at a compromise by reducing the charges against the defendant or recommending a reduced sentence in exchange for a plea of guilty.

The concept of the plea bargain may strike some as a gift to the defendant or a reward for not going to trial. In fact, the plea bargain is a valuable tool of the prosecutor. Obtaining a guilty plea saves the prosecutor's office many hours of attorney time. A negotiated plea moves cases more quickly than via trial and thereby reduces the backlog of cases in the system. It eliminates the formality and expense of a trial in "open and shut" cases and helps maintain a high conviction rate. Perhaps most importantly, a plea bargain saves substantial amounts of money that would have to be raised through taxes. It can also be a great help to the prosecutor when an essential element of his case is weak, either inherently or from unanticipated problems arising from witnesses or other evidence. In return, the guilty defendant usually receives a more lenient sentence, avoids a public trial, and gains a measure of certainty and control over his ultimate punishment.

Consider the actual culprits in our scenario with Bill, the innocent defendant. Assuming that Ed and Mike are eventually charged with robbery and murder, plea negotiations would offer them the best chance to decrease their punishment. If Ed was the actual shooter, Mike may have his own sentence reduced by providing testimony against Ed. The district attorney would be more likely to seek Mike's cooperation if his case against Ed is weak.

The Criminal Trial

At the trial of a criminal defendant, the prosecutor acts on behalf of the citizenry. Whether he represents a county, state, district or parish, the prosecutor represents "the people" of the political subdivision by which he is elected or appointed. At trial he presents the case against the defendant. As the prosecutor represents the charging party, the prosecutor presents his case first.

Before he begins to present any physical or testimonial evidence, the criminal prosecutor makes an opening statement. The opening statement is an address directly to the jury after the jury is selected, or to the judge in a bench trial, wherein the prosecutor outlines what he is going to prove and how. There can be no surprise proof or witnesses in a criminal prosecution. If the outline of the case against the defendant as set forth in the opening statement is not proved, the defense can move to have the charges dismissed at the end of the prosecution's evidence.

After opening statements by both sides, the prosecution presents its case to the trier of fact. This is done through the production of exhibits and the testimony of witnesses. If, at the conclusion of prosecution evidence, the prosecution has not proved *prima facie* that the defendant is guilty,[5] then the defense can move the court for a dismissal without presenting any proof at all.

After the prosecution presents its case, the defense may present evidence in its favor or may instead rely on the presumption of innocence and choose not to defend in the action. Regardless of how the defense decides to proceed, the prosecutor must prove his case beyond a reasonable doubt, as discussed earlier. If the prosecution has not met its burden of proof, to show beyond a reasonable doubt that the defendant committed the crime, the defendant must be acquitted.

Recognize that the criminal defendant has nothing to prove, in theory. He has no burden of proof whatsoever. The Constitution provides that the criminal defendant

---

[5]The evidence presented is sufficient to demonstrate guilt, if uncontradicted.

can sit mute throughout his trial, offer no testimony or other evidence, and need not even address the jury through opening or closing statements. And where a defendant does nothing on his behalf, the jury will be told that the defendant is fully within his right to do so, and the jury may not draw any negative inference from his silence. The prosecution may not even allude to the defendant's silence to help prove its case. If the prosecutor has not proved that the defendant committed the crimes with which he was charged beyond a reasonable doubt, the jury must find the defendant not guilty. The criminal arena is the only area of law where this absolute burden of proof applies.

THE POST-TRIAL PHASE

In the post-trial phase the prosecutor also has responsibilities and duties. The prosecutor is often invited to recommend a penalty range after a defendant pleads guilty or is found guilty after trial. The court has the authority to sentence convicted criminals to fines, restitution, community service, therapy, probation, home confinement, jail, and in certain states, the death penalty.

In capital cases the prosecutor must determine early on if the death penalty will be sought, and provide the defendant with notice soon after arraignment.[6] The filing of this notice advises the defendant that at the conclusion of the trial the prosecutor will argue for the death penalty if the defendant is convicted of murder in the first degree.

After a conviction for first-degree murder, the trial court will promptly conduct a separate hearing to determine if the defendant will be executed or sentenced to life without parole. The same jury that found the defendant guilty will usually hear the sentencing argument. The argument essentially encompasses whether or not there existed aggravating factors to the crime which would warrant the ultimate penalty; such as in the killing of a witness, police or peace officer, or a person killed during the commission of another serious crime (felony murder). The aggravating factors can be presented by the prosecutor only if they are proved beyond a reasonable doubt and if the prosecutor has previously advised the defendant of the intent to offer the aggravating factor.

After the presentation of the people's argument, the defendant presents mitigating factors for the jury to consider. The prosecutor will then make a summation to the jury asking that they vote for the death penalty. The defense will then argue against it.

The prosecutor will also be involved in post-trial motions by the defendant challenging the conviction or sentence. When a convicted criminal applies for early release from incarceration or probation, the prosecutor often takes part to represent the rights of victims, or society as a whole, to see that properly convicted criminals

---

[6]We will base our discussion on the rules recently enacted in New York for capital cases. New York is one of the most recent states to adopt the death penalty.

who are a danger to society are not improperly released before they have served their sentences.

GENERAL LEGAL OBLIGATIONS THAT IMPACT THE PERFORMANCE OF THE CRIMINAL PROSECUTOR

The Presumption of Innocence

One of the most important features of American criminal jurisprudence is the concept that a criminal defendant is innocent until he is actually proven guilty of a specific crime. The judge or jury must accept the defendant's innocence until it is proven beyond a reasonable doubt that the defendant committed the crime as charged. Similarly, the obligations of the criminal prosecutor toward the accused are also affected by the presumption of innocence.

The accused is innocent until proven guilty during all stages of a criminal prosecution up to an actual conviction, whether that conviction comes after trial or by plea of guilty. It may appear that criminal defendants are granted more than their fair share of rights and have a seemingly unfair advantage when compared with the strict requirements levied upon the police and prosecutor.[7] However, remember that until there is a conviction the criminal defendant is entitled to the same rights and the same level of protection from unfairness as any other citizen. The mere fact that an accusation has been made and charges brought does not dilute that protection.

Zealous Advocacy

One of the long accepted principles enumerated in the Model Rules of Professional Responsibility,[8] and its predecessors[9] the Model Code and the Code of Professional Responsibility, is that a lawyer has a duty of undivided loyalty to his client. Moreover,

---

[7]It has become popular to decry the "liberal" way in which criminals accused are treated. They must be read their rights, given a free attorney, released on "technicalities," etc. Yet, these are the rights given to every citizen. It should be remembered that anyone can make a mistake, or be wrongly charged with a crime. It is to protect all of us that these "liberal" protections exist.

[8]The American Bar Association has created the Model Rules of Professional Conduct, which codifies the general ethical rules under which lawyers must practice. The model rules are not a strict statutory scheme, such as a penal code which enumerates with specificity each act that is prohibited. Rather, it is a set of general guidelines intended to demonstrate to the lawyer his or her obligations in broad strokes. Attorney regulatory schemes are not intended to specifically address every act prohibited. See McDonough, Chris and Epstein, Michael. (1995). Regulating attorney conduct: Specific statutory schemes v. general regulatory guidelines. Touro Law Review, 609 (11).

[9]Nearly 40 states have adopted the Model Rules of Professional Responsibility. Other states, such as New York, continue to utilize a form of the Code of Professional Responsibility, which is the predecessor to the model rules.

a lawyer must guard his client's confidences and secrets, and zealously advocate on behalf of a client. These rules apply to all lawyers.

Zealous advocacy and client loyalty are a consequence of the adversarial system by which our courts hear cases. Generally what this means is that both sides of a case present their clients' positions as strongly as possible without concern for whether their argument is 'fair' to the other side, or whether they possess information or evidence that they are not obligated to disclose to the other side. This system of requiring all sides to present their positions as strongly as possible is intended to allow the trier of fact to have all the relevant available information. The adversarial system endeavors for a free flow of information so thorough that the judge or jury will have all the facts necessary to make the best possible decision.

In recognition of the way in which American jurisprudence operates, the model rules require that lawyers seek the lawful objectives of their clients, without engaging in any activity which could result in prejudice to their client's cause.[10] For example, even when a client has lied on the witness stand or otherwise engaged in fraud before the court, a defense lawyer or civil lawyer cannot reveal that fraud to the court or anyone else without the client's consent or waiver of the attorney's obligation of confidentiality.[11]

How is it that a criminal defense attorney is protected from discipline for not revealing to a court that his client has lied under oath on the witness stand—and would be disciplined for making such a revelation without client consent, yet a prosecutor has to be so scrupulously honest that he must turn over evidence to the defense that will damage his case? Where does this special standard for criminal prosecutors come from?

Obligation to Justice

The prosecutor's ethical obligations run deeper than in most lawyers, and reach beyond a duty to the people who elected him and whom he represents. Moreover, the prosecutorial role is more complex than simply convicting people believed to have committed crimes. The prosecutor must seek justice, while at the same time zealously advocating on behalf of "the people." He must perform this difficult balancing act within the guidelines erected by the U.S. Constitution and the applicable ethical code regulating his conduct as an attorney.

In *Berger v. United States* the Supreme Court of the United States held that

> The [prosecutor] is the representative not of an ordinary party to a controversy, but of a sovereignty whose obligation to govern impartially is as compelling as its obligation to govern at all; and whose interest, therefore, in a criminal prosecution is not that it shall win a case, but that justice shall be done. As such, he is

---

[10]Note that conduct which is frivolous or otherwise unrelated to his client's cause is not given this blanket protection by the ethical rules. ABA Model Rules of Professional Responsibility 3.1.

[11]New York Code of Professional Responsibility, DR 4-101.

in a particular and very definite sense the servant of the law, the twofold aim of which is that guilt shall not escape or innocence suffer. He may prosecute with earnestness and vigor—indeed, he should do so. But while he may strike hard blows, he is not at liberty to strike foul ones. It is as much his duty to refrain from improper methods calculated to produce a wrongful conviction as it is to use every legitimate means to bring about a just one.

As eloquently stated by the Court, a prosecutor must attempt to achieve justice by striving equally as hard to avoid prosecuting an innocent man as trying to convict the guilty. In short, the prosecutor must treat criminal defendants fairly. He can be said to have achieved a "quasi-judicial" role, because the prosecutor is more than a litigant, he is essentially an administrator within the criminal justice system.

Conflicts Between Zealous Advocacy and the Duties Owed to the Accused

A prosecutor has a duty to represent his client strongly and must be loyal to the lawful goals and desires of the people he represents, as do all lawyers. Yet, as we have seen, the criminal prosecutor has the added obligation to do justice, which other lawyers do not. Factor into the mix the fact that a prosecutor must also respect the fact that a criminal accused is innocent until proven guilty, and it would appear that the criminal prosecutor is enmeshed in an unresolvable conflict. Not only do these obligations conflict with each other, but they also run contrary to the seemingly clear aims of society—to bring criminals to court, convict them, and put them in jail.

In sum, a prosecutor must represent the interests of his clients strongly and see to it that criminals are punished. At the same time, the prosecutor must treat the accused in a fair and forthright fashion and respect his mantle of innocence. The prosecutor is held to a difficult and absolute burden of evidentiary proof beyond a reasonable doubt. He must divide his loyalty between his obligation to his client and his obligation to do justice—seemingly in direct contrast to the philosophy of the adversarial system of American jurisprudence. No such conflicting and confusing duties are imposed on the civil lawyer or the criminal defense attorney; nor could they be under the general requirements of client loyalty and zealous advocacy.

Why must the prosecutor be concerned with the interests of the defendant at all, when our courts embrace the adversarial system and the attorney codes of conduct demand that a lawyer usually act only in the best interest of his client—regardless of the truth? The reason is that while the criminal prosecutor does represent a client, the relationship with that client is very different from the normal attorney client relationship.

CONCLUSION

The criminal prosecutor is not an ordinary lawyer representing an ordinary client. The criminal prosecutor represents "the people" by whom he is appointed or elected.

In short, he represents the government. The government's obligation to govern fairly is as important as its obligation to govern at all, hence the focus of the prosecutor in a criminal prosecution "is not that it shall win, but that justice shall be done".[12]

The obligation to govern fairly runs to the accused the same as it does to any other citizen. United States Supreme Court Justice Hugo Black wrote that "[t]he worst citizen no less than the best is entitled to equal protection of the laws of his State and of his Nation."[13] By protecting the rights of those citizens who are charged with breaking society's laws, the "worst citizens," we ensure that the rights of the law-abiding are best protected.

The prosecutor therefore, as a "quasi-judicial" representative of the government, must maintain a higher ethical and professional standard than other lawyers because his obligations run to the accused whom he prosecutes as well as the people he represents. He must act in an open, honorable, and fair manner toward all citizens; including those accused of committing crimes.

Cases and Opinions:

Arizona v. Noriega, 690 P. 2d 775 (1984).

Bell v. Maryland, 378 U.S. 226, 328 (1964).

Berger v. United States, 295 U.S. 78, 55 S. Ct. 629, 79, L. Ed. 1314 (1935).

Brady v. Maryland, 373 U.S. 83, S. Ct. 1194 (1963).

People v. Carter, 77 N.Y. 2d 95, 107, Titone, J. dissenting (1990).

---

[12] *Arizona v. Noriega,* 690 P. 2d 775 (1984).
[13] *Bell v. Maryland,* 378 U.S. 226, 328 (1964).

Chapter 6

PROSECUTING FOR SAFETY'S SAKE

Hal Pepinsky

WHAT PROSECUTORS DO

"Prosecutors" go by many different names in different legal domains. In the United States federal courts, they are called "U.S. Attorneys." There are various levels of U.S. Attorneys, each serving various prosecutorial roles. In the states, prosecutors may be called "prosecutors," "district attorneys," or "state's attorneys." There too, lead prosecutors for state systems or in the federal system are called "attorneys general." Prosecutors invariably are authorized to perform many legal duties beyond prosecuting crimes, such as presenting family courts with evidence that children need state services. Prosecutors are best known, though, for their role in criminal law enforcement—the focus of this chapter.

In some states or nations, those paid to prosecute criminal charges have much broader duties than in the Anglo legal tradition. For instance, in legal systems developed in the Soviet Union's political axes, "procurators" might have the power to discipline and correct judges as well as duties we call "criminal prosecution" in the United States. In the Navajo legal tradition which emphasizes peacemaking, no prosecutor position exists. (Yazzie, 1998, and Zion, 1998).

I encourage readers not to take for granted that "prosecution" as I know it at home in the U.S. Midwest represents the only way that civilized officials respond to crime and violence. For current law and legal commentary on ethics of prosecution in the United States alone, I found it necessary to be adaptive to uncover references. For electronic word searches, the most fruitful version of the term was "prosecuting." Do not assume that criminal prosecution is something only "prosecutors" do. In fact, it is a mistake to think that "prosecutors" are legally or ethically required to seek punishment of offenders. The choice whether to punish is the basic ethical choice discussed in this chapter. Prosecutors have free discretion in all U.S. jurisdictions, virtually unchecked, to decide whether to file criminal charge and start criminal court proceedings against anyone. In England and in Kentucky, to cite rare common-law exceptions, a private person may initiate criminal charges against her or his personal assailant. But in most U.S. jurisdictions, if no one in the prosecutor's office will file charges, a criminal case cannot be initiated in a court. In most states, prosecutors are elected to office, and appoint all others who do prosecutorial work in the county. Although personal appeals and other pressures may be exerted on anyone who does prosecutorial work, prosecutors enjoy broad powers to exercise state power over people.

Once criminal prosecution is initiated, U.S. prosecutors have virtually unbridled discretion to make a motion for dismissal or to negotiate plea bargains with defendants. In courtrooms, at trial, and at hearings of motions that I have attended, prosecutors wax sanctimonious about the inexcusability of the behavior of those they prosecute, but no formal ethics require them to do so. Nor are prosecutors required by law to preach that convicts "need consequences" for having behaved so badly. In fact, their formal ethical standards are remarkably vague. Fisher (1988, 197) leads off an extended discussion of "virtuous" prosecution in the United States this way:

> Questions about the scope and content of the duty to "seek justice" pervade prosecutorial work. Prosecutors are required to serve in a dual role: they are both advocates seeking conviction and "ministers of justice."

Formally in Anglo-American law, prosecutors are given greater responsibility than other lawyers, even though all lawyers are held to have duties as "officers of court" above and beyond duty to individual clients. Instead of serving individual clients, prosecutors are considered "ministers of the public interest," who "seek justice." That is the folklore, although formal law remains silent about such lofty ideals. For example, the Constitution or "supreme law" of my home state of Indiana (Art. 7, sec. 16) authorizes prosecutors to exercise whatever powers the legislature grants them. The legislature in turn merely requires prosecutors to take an oath to "support" Constitutions of Indiana and the United States and "[to] faithfully discharge the duties of such office" (Indiana Code, sec. 5-4-1-1(a)). Rule 3.8 of the Indiana Rules of Professional Conduct Requires that the "prosecutor in a criminal case shall:

(a) refrain from prosecuting a charge that the prosecutor knows is not supported by probable cause;
(b) make reasonable efforts to assure that the accused has been advised of the right to, and the procedure for obtaining, counsel and has been given reasonable opportunity to obtain counsel;
(c) not seek to obtain from an unrepresented accused a waiver of important pretrial rights, such as the right to a preliminary hearing;

(d) make timely disclosure to the defense of all evidence or information known to the prosecutor that tends to negate the guilt of the accused or mitigates the offense, and, in connection with sentencing, disclose to the defense and to the tribunal all unprivileged mitigating information known to the prosecutor, except when the prosecutor is relieved of this responsibility by a protective order of the tribunal; and

(e) exercise reasonable care to prevent investigators, law enforcement personnel, employees or other persons assisting or associated with the prosecutor in a criminal case from making an extrajudicial statement that the prosecutor would be prohibited from making under Rule 3.6 [as a lawyer or "officer of court"]."

In other words, formal legal constraints on how hard prosecutors work to obtain convictions and on how harshly they seek to vilify and punish convicts are specific and few. Elaboration of what is meant generally for a prosecutor to serve the public interest or to seek justice is absent from the law itself and rare in legal commentary. The elaboration that does exist focuses on the duty of prosecutors to exonerate the innocent as a companion to a duty to obtain the conviction and sanction of the guilty (see, e.g., Fisher, 1988; Green, 1999; Levenson, 1999).

Prosecutors work in a machine which has come to be known as the criminal justice system. In my home county in Indiana with a population of about 120,000, for instance, prosecutors have told me and my students that they recognize that they have room on the local court calendar to bring 25 to 30 criminal cases a year to jury trial, less than one percent of the cases they prosecute. They have to be highly selective about prosecuting cases which they believe that they can "win" at trial against defendants resistant to guilty pleas. I argue in this essay that the imperative to win means on one hand that prosecutors back off cases in which victims are in greatest danger of recurrent personal violence, and that in cases they do pursue that they become inordinately sanctimonious about showing that the few offenders they do prosecute deserve to "receive consequences"—to be punished. Hence,

> Observers have complained about a tendency on the part of prosecutors to prefer. . .[seeking conviction to seeking justice]. This is commonly described as a tendency to behave overzealously or according to a "conviction psychology" (Fisher, 1988, 198).

Regardless of how one feels about the exercise of prosecutorial discretion, it is obvious that prosecutors are highly selective in filing charges, let alone on holding out for conviction of certain offenses or for punishment.

I have known many prosecutors and have invited several to speak to my classes repeatedly. I have supported some candidates for prosecutor, some even for re-election. I am aware that prosecutors exercise their discretion in many ways, including often doing as I propose in this essay. At the same time, I confess to having thought for years as a criminologist that the only good prosecutor was an ex-prosecutor. I was a student public defender in law school. I still believe more in working out alternatives to incarceration and punishment for criminal defendants than in putting offenders away. More than 30 years ago, this was a gut-level conviction. I now feel able to articulate ethical principles that lie behind my bias, and to recommend that these principles be adopted by anyone in any interaction, including prosecutors at work.

Many lawyers go to work as deputy or assistant prosecutors directly out of law school, and build a base and reputation upon which to leave for private legal practice of many sorts. But for those who occupy senior prosecutorial positions such as U.S. Attorney or as the elected prosecutor of a state's county, prosecution becomes a political springboard—a chance to show one's capacity to strike blows for law and order. Politically ambitious prosecutors also resist being embarrassed by their assistants. It is tempting for prosecutors to go on moral crusades against categories of "offenders" who "need to be brought to justice," such as those who fail to pay child support or those caught selling crack cocaine on street corners. Whatever rationale for prosecution one adopts, it seems to me that it requires attention to more than politically convenient targets. In this essay I develop politically disinterested criteria that prosecutors might apply to serve our common public interest.

WHY PROSECUTE?

I entered a so-called premium law school with a vision that somehow as a lawyer I would be able to make life more just for all. I would help myself and others gain the satisfaction of seeing each other do the *right* things, the things that make us *trustworthy* rather than threatening. Since graduating, I have periodically and informally written out rules that various groups have adopted. My most spectacular rule-writing failure was my first major "legislation"—a grading system for doctoral exams in which the passing score combined course grades and exam marks. The new exam system was part of a set of terms I had a big hand in drafting, which ended a sit-in strike by sociology graduate students. The very specificity of the rules was so threatening that only two students with nearly straight As used them, instead of opting out under a "grandfather clause" as I and a host of others did.

My most enduring successes in rule-writing have been in designing models of governance inspired by the system which Leslie Wilkins tried to build into the earliest national parole guidelines in the United States (as described in Pepinsky, 1980, 295–96). My child's daycare and a workplace of mine have adopted frameworks that I have offered to set annual salary raises. The workers in each case would specify variables and weights for those variables to calculate annual raises using simple linear algebraic equations. Ideally, those who apply the guidelines also allow themselves to make exceptions for equity's sake, and write out reasons for these exercises of discretion to look back on later. Each year, the groups can consider whether they want to develop new criteria, delete old ones, or modify any weights. The weights and measures for salary increases evolve over time, in ways that depend on open review of each year's experience with the guidelines. Ideally, weights and measures change because workers listen and learn from their own feelings as to who has been fairly or unfairly treated, and why.

I used to think of this as a process by which people create "just" decisions—a process for doing "justice" which could be applied to any realm of social investment

(Pepinsky and Jesilow, 1992, 127–52). I still think that the process is fine, but I worry about a connotation that the term "just" or "justice" has most of the time I hear the term. We presume that "just" results are derived from fixed principles, so that anyone knowing any case and applying the principles would achieve the same result—taking an eye for an eye, for example. We presume that the result "solves" a social problem so that we can "leave it behind." Correct outcomes end our social problems so that we can forget the problems and go on with other matters.

In the salary systems I helped create, you learn from and build upon prior experience rather than leaving it behind. You remain open to learning from continuing experience; you continue responding to a problem rather than solving it—recognizing that *all* "solutions" are equally "final" by definition, and hence, in principle, as problematic as any other "final solution." As long as the process allowing experience to inform policy continues, no one can foresee, let alone preordain, the correct result. For instance, you cannot spell out in advance what reasons candidates for salary increases might give, specifying exceptions that those who apply rules openly and democratically will decide to make for equity's sake, or predict how the salary policy itself will be changed. It is equally impossible, logically let alone empirically, to draw up a code which makes the punishment fit the crime (Pepinsky and Jesilow, 1992, 116–26). To follow the democratic process of learning from one another's experience, participants in the process have to let go of attachment to outcome, and let themselves discover what outcomes they accept after they have listened and learned.

I think of my own success and failure in laying down rules for others to follow when I try to answer the structural question: Why prosecute? It is axiomatic to me as a "scientist" of crime and violence that what works and does not work for me personally works likewise in groups of whatever larger size—from personal to global levels.

When I apply my personal rule-making experience to the notion of legislators telling prosecutors what punishment of offenders to push for, the absurdity is glaring. How on earth can some happenstance majority of legislators foresee what victims, offenders, and others among whom they both live will honestly and fairly want and need to become stronger and safer in the wake of crime and violence? What extraordinary magic do we believe in that makes us think that a legislator ought to be telling a prosecutor what ought to happen to entire categories of criminals? How have we come to believe so deeply in the knowledge and wisdom of lawmakers who are so very far removed from cases in which the law is applied?

It seems to me "elementary," as Sherlock Holmes would say, that the penal code is not an adequate excuse for anything a prosecutor does. Serving the public interest, seeking the kind of justice that seems to make people really safer, more trusting, and more trustworthy, requires learning from the people involved in the case what will leave them safer and more aware of what won't. There is no higher social purpose a prosecutor can serve then helping victims at hand gain safety in their own terms.

Howard Zehr (1995), one of the more experienced mediators and widely attended theorists of a worldwide criminal justice movement for mediation and reconciliation known as "restorative justice," warns me that "safety" itself has taken on connotations that promote isolation, peril, and violence. Such is the case, for instance, when we use isolated, perhaps adult-provoked, violence by youths to justify a war on children, especially adolescents, who in fact are far less violent and criminal than men who are their fathers' ages (Males, 1999). It promotes violence to turn our schools more and more into police states in the name of "safety." The measures being taken in schools right now, like forcing students to wear id tags, go through metal detectors, and dress uniformly, to say nothing of bringing in dogs for locker and parking lot sweeps, would not, as far as I can see, have prevented a single one of the school shootings that has become a pretext for this absurdity. Here again is magical thinking, which has both unfair and dangerous results. People shut down when they are closely watched and monitored for safety's sake. In this climate predators feel a necessity to inflict greater terror on their victims to keep them from talking to outsiders. In general, a tough law and order climate isolates and silences its subjects.

In the realm of prosecution, where virtually all cases are plea bargained and where the better part of legal wisdom is for defendants to admit nothing to anyone, prosecutors and others, such as probation and parole officers, do not have much chance to get to know what is really going on in defendants' lives, let alone how intervention will affect defendants. How can you know about perpetrators if the very process you are applying makes it advisable for perpetrators NOT to own up to their offenses and deal honestly and openly with what triggers their violence? Tough enforcement can shut down and shut out victims too. Consider for instance a typical situation prosecutors often face of what to do when a woman decides she does not want to continue prosecution of her husband or boyfriend for battering her. Some prosecutors, as a matter of policy, threaten to prosecute these complainants themselves if the complainants fail to appear to testify and repeat their earlier complaints.

Meanwhile, those who work as advocates know that safety and healing for victims depends most crucially on victims taking control of their own lives, including the handling of their own cases. Anyone who would help victims ought to resist strongly, in principle, repeating or doing anything else with victims' stories without their permission, and ought to seek victims' guidance on what to do next with their stories, as therapists do with their clients. Survivors of personal violence and victims' advocates like Susie Hall, vice president of the Alliance for the Rights of Children have taught me that when, without taking over, you can just listen to stories of victimization and say, "I'm so very sorry," you validate and help victims the best you can, and learn more than those who try to do something else. In one case, I heard a mother give solid bases for believing that her ex-husband, a deputy prosecutor who headed his county's child protection team was probably raising his children in satanic ritual violence, enough to split the young children into multiplicity, and that the mother who was trying to get her children away was probably about to have a judge take custody from her and give custody to the father.

I hear of many such cases in which it is too politically inconvenient for prosecutors to listen to victims, all the more so as the seriousness and extent of the violence and betrayal of trust increases. Sometimes the evidence in such cases gets published, as by DeCamp (1992). Like Rosen and Etlin (1996), I have heard from parties involved and received documentation in cases in which, after their parents have separated, children apparently feel safe enough to let adults know that one parent is sexually assaulting, sometimes even torturing them. When "protective parents," so called because they are trying to free their children from another parent's violence, try to restrict visitation, they almost always lose custody and, ultimately, contact with their children to the apparent assailant if they resist letting the children stay alone with the apparently offending parent. The worse the violence and the more organized it becomes, the harder it becomes for any child, or any adult remembering what happened, to make people believe that any violence happened at all. Those whose advice I most respect, who treat survivors of adult violence to children politely called "incest," recommend that survivors of sexual betrayal in childhood (Freyd, 1996) NOT confront their "abusers" until strong enough to be unfazed by flat denial that the violence occurred. With no guarantee that any legal action against their abusers would succeed, there is no therapeutic justification for forcing victims to confront domestic assailants at all, let alone to become prosecution witnesses. Happily, there is a great deal that victims of "betrayal trauma" can do and, in fact, do to become safer and less guarded in the aftermath, without regard to what happens to their perpetrators (Whitfield, 1995).

To me, serving the public interest requires that prosecutors take account of how people will be left when prosecution and punishment are over. This includes helping victims prepare to be safer after their assailants get out of jail or prison. Doing things to offenders which theoretically and temporarily keeps offenders from victimizing people in the abstract, is no excuse for doing things to offenders that leave actual victims more frightened and vulnerable than they have already become.

I conclude that the highest public purpose prosecution can serve is to leave those involved in crime and violence, those already most victimized and isolated first, safer and stronger than before prosecution. Even though U.S. inhabitants are incarcerated at world record rates that have grown steadily since 1975. This growth is largely the result of U.S. jail and prison sentences are long by world standards and getting longer. Beyond effects on those already victimized, the overriding public interest in how offenders are prosecuted lies in what makes offenders safer to themselves and others after they have done whatever time the prosecutor helps get them for the crime. Prosecution is a powerful, blunt instrument, which can as easily damage victims, offenders, and the public that they serve. In the remainder of this essay I explore how prosecutors can serve the most fundamental public interest in leaving those most involved in offenses safer rather than sorrier.

Balancing Conversations is What Works

There is a clear, sharp boundary between relating to people in ways that leave them safer from structural and personal violence and relating to people in ways that leave them in greater fear, anger, and risk of violence. I and others call the former ways of relating to people "peacemaking," and the latter "warmaking" (Pepinsky and Quinney, 1991; Fuller, 1998). This boundary applies to relating to others anywhere, anytime. Let me describe the two approaches to relating to others generally, and apply the model to illustrating how prosecutors can make peace rather than war in their work.

The process of making peace is beautifully described as the philosophy that lies behind the Navajo peacemaker court—an alternative to Anglo-style prosecution available today in the Navajo Nation, as a creature of the Navajo Supreme Court (Yazzie, 1998, and Zion, 1998). The beauty of Navajo description is that it highlights what all of us outside the Navajo Nation do as well to make peace or war in our own lives.

In Navajo tradition all violence inevitably results from imbalances in all our relations. There is growing recognition among scientists from other intellectual traditions that this is so. Global warming is one of the physically largest and highest imbalances we worry about—too much heat and waste gas without enough nurture of mother earth's capacity to restore life-sustaining atmospheric balance. It is generally recognized that if in global agribusiness farmers are forced to plant but one genetically uniform variety of a foodstuff like wheat, one bug, one poison, or one cutoff of supply at the source spells disaster for all. Darwin pointed out that species and ecosystems survive longer the more variety they contain. Urban ecologists (Jacobs, 1961) and criminologists (Brantingham and Brantingham, 1975) have long since pointed out that the healthiest, safest, most open and caring neighborhoods are those which contain the greatest variety by virtually any demographic indicator, as well as by age, size, and mixture of types of occupancy in buildings. In this physical and social environment no type of person, group, activity or structure dominates others.

About a decade ago when I was the only non-African in a neighborhood in Dar es Salaam where people poorer that I had ever known up close lived around me, took me in, and befriended me, I took off my $20 wristwatch and took little cash with me when I went out to catch a bus. I did not want to tempt violence or theft by flaunting an imbalance between my wealth and my neighbor's poverty. I visited friends in an embassy residence that had shards of glass embedded in the top of the walls surrounding the compound, and a guard stationed at the gate at all times. The experience reminded me that a growing gap between rich and poor, or between decision-makers and their subjects, promotes fear and violence.

At a personal level, the explosively jealous husband who beats, terrorizes, and isolates his wife is a sort of caricature of Navajo ideas of what lies at the root of violence: He has all the power, and she has none. That is not only how Navajos would see the problem. The image of imbalance makes me think of Lady Justice, holding her scale in her left hand. The goal in using a balance is to make the unknown weight on one side equal the known weight on the other. Balancing social forces through law by beating offenders down lower and humbler than their victims simply reverses imbalance, rather than moving toward the balance of human power that Lady Justice and the Navajo seek.

People get terrorized by coming home and finding that strangers have trashed and stolen from their homes. Whey do they change their locks or wake up alarmed in the aftermath? Because they fear that burglars might come back, and I think, too, because they haven't had a chance to tell the burglars how they make them feel. Burglary victims are paradigmatic success stories in literature on victim-offender mediation or reconciliation (like that by Van Ness and Strong, 1997 and by Zehr, 1995). When burglary victims are able safely to ask their questions toward their offenders, they commonly report feeling considerably safer.

Like people who talk about "discourse" (such as Wagner-Pacific, 1993), I see these encounters—burglaries and mediation alike—as moments of human conversation. In the relationship between burglars and their victims, the threat comes from having the burglars in effect do all the talking and none of the listening. They pay no attention to what their victims might feel. In fact, burglars strive to avoid any contact with their victims whatsoever. That certainly gives the burglars the first and last word. So burglaries leave us with wide power gaps in social relations which burglars have initiated and victims can't stop feeling threatened just because the burglars have left. Victims fear someone's relentless pursuit of a personal agenda that affects them deeply—an agenda unaffected by how the victims feel. What is true for burglars is all the more obviously true of personal assailants. Rape victims commonly report terror during the act ("He might be killing me!"), compounded by their assailants' failure to be moved by the terror. The encounter is all action on one side and no interaction even in a victim's moment of extreme emotional crisis. The rapists are doing all the talking and none of the listening. This terror haunts victims long after the rape itself.

It is relatively easy for burglars to reassure their victims that their home was selected by chance and that the last thing in the world the burglars would want to do is go back. I have come to share the belief that the most deeply and enduringly traumatizing violence—that which produces lasting fear and anger—comes from those we in childhood turn to for love and nurture, who time and again betray our trust with their violence—the kind of violence they make sure no one who cares will see or hear, the kind of violence where they threaten their victims that they had better not tell (Freyd, 1996). These are the very assailants whom therapists warn us even as adults not to confront until we are already long-since validated enough not to depend on the response we get from them.

I once asked a prosecutor and county attorney to intervene in juvenile court on behalf of having medical attention for children I thought were in danger of continuing parental sexual violence, and on behalf of finding them a place where they could talk with adults that they might grow to trust about to arrange to live more safely. I was turned down, but the law did, as far as I could see, authorize the prosecutor to take this initiative, which might really have helped the children. The prosecutorial view seemed to be that either there was enough evidence to prosecute the father for felonies or there was no point in doing anything. I concur with the prosecutorial view that in these cases, it would have compounded tragedy to try to bring the fathers to criminal trial, where the children would have faced cross-examination in front of their father (or as happened to one case in my hometown, cross-examination by her father because he was serving as his own attorney). Experience tells me that between complaining children and parents who protest that they would never hurt the children, the prosecutors and law enforcement officials often think that children are making things up, exaggerating, or letting their imaginations run away with them. A local prosecutor told one of my classes that he only prosecuted child abuse cases against parents when he was confident of getting a guilty plea. A police detective told the class that he felt that he needed a confession to make a child abuse case prosecutable. They feared the prospect of failing to resolve all "reasonable doubts" that jurors might use to acquit. They hated putting children through the prosecution process. They realized, too, that acquittal would almost certainly be taken as legal exoneration, so that parents would be granted as much unrestricted time with their children as they wanted, no further questions asked.

I have met many young children in the past several years who apparently have no legal recourse but to go back to visit or stay with a parent who probably will continue to hurt them terribly. I have even tried to help comfort one or two such children when they were screaming inconsolably.

Only once did I ever ask any of these children what their apparent abuser had done to them (and I regret that I did so once to prepare a child to testify). I reassured some of these children that someone else had told me about stuff the children had earlier reported, and that I believed them and was sorry it had happened—no specifics, just a general statement. I later learned that such simple reassurance made a lasting impression on children who used this type of reassurance to become strong enough to resist the abuse.

Imagine how you would relate to such a child if you had received the kind of documentation I see in cases like this and were meeting the child for the first time. If you respond the way many of my students do when I ask them what they would first say to someone who told them that they had just been raped, you will want the child to tell you who did what, when, and where. You will want to know what the child did. (Sadly, many people seem to believe that children can actually want and seduce their parents into sex acts, for instance, and we often, by reflex, ask questions implying that victims might have been to blame.) I also hear from students who would first ask, "How are you doing? Is there anything I can do to help?" That invitation to an apparent victim to take the lead in telling the interviewer what they should talk about next is the peacemaking approach. Prosecutors can take this approach as well as anyone else. They can try to open avenues for child victims to talk to other adults safely and privately—adults whom the prosecutors can consult during the process of deciding what to do next. Prosecutors can help create opportunities for child victims to talk and be heard in daily conversations such as talking with teachers and school counselors about whether violence continues.

This is the process used by the facilitators in the Navajo peacemaker court. There may come a point when everyone involved has already managed to talk the situation out with each other and to be in safe company as a result of a series of balancing conversations, before any formal ceremony is held. When the Navajo peacemaking court process extends to a formal culmination, the facilitator convenes a circle big enough to include victims, offenders, their relations, friends, and supporters. Beginning and ending with a prayer that higher wisdom will guide their conversation, facilitators simply keep the conversation going around the circle, time and time again, until everyone in the circle has said all that she or he cares to, and until the facilitator has guided the conversation from what happened to what each member of the circle feels and proposes to do in the aftermath.

It is a cardinal belief of the Navajo that it only aggravates imbalance to try to make anyone do anything. In this view, the only actions we can trust are those we freely choose, those for which we accept personal responsibility, those which honestly emanate from our own hearts, unencumbered by others' demands. It is vital to Navajo peacemaking that victims and others who are hurt and threatened have a chance to say so and be heard. It is anathema to Navajo peacemaking to tell others what to do. Rather it expects spontaneous declarations of what responsibility individual circle members are prepared to assume themselves. It is a goal of Navajo peacemakers to balance everyone's participation in a circle between talking and listening. If the peacemaking circle does its job, members leave the circle being more mindful of the violence that has happened, and being responsible for creating social relations where violence no longer flows from the same source, or against the same victims. The very diversity and individuality with which people carry on and leave this conversation are a source of the circle's capacity to make peace out of violence, reducing risk of revictimization and reoffending at the same time.

Because I think the ethical principle is so important, I have mentioned that those who have been victimized should not necessarily be forced to confront their victimizers. It is important to note, however, that communication does not require confrontation. Thus, for instance, it would be a step toward balancing the conversation for prosecutors to offer to convey any messages complainants cared to deliver to their alleged victimizers, including requests for answers to questions like, "Why did you do this to me?" Defendants who were pleading guilty, if no one else, would certainly have everything to gain by responding empathetically. In the prevailing warmaking climate of prosecution, victims are kept from communicating in any manner with offenders. Even after prosecution, prisoners and victims often appear separately before parole boards. That is a loss for victims.

Awesome as the power of prosecutors is to affect people for life, whatever the prosecutor does is, on the whole, a brief episode in people's lives. The prosecutor cannot hope to know better than victims and offenders what is best for them. The prosecutor can help victims and offenders alike to assume more open, honest, safe, and respectful lives among those with whom they will continue to live.

It is only insofar as prosecutors help victims and offenders gain greater control of their own lives that prosecutors make peace.

In prosecution as in intervening anywhere in daily life, facilitating balance entails reaching out first to listen to the most obvious victims at hand, to hear their stories, and to let a sense of what victims would prefer to do next, be the primary continuing guide to action. No law or rule prohibits prosecutors from proceeding this way. In the process they can use a peacemaking principle to "minimize the [use of] force necessary to keep the peace" (originally stated in the closing chapter of Pepinsky, 1991). I have left friends in jail on a couple of occasions when I could have tried to bail them out because for the moment, among available options, I have found them safer to themselves and to others in jail than anywhere else immediately available. Beyond such moments, peacemaking calls for helping create places for defendants or convicts other than in cages which these days might cost $100,000 per cell to build and half that much to operate for a year. The challenge beyond the momentary emergency in which we confine people is to help them build safe, open, responsible lives free of confinement, rather than becoming further disabled from getting legitimate jobs and getting help. Prosecutors do not have to make all the arrangements themselves, but they should be oriented toward obtaining services of those who could help arrange non-custodial lives for defendants and convicts that leave victims feeling safer.

What if prosecutors cannot identify any concrete person who is victimized, or who like members of Mothers Against Drunk Driving is ready to speak on behalf of the kind of personal victims an offender creates? I have a hard time imagining something that scares and hurts people enough to justify a prosecutor's attention that would not present concrete, personal victims, or at least those who would speak on behalf of victims that they have known personally. Accordingly, I have a hard time imagining peace arising out of most drug enforcement, which today accounts for a third of those incarcerated around the world. Drug enforcement creates victims by driving users deeper into addiction and further from getting help, and encourages corruption, which has led me and many others to conclude that our own CIA and its predecessor the Office of Strategic Services, and the U.S. military were the prime movers in global trafficking in illegal arms and drugs from World War II on (see Chambliss, 1988, for one review of evidence). On the whole, the drug war distorts, impairs, and corrupts our capacity to reduce drug abuse and protect its victims. When personal victims of drug abuse present themselves including people trying to get help with their own addictions, prosecutors let victims guide them toward peace as in any other case.

In sum, from a peacemaking perspective, there is no higher calling for prosecutors than to balance the relations of those whose social ties have been ruptured by violence, primarily victims and secondarily, offenders. The most basic requirement of responses to offenders or suspects is that victims gain control of and guide the process. What prosecutors do to or with offenders and suspects within those limits should be aimed at establishing relations within which offenders and suspects can participate empathetically, responsibly, and equitably, without either subordinating or being subordinated by others. In the peacemaking frame, incarceration for safety's sake at the moment is no excuse for tearing down offenders' capacity to participate in balanced social conversations in the future. Although there may be no alternative to momentary force to prevent an imminent threat that people will continue to hurt themselves or others, the principle of "minimizing the force necessary to keep the peace" applies.

From a peacemaking perspective, a higher moral purpose for a prosecutor than this is moral pretense. One can suppose that since we are all connected such that violence begets violence and peacemaking builds safety—such that karma operates—we collectively get our just desserts from how we relate with one another. But there is no cosmic scale in which power fails to corrupt some of us who divine for others how much punishment subjects of the law deserve. Violence has consequences enough, first and foremost to victims, to respond to without anyone having to "give" consequences in addition. Better that offenders should pay attention to the consequences of their own actions at hand than that we should create new consequences to distract their attention. On the whole, as theorists of restorative justice like Howard Zehr (1995) propose, we do better healing from and preventing violence when we concentrate first on real harm done—real fear and pain caused—rather than paying attention to whether abstract rules have been broken. This is true for all of us, prosecutors included.

MORALIZING AND CREATING SAFETY

I recently listened to a radio talk show on drug enforcement in sports. A physician pointed to the absurdity that as many controlled or prohibited performance-enhancing drugs can be bought over the counter as nutritional supplements, which are untested as to purity or effect. This physician recommended setting up a covert random testing and surveillance system to ensure that athletes are not taking what is prohibited. The reason for the recommendation is that it is somehow vital to ensure that outcomes of sports contests are "fair" because they are "unaided." I found myself thinking: We are talking about people playing games, going home after the final score, entertaining people. Why are we so invested in believing that the outcome of these games is fair, so invested that we would spend inordinate sums on drug enforcement. Why do we care so?

I do not presume to know why we care so, except that we are vulnerable to scapegoating public enemies in a vain displacement of anger at our personal victimizers. I do know that in this radio conversation, I kept thinking that the primary failure of safety at hand was the lack of information about nutritional supplements. Would it not be a much greater public service to match drug or nutritional supplement advertising and enticement with public service announcements of problems people had encountered using these substances, helping to ensure that people at least know what is in the stuff they use, and advertising ways to help to free oneself from unwanted addictions?

Enough of moralizing. More than two hundred years ago Cesare Beccaria (1968 [1764]) warned that trials aimed at achieving just retribution were "spectacles" which merely distracted people from real threats to personal safety. Wars on crime are fictional caricatures of the violence that most nearly and dearly threatens and victimizes us. Instead of turning prosecution into some morality play and political spectacle, I propose that prosecutors let victims know they can come for help without being revictimized. That may be hard. Suppose a young student who was sexually abused by a teacher is later prepared to confront that teacher, and in a small community is unprepared to enter the public spotlight or risk the consequences, but would like to insist that the offender seek treatment. Under mandatory reporting laws in force today throughout the United States, any counselor or therapist who talked to the offender would be obliged to report that confession to forces of law enforcement, or else face loss of license and other liability if the offender reoffended without the notification. I know someone in that position, and he can't see a viable alternative to staying totally quiet and letting the teacher stay on the job. Fortunately, there are few such legal restrictions on prosecutors and others. As a prosecutor, it seems to me that you can legally say that such a reporting obligation has already been fulfilled. . .by reporting it to you. You might be satisfied if the offender selected a competent therapist who promised to let you know if the offender were about to re-offend, or had re-offended, who had no need to share whatever the offender said about prior conduct. My greatest satisfaction as a student public defender came in arranging plans with defendants to present to judges as alternatives to incarceration. These plans often included a pledge to be in therapy. Judges invariably adopted my plans, grateful to have alternatives to dead time in prison or in a hospital for the criminally insane. I see no reason why prosecutors would not do likewise, to serve the public interest, to arrange for offenders to become safer and saner in the community rather than more socially disabled after walking out of prison. Moralizing aside, I do believe that prosecutors can help people become safer in the wake of crime and violence.

Peacemaking is an attitude anyone can apply when responding to violence anywhere, anytime. I hope readers enjoy the fruits of adopting that attitude, as I have. May we all find safety in one another's midst.

REFERENCES

Beccaria, C. (1968 [1764]). *On crimes and punishments* (H. Paolucci, Trans.). Indianapolis: Bobb-Merrill Reprints

Brantingham, P., and Brantingham, P. (1975). Residential burglary and urban form. *Urban studies*, 12, 273–84.

Chambliss, W.J. (1988). *On the take: From petty crooks to presidents.* Bloomington, IN: Indiana University Press.

DeCamp, J.W. (1992). *The Franklin cover-up: Child abuse, satanism, and murder in Nebraska.* Lincoln, NE: AWT, Inc.

Fisher, S.E. (1988). In search of a virtuous prosecutor. *American journal of criminal law, 15,* 197–261.

Freyd, J.J. (1996). *Betrayal trauma: The logic of forgetting childhood abuse.* Cambridge, MA: Harvard University Press.

Fuller, J.R. (1998). *Criminal justice: A peacemaking perspective.* Boston: Allyn and Bacon.

Green, B.A. (1999). Why should prosecutors "seek justice"? *Fordham urban journal, 26,* 607–43.

Jacobs, J. (1961). *The death and life of great American cities.* New York: Random House.

Levenson, L.L. (1999). Working outside the rules: The undefined responsibilities of federal prosecutors. *Fordham urban journal, 26,* 553–71.

Males, M.A. (1999). *Framing youth: Ten myths about the next generation.* Monroe, ME: Common Courage Press.

Pepinsky, H.E. (1980). *Crime control strategies: An introduction to the study of crime.* New York: Oxford University Press.

Pepinsky, H.E. (1991). *The geometry of violence and democracy.* Bloomington, IN: Indiana University Press.

Pepinsky, H.E., and Jesilow, P.D. (1992). *Myths that cause crime* (3rd ed.). Santa Ana, CA: Seven Locks Press.

Pepinsky, H.E., and Quinney, R. (1991). *Criminology as peacemaking.* Bloomington, IN: Indiana University Press.

Rosen, L., and Etlin, M. (1996). *The hostage child: Sex abuse allegations in custody disputes.* Bloomington, IN: Indiana University Press.

Van Ness, D., and Strong, K.H. (1997). *Restoring justice.* Cincinnati, OH: Anderson Publishing Co.

Wagner-Pacific, R. (1993). *Discourse and destruction: The city of Philadelphia versus MOVE.* Chicago/London: University of Chicago Press.

Whitfield, C.L. (1995). *Memory and abuse: Remembering and healing the effects of trauma.* Deerfield Beach, FL: Health Communications, Inc.

Yazzie, R. (1998). Navajo peacemaking: Implications for adjudication-based systems of justice. *Contemporary justice review, 1,* 123–31.

Zehr, H. (1995). *Changing lenses: A new focus on crime and justice (2nd ed.).* Scottsdale, PA: Herald Press.

Zion, J.W. (1998). The use of custom and legal tradition in the modern justice system. *Contemporary justice review, 1,* 133–48.

Chapter 7

JUDICIAL ETHICS

Victor M. Ort

Charles R. Goldburg

Abstract

This chapter deals with the rules of the judiciary. It focuses on the integrity and independence of the members of the judiciary. Judges need to avoid impropriety and its appearance. Their social activities are limited under the rules of ethics. They may not belong to organizations that are discriminatory in nature. They must perform their duties impartially and with diligence. They need to keep order and a proper decorum in their courtrooms at all times. Judicial duties have to take precedence over all other activities. The judge is required to accord the right of every person to be heard. Both sides must have the opportunity to be heard. All matters have to be disposed of promptly and efficiently. Judges are not allowed to commend or criticize jurors, and they have to refrain from inappropriate political activity. Judges are, for the most part, restrained by the parties' claims and at all times the judge must have control of the trial.

This chapter considers judicial ethics from the point of view of both positive rules that are imposed on a judge by governmental authority and a judge's own view of judicial philosophy and how it impacts on the decision-making process. The positive rules that will be discussed are those applicable primarily to state judges in New York, Part 100 of the Rules of the Chief Administrator of the Courts Governing Judicial Conduct (hereinafter cited as the "RCA") but are representative of the rules throughout the country.

The RCA are intended to provide guidance to judges in establishing and maintaining high standards of judicial and personal conduct and to provide a structure for regulating such conduct through disciplinary agencies.[1] Although the RCA are not designed to impinge on the independence of judges in making judicial decisions,[2] they nonetheless have the effect of providing a set of ethical rules which not only bear upon the judicial process generally but also affect the administration of justice in individual cases.

First among these rules is the precept that a judge shall uphold the integrity and independence of the judiciary.[3] Decisions of the court will not be accorded respect and legitimacy unless they are handed down by judges who are themselves models of ethical and moral conduct. Moreover, the integrity of an individual judge reflects on the public's confidence in the judiciary generally. The conduct of a judge in his personal affairs is considered to be highly relevant in evaluating the integrity of the judge in the performance of his judicial office. Finally, public confidence in the judiciary requires that judges independently decide cases solely on the law and the facts presented to them and not be influenced by outside persons or the judge's own personal advantage. As an example, a judge should not be influenced by the fact that a lawyer contributed to judge's election or re-election campaigns.

A judge shall avoid impropriety and the appearance of impropriety in all of the judge's activities.[4] A judge must not be influenced by any improper motives. Thus, a judge shall not allow family, social, political or other relationships to influence the

---

[1] Preamble to the RCA; Code of Judicial Conduct Preamble (1990); See *In re Seaman*, 133 N.J. 67, 95, 627 A.2d 106, 120 (NJ 1993) (Canons direct each judge in conducting himself or herself in office, and guide the court in determining when judicial misconduct has occurred.); *cf. Disciplinary Counsel v. Campbell*, 68 Ohio St.3d 7, 10, 623 N.E.2d 24, 27 (OH 1993) (Code of Judicial Conduct serves to insure a legal system of the highest caliber and maintain public confidence in that system); See also *Counsel v. Stafford*, 626 N.E.2d 577, 579 (IN App. 5th Dist. 1993) (Code of Judicial Conduct and Canons intended to establish standards for the ethical conduct of judges, the violation of which may result in disciplinary proceedings).

[2] Preamble to the RCA; Code of Judicial Conduct Preamble (1990); *cf. In re Seaman*, 133 N.J at 95, 627 A.2d 121 (the Canons, although rules to be enforced, exhibit an aspirational and horatory character yet are not mere platitudes).

[3] RCA 100.1; Code of Judicial Conduct Canon 1 (1990); See *In re Inquiry Concerning a Judge re Wright*, 694 So.2d 734, 735 (FL 1997) (rude language and tone by the judge to Assistant State Attorney lessened public confidence in the integrity of judiciary resulting in reprimand); See *In re Kroger*, 702 A.2d 64, 66, 68, 72 (VT 1997) (judge who lied at a public hearing while under oath injured the integrity of the judicial system, and was consequently reprimanded and suspended); See *In re McClain*, 662 N.E.2d 935, 944 (IN 1996) (judge's participation in harassment of court employee's key writing letters and making telephone calls served to diminish the integrity of the court); See *Inquiry Concerning Davey*, 645 So.2d 398, 407, 408 (FL 1994) (judge who continues to handle case after being appointed to bench undermines integrity and independence of judiciary)

[4] RCA 100.2; Code of Judicial Conduct Canon 2 (1990); See *Matter of Justin*, 577 N.W. 2d 71, 72 (MI 1998) (judge who had ongoing dispute with the City of Jackson, mishandled court funds in protest to the city's actions, and was engaging in conduct involving impropriety and the

judge's judicial conduct or judgment.[5] To do so would be improper. Moreover, the judge must not even appear to be influenced by any improper considerations. Thus, a judge who was in the process of going through a hotly contested divorce should avoid sitting in a matrimonial case. A judge with extensive real estate holdings should avoid hearing zoning matters or landlord-tenant disputes.

With regard to social activities, a very delicate balance must be struck. Judges are frequently invited to law firm golf outings, annual Christmas parties, and weddings. If one of the hosts were to appear before the judge as an attorney or litigant, the judge must not favor them. On the other hand, the judge must not "bend over backwards" to avoid looking like she is favoring the host and thereby treat them less fairly. A judge shall not lend the prestige of judicial office to advance the private interests of the judge or others.[6] To do so would convey the impression that the judge might allow her personal interests to influence judicial decisions or that the other person whose interests were advanced by the judge might be in a position to influence her. For example, joining a local environmental group may call into question a judge's objectivity, should the judge be assigned to any case concerning sensitive environmental questions.

A judge shall not hold membership in any organization that discriminates on the basis of race, religion, gender, or national origin.[7] For a judge to belong to any such organization might give the impression that the judge himself harbors bias toward members of the group discriminated against by the organization. This is particularly troublesome with respect to country clubs or yacht clubs which traditionally recognize only males as members. Does this mean a judge should avoid such organi-

---

appearance of impropriety); See *In re Case of Snow*, 140 N.H. 618, 626, 674 A.2d 573 (NH 1996) (judge creates appearance of impropriety when he makes phone call to fix brother's speeding ticket); See *In re Disciplinary proceeding against Ritchie*, 123 Wash.2d 725, 735–36, 820 P. 2d 967, 972 (WA 1994) (judge who submitted misleading travel vouchers seeking reimbursements for different trips over a 5-year period which were only incidentally related to judicial business engaged in unacceptable impropriety).

[5]RCA 100.2(B); Code of Judicial Conduct Canon 2(B); See *Matter of McKinney*, 324 S.C. 126, 127, 478 S.E.2d 51, 53 (SC 1996) (judge acted improperly and was consequently removed from office when he issued arrest warrants at the request of his daughter); See *In re Trettis*, 577 So.2d 1312, 1313 (FL 1991) (improper for judge to let personal relationships influence judicial conduct in connection with estate activities); See *Matter of Cox*, 532 A.2d 1017, 1019 (ME 1997) (judge's conversation in his chambers with police officer assigned to his court regarding the officer's arrest of his son was improper).

[6]RCA 100.2(C); Code of Judicial Conduct Canon 2(B) (1990); See *In re Inquiry Broadbelt*, 146 N.J. 501, 514, 683 A.2d 543, 549 (NJ 1996) (judge's regular appearances on television show served to improperly lend the prestige of the judiciary to the show to advance the show's interest); See *In re Lorona*, 178 Ariz. 562, 566–67, 875 P.2d 795, 798–99 (AZ 1994) (justice of the peace lent prestige by fixing traffic tickets of friends and family and was consequently suspended); See *In re Fogan*, 646 So.2d 191, 191–194 (FL 1994) (judge improperly lent prestige and consequently received reprimand for writing a letter of character reference to court for a friend awaiting sentencing).

[7]RCA 100.2(D); Code of Judicial Conduct Canon 2(C) (1990).

zations as the Y.M.C.A., N.O.W., United Jewish Appeal, or even ethnic bar associations such as the Catholic Lawyers Guild, Jewish Lawyers Association, Women's Bar Association, or the Black Bar Association? Or for that matter, any bar association at all given it is open only to lawyers. Likewise, an argument could be made to the effect that a judge should not belong to the American Association of Retired Persons since it is discriminatory with respect to age. It is reason and logic that governs so the rule against a judge's belonging to an organization which fosters racial or ethnic bias should not be interpreted to require a judge to rescind from all forms of association. Stated otherwise, a judge is not required to become a hermit once he or she is elevated to the bench.

A judge shall perform the duties of judicial office impartially and diligently.[8] The obligation to decide cases impartially imposes a duty to decide cases upon the law and the facts and not be influenced by any other factors. Clearly, every judge enters the courtroom with his or her "baggage," that is no judge exists in a vacuum, free from life experiences and impressions which shaped the way that person views things. What must be done is to make every attempt to segregate those things from the case itself and decide the case only on the evidence adduced before the court. A judge shall perform judicial duties without bias or prejudice against or in favor of any person.[9]

A judge shall not be swayed by public clamor or fear of criticism.[10] This requirement is particularly difficult in this day and age of mass media and public fascination with the judicial system. In states where televised trials are no longer permitted, such as New York, the task is somewhat easier. Where televised trials do exist, problems persist. However, one would be hard pressed to conceive of a judge who does not agonize about certain situations which have received media attention in the recent past. Prime examples are cases dealing with domestic violence and/or sexual predators, particularly when the perpetrators have shown a propensity to repeat their offenses

---

[8]RCA 100.3; Code of Judicial Conduct Canon 3 (1990); See *In re Smith*, 687 A.2d 1229, 1240 (Pa.Ct.Jud.Disc. 1996) (judge who fails to render timely decision in 61 cases when they were ready to be adjudicated failed to perform diligently); See *Inquiry Concerning Steinhardt*, 663 So. 2d 616, 617 (FL 1995) (judge who refused to hear cases of a police officer because that officer issued a parking ticket did not perform his duties impartially and diligently).

[9]RCA 100.3(B)(4); Code of Judicial Conduct Canon 3 (B)(5)(1990); See *State v. Pattno*, 254 Neb. 733, 737, 579 N.W.2d 503, 506 (NE 1995) (judge who made disparaging remarks about homosexuals during sentencing did not perform his judicial duties without bias); See *Dodds v. Commission on Judicial Performance*, 12 Cal. 4th 163, 171, 176, 906 P. 2d 1260, 1266, 1269, 48 Cal. Rptr. 2d 106, 111, 114 (CA 1995) (judge told joke suggesting bias toward litigant. Prejudging of case by stating to plaintiff upon hearing figure she was seeking that she should get out of his chambers and it would not settle constituted prejudicial conduct).

[10]RCA 100.3(B)(1); Code of Judicial Conduct Canon 3 (B)(2)(1990); See *In re Bell*, 894 S.W. 2d 119, 123, 131 (TX Spec. Ct. Rev. 1995) (judge received public admonition for responding to personal criticism voiced out of court concerning finding of contempt); *cf. In re Charge of Judicial Misconduct*, 47 F. 3d 399, 400 (10th Cir. 1995) (judge holding press conference and appearing in several television shows because of high profile case should not have been caught up in public clamor); See *Matter of Boles*, 555 N.E. 2d 1284, 1287 (IN 1990) (judge suspended for responding to public clamor and fear of criticism by vacating judgment awarding attorney's fees in response to letter received by court).

but are nevertheless entitled to be released. Although preventive detention is ordinarily not the purpose of bail, judges do have a legitimate concern to protect the public against future harm.[11] An ameliorating influence are statutes such as Megan's Law that provide for registration of the sexual offender and notification to the community prior to his release.[12]

A judge shall be patient, dignified, and courteous to litigants, lawyers, jurors, and witnesses.[13] To be sure, there are certain lawyers who thrive on "baiting" judges. But to be rude or impatient with any of these individuals might suggest that the judge was biased and not impartial. A judge shall require order and decorum in proceedings before the judge.[14] This requirement also promotes the dignity of the court, public confidence in the court system, and the appearance of impartiality and fairness.

The judge's responsibility to perform the duties of his office diligently requires that the judge's judicial duties take precedence over all the judge's other activities.[15] A judge shall be faithful to the law and maintain professional competence in it.[16]

---

[11] *United States v. Salerno*, 481 U.S. 739 (1987)

[12] See, e.g. Correction Law Article 6-C (McKinney 1997)

[13] RCA 100.3(B)(3); Code of Judicial Conduct Canon 3 (B)(4)(1990); See *Matter of Brown*, 427 MA 146, 148–154, 691 N.E. 2d 573, 576–579 (MA 1998) (judge's derisive comments regarding labor union, union president, and his family involved in matter before judge warranted reprimand); See *In re Millard*, 63 Ohio Misc. 2d 475, 477-484, 631 N.E. 2d 224, 225–230 (Ohio Comm. of Judges 1994) (judge who demeaned lawyer in front of jury did not uphold her duty to be dignified and courteous to those in front of the court); See *Matter of Jenkins*, 503 N.W. 2d 425, 426 (Iowa 1993) (judge who made demeaning comments about people in front of the court was reprimanded for that conduct).

[14] RCA 100.3(B)(2); Code of Judicial Conduct Canon 3(B)(3)(1990); See *Matter of Bozarth*, 127 N.J. 271, 272–278, 604 A. 2d 100, 101–105 (NJ 1992) (judge who dealt inappropriately with defendants, trivialized defendant's right to counsel and implemented inappropriate method for handling tardy defendants warranted public reprimand); See *Matter of Disciplinary Proceeding against Berittenbach*, 167 Wis. 2d 102, 105–106, 113, 482 N.W. 2d 52, 52–53, 56 (WI 1992) (judge engaged in courtroom behavior that was loud, angry, discourteous and lacking in dignity or decorum warranted suspension from office); See *Matter of Anderson*, 168 Ariz. 432, 435, 814 P. 2d 773, 776 (AZ 1991) (justice of the peace who used telephone in courtroom to obtain advice on cases for "friends of the court" manifested a lack of decorum in proceedings in front of him and was censured).

[15] RCA 100.3(A); Code of Judicial Conduct Canon 3(A)(1990); See *Hunter v. Supreme Court of New Jersey*, 951 F. Supp. 1161, 1167 (NJ 1996) (judge who refused to extend court session to allow a witness with special medical needs to complete her testimony was reprimanded); But See *Matter of Verbage*, 200 W. Va. 504, 506, 490 S.E. 2d 323, 325 (WV 1997) (judge who failed to consider domestic violence problem while on duty as "on-call" magistrate was guilty of misconduct, no sanction warranted because of mitigating factors of illness and another judge being on hand to take care of his responsibilities).

[16] RCA 100.3(B)(1); Code of Judicial Conduct 3 (A)(1990); See *In re Bell*, supra, 894 S.W. 2d 119, 123, 131 (TX Spec. Ct. Rev. 1995) (judge received public admonition for responding to personal criticism voiced out of court concerning finding of direct contempt); See *Mississippi*

A judge shall accord the right to be heard to every person who has a legal interest in a proceeding.[17] One difficult area is when a criminal defendant files a motion on his own behalf, the court's patience is frequently tested. Even though he has access to the law library in the jail, the defendant is unskilled in the law and may misinterpret the applicable statutes. He may also be inarticulate in presenting his claim to the court. Prisoner petitions often border on the frivolous, and jailhouse lawyers occasionally submit multiple petitions to the court repeating the same claim. Nevertheless, the court has an obligation to decide a prisoner's *pro se* motion on the merits. Every litigant has a right to be heard, even when it occasionally becomes an imposition on the court.

It is a fundamental principle of American jurisprudence that fairness requires that both sides have an opportunity to be heard. Thus, as a general rule, a judge shall not permit or consider *ex parte* communications, that is communications from one side while the other side is not present.[18] This rule, however, is not absolute. *Ex parte* communications that are made for scheduling or administrative purposes are authorized, provided that no party gains a procedural advantage, and the party not included in the communication is promptly notified. A judge, with the consent of the parties, may also confer separately with the parties and their lawyers on agreed upon matters. As long as the party who was not involved in the communication is ultimately advised as to its substance, no unfair advantage to her adversary will be obtained.

A judge shall dispose of all judicial matters promptly and efficiently.[19] Justice delayed is justice denied. If proceedings become unduly protracted, cost to the litigants

---

Com'n on Judicial Performance v. Milling, 651 So. 2d 531, 537 (MS 1995) (judge was not faithful to the law when she let person drive her car after she suspended his license); See *In re Martin*, 333 N.C. 242, 242–244, 424 S.E. 2d 118, 118–120 (NC 1993) (judge not faithful to the law when he charges drivers with reckless driving when they should have been charged with driving while impaired).

[17]RCA 100.3(B)(6); Code of Judicial Conduct 3(B)(7)(1990); See *In re Inquiry Concerning a Judge re Wright*, 694 So. 2d 734, 735 (FL 1997) (judge denied ADA right to be heard and precluded crime victim from making statement); See *In re Thoma*, 873 S.W. 2d 477, 505 (TX Rev. Trib. 1994) (judge's *ex parte* waiving of balance of fines and fees owed by probationer violated canon requiring judge to accord every legally interested person the full right to be heard); See *In re Mallard*, 63 Ohio Misc. 2d 475, 478–479, 631 N.E. 2d 224, 226–227 (Ohio Comm. Of Judges 1994) (judge who accepted guilty pleas without defendant's attorney being given the chance to speak on behalf of his client violated canon requiring every interested person a right to be heard).

[18]RCA 100.3(B)(6); Code of Judicial Conduct Canon 3(B)(7)(1990); See *Miss. Com'n on Judicial Performance v. Sanders*, 708 So. 2d 866, 877 (MS 1998) (judge reprimanded and fined for engaging in *ex parte* communications with several parties while sentencing matter was pending); See *Matter of Sanders*, 674 N.E. 2d 165, 166 (IN 1996) (judge guilty of misconduct in participating in *ex parte* communications with criminal defendant who had case pending before judge); See *In re Martin*, 340 N.C. 248, 456 S.E. 2d 517 (NC 1995) (judge censured for *ex parte* communications with law enforcement personnel and court personnel concerning child of friend who had been taken into custody).

[19]RCA 100.3(B)(7); Code of Judicial Conduct Canon 3(B)(8)(1990); See *In re Daghir*, 657 A. 2d 1032, 1034–1035 (PA Ct. Jud. Disc. 1995) (judge censured for engaging in a pattern of

is increased which discourages people from asserting their rights. The legal system itself may impose time constraints within which matters have to be resolved. For instance, the New York Criminal Procedure Law requires that, with certain exceptions, felony cases must be resolved within six months.[20] However, notwithstanding compliance with timeliness standards imposed either by statute or court rule, a judge should remember that promptness should not be an end unto itself. The case before the court belongs to the parties. It is their dispute, and, if both sides seek a reasonable delay, every effort should be made to accommodate their request.

A judge shall not make any public comment concerning her own pending cases or the pending cases of any other judge.[21] Public comment by the judge might suggest that the judge was either influenced by public opinion or that she desired to influence another court or jury.

A judge shall not commend or criticize jurors for their verdict.[22] To do so might suggest that the judge had an interest in the case or might influence the jurors in subsequent jury service. Here, too, a delicate balance must be struck. Every human being, jurors included, craves the knowledge that he or she "did the right thing." When speaking to a jury after its verdict, it is reassuring to them to go over certain of the key facts and say something like: "if once you determined x, it was a logical conclusion that y followed," rather than "yes, I thought he was guilty too" or "I agree the People failed to prove their case" or the like. Other issues that frequently arise when discussing cases with jurors are the defendant's prior criminal record or the sentence faced by defendant. If a juror learns after the verdict that a defendant who did not testify had a criminal record, the juror may be unable in a future case to accord the presumption of innocence to a defendant who does not testify. On the other hand, a juror who learns that a defendant faces a much stiffer sentence than he realized may be reluctant to convict a defendant in a subsequent case.

---

unreasonable and unjustifiable delay in the disposition and decision of six cases pending before judge); See *In re Braun*, 180 Ariz. 240, 241, 883 P. 2d 996, 997 (AZ 1994) (judge who was habitually tardy in the conduct of court business and who failed to decide cases in a timely manner was suspended); See *Doan v. Com'n on Judicial Performance*, 11 Cal. 4th 294, 335, 902 P. 2d 272, 293 45 Cal. Rptr. 254, 275–76 (judge's habitual tardiness in commencing court sessions, despite complaints and advisements was in violation of canons of ethics).

[20]See CPL § 30.30 (McKinney, 1992)

[21]RCA 100.3(B)(8); Code of Judicial Conduct Canon 3(B)(9)(1990); See *In re McCully*, 942 P. 2d 327, 330, 332 (UT 1997) (judge reprimanded for allowing a litigant to submit a sworn affidavit signed by judge concerning the court system and conclusions about a case pending before another judge); See *In re Conduct of Schenk*, 318 Or. 402, 428, 870 P. 2d 185, 201(OR 1994) (judge's letters to newspaper criticizing district attorney and guest editorials about pending or impending cases violated canon prohibiting public comment); See *Goldman v. Nevada Com'n on Judicial Discipline*, 108 Nev. 251, 296, 830 P.2d 107, 136 (NV 1992) (judge violated canon by making improper public comments to news media concerning contempt citation and jailing of public officer).

[22]RCA 100.3(B)(9); Code of Judicial Conduct Canon 3 (B)(10)(1990).

To avoid the appearance of impropriety, a judge shall disqualify himself in a proceeding in which the judge's impartiality might reasonably be questioned.[23] This includes, but is not limited to, situations where

1. The judge has a personal bias or prejudice concerning a party.
2. The judge has personal knowledge of disputed evidentiary facts.
3. The judge has served as a lawyer in the matter in controversy.
4. A lawyer with whom the judge previously practiced law served during such association as a lawyer in the matter.
5. The judge has been a material witness in the matter.
6. The judge, or his spouse or minor child, has an economic interest in the matter or any other interest that could be substantially affected by the proceeding.
7. The judge, the judge's spouse, or a relative within the sixth degree of consanguinity of either of them, or the spouse of such person, is a party to the proceeding, has an interest that could be affected, or is likely to be a material witness.
8. The judge, her spouse, or a person within the fourth degree of relationship to either of them, or a spouse of such person, is a lawyer in the proceeding.[24]

If after a matter is assigned to the judge, the judge discovers that he or his spouse or child has such an economic interest in a party to the proceeding, disqualification is not required if the judge divests himself of the interest that provides the grounds for disqualification.[25] Where a judge does not have an actual bias or interest which would

---

[23]RCA 100.3(E); Code of Judicial Conduct Canon 3(E)(1)(1990); 28 U.S.C. §455(a); see *Mississippi Com'n on Judicial Performance v. Sanders*, 708 So. 2d 866, 873, 876 (MS 1998) (judge should have disqualified herself in proceeding involving client she previously represented as an attorney); See *In re Cooks*, 694 So. 2d 892, 901 (LA 1997) (judge censured for failing to recuse herself from case where she had a close personal relationship with litigant); see *In re Zoarski*, 227 Conn. 784, 791, 632 A. 2d 1114, 1118 (CT 1993) (judge who had neighborhood and legal relations with defendant should disqualify himself in a proceeding in which his impartiality might be reasonably questioned).

[24]RCA 100.3(E); Code of Judicial Conduct Canon 3(E)(1)(a-d)(1990); 28 U.S.C. § 455 (b)(1–5); see *Mississippi Com'n on Judicial Performance v. Sanders*, supra, 708 So.2d 866, 873, 876 (MS 1998) (judge should have disqualified herself in proceeding involving litigant whom she previously represented as an attorney); See *State v. Vidales*, 6 Neb. App. 163, 173, 571 N.W. 2d 117, 123, 124 (NE 1997) (judge should have disqualified himself when spouse-attorney brought case in front of his court); See *Matter of Sanders*, 674 N.E. 2d 165, 166–167 (IN 1996) (judge suspended for refusing to recuse himself from criminal trial after meeting witness who was working with the state).

[25]RCA 100.3(E); 28 U.S.C. § 455(f); See *Baldwin Hardware Corp. v. Franksu Enterprise Corp*, 78 F. 3d 550, 556 (Fed. Cir. 1996) (judge who was beneficiary of trust divested himself of shares of corporation thus eliminating conflict); See *Perpich v. Cleveland Cliffs Iron Co.*, 927 F. Supp. 226, 231 (E.D. MI 1996) (judge who owned stock in two corporate defendants was not required to

require disqualification as a matter of law, the trial judge himself is the sole arbiter of recusal and must be guided by personal conscience.[26]

A judge must conduct her extra-judicial activities so as to minimize the risk of conflict with judicial obligations which would require disqualification.[27] Thus, a judge shall not appear at a public hearing before an executive or legislative body except on matters concerning the legal system.[28] A judge shall not accept appointment to a governmental committee or commission concerned with issues of policy other than the improvement of the law.[29] A judge shall not serve as an officer or director of an organization that is likely to be engaged regularly in litigation.[30] A judge shall not engage in frequent financial or business dealings with individuals likely to come before the court on which the judge serves.[31] A judge shall not receive gifts or loans

---

disqualify himself in personal injury action when he immediately divested himself of interest upon learning of conflict and took no action after motion for disqualification was filed).

[26] *People v. Moreno*, 70 N.Y. 2d 403, 405 (1987)

[27] RCA 100.4; Code of Judicial Conduct Canon 4 (1990); See *In re Arrigan*, 678 A. 2d 446, 448–449 (RI 1996) (judge who engaged in fund-raising activities with attorneys by soliciting their contributions was censured); See *Matter of Handy*, 254 Kan. 581, 585–586, 867 P. 2d 341, 345–346 (KS 1994) (judge who purchased property from estate after signing order admitting will to probate, and presiding over cases in district court in which city was a party while sitting as municipal court judge in same city has not minimized the risk of conflict); See *Mississippi Com'n on Judicial Performance v. Atkinson*, 645 So. 2d 1331, 1334, 1336 (MS 1994) (judge failed to regulate his extra judicial activities so as to minimize conflict by setting a bail bond for a defendant as municipal judge, and then serving as attorney for defendant in petition to reduce the bail).

[28] RCA 100.4(C)(1); Code of Judicial Conduct Canon 4 (C)(1)(1990); See *Inquiry concerning a Judge*, 822 P. 2d 1333, 1341–1343 (AK 1991) (judge's meeting with governor to address issue of whether governor could intervene on judge's behalf in a personal matter was one of the reasons for judge's private reprimand); See also *In re Kroger*, 702 A. 2d 64, 66 Fn.l (VT 1997) (the participation of two judges at an unauthorized public hearing, and particularly their raising questions about the integrity of a fellow judge, may have violated canon of ethics requiring judges generally not to appear at public hearings).

[29] RCA 100.4(C)(2); Code of Judicial Conduct Canon 4(C)(2)(1990); See *Matter of Disciplinary Action Against Grenz*, 534 N.W. 2d 816, 819 (ND 1995) (judge who accepted appointment and served as member of airport authority warranted censure); but cf. *Mistretta v. U.S.*, 488 U.S. 361, 403, 109 S. Ct. 647, 671 (1989) (judges are not *per se* disqualified from working on administrative committees, in this case a sentencing commission, as long as there is no conflict or overlap when performing each role. The ultimate inquiry is to determine whether extra judicial assignment undermines the integrity of the judiciary).

[30] RCA 100.4(C)(3); Code of Judicial Conduct Canon 4(C)(3)(A)(1990); cf. *Matter of Imbriani*, 139 NJ 262, 263–66, 652 A. 2d 1222, 1222–1224 (NJ 1995) (judge removed for managing affairs of a corporation and receiving compensation); cf. *Matter of Ford*, 404 Mass. 347, 353, 535 N.E. 2d 225, 229 (MA 1989) (judge censured for being an officer, director and manager of corporation).

[31] RCA 100.4(D)(1); Code of Judicial Conduct (4)(D)(1)(b)(1990); See *Matter of Davis*, 946 P. 2d 1033, 1043–1044 (NV 1997) (judge removed from office for reasons including using chambers to conduct his antique business and selling those antiques to people he came in contact

except from relatives and friends on special occasions.[32] A judge shall not serve as a trustee except for the trust of a family member.[33]

A judge shall refrain from inappropriate political activity.[34] In particular, a judge may not hold office in a political organization, engage in partisan political activity except in support of his own campaign, permit his name to be used in connection with political activity, publicly endorse a candidate, make speeches on behalf of a candidate, solicit funds, make a contribution, or even attend a political gathering.[35]

These objective rules and prohibitions are designed to ensure fairness and public confidence in judicial decisions. Judicial ethics also involves matters of judicial philosophy which call into question the proper function and role of the judge himself.

---

with at courthouse); See *In re Johnson*, 683 So. 2d 1196, 1197–1201 (LA 1996) (judge removed from office who continues to engage in business of operating a telephone service for jail inmates while on bench); See *Adams v. Commission on Judicial Performance*, 10 Cal. 4th 866, 885–901, 897 P. 2d 544, 552–562, 42 Cal. Rptr. 606, 614–624 (CA 1995) (judge removed from office for reasons including engaging in business activities with parties in the automotive business who were litigants in front of judge).

[32]RCA 100.4(D)(5): Code of Judicial Conduct Canon (4)(D)(5)(d)(1990); See *Adams v. Commission on Judicial Performance*, 16 Cal. 4th 866, 887–90, 897 P. 2d 544, 560–62, 42 Cal. Rptr. 2d 606, 622–624 (CA 1995) (judge removed from office for reasons including receiving gift from counsel who had cases in front of him); See *Matter of Pekarski*, 536 Pa. 346, 350–355, 639 A. 2d 759, 760–763 (PA 1994) (judge removed for accepting loans from people with whom she had social relationships and from people who came or were likely to come before her in court); See *Matter of Drury*, 602 N.E. 2d 1000, 1004–06 (IN 1992) (judge removed for accepting loans under guise of campaign contribution from attorney practicing in his court).

[33]RCA 100.4(E)(1); Code of Judicial Conduct Canon (4)(E)(1)(1990); cf. *Matter of Loyd*, 424 Mich. 514, 531, 384 N.W. 2d 9, 17 (MI 1986) (judge removed for reasons including failure to withdraw as conservator for children who were not hers).

[34]RCA 100.5; Code of Judicial Conduct Canon (5)(1990); See *In re Glickstein*, 620 So. 2d 1000, 1001, 1002 (FL 1993) (judge sanctioned for writing letter which supported the candidacy of a fellow judge); See *Matter of Buckson*, 610 A. 2d 203, 227 (DE Jud. 1992) (judge who attended and spoke at political gathering and publically declared his candidacy for the office of governor without resigning judicial office was censored and removed); See *Matter of Katic*, 549 N.E. 2d 1039 (IN 1990) (judge sanctioned for acting as leader for Democratic party and letting his views about candidates be publically known).

[35]RCA 100.5(A); Code of Judicial Conduct Canon (5)(A)(1)(a-e)(1990); See *Matter of Davis*, 946 P. 2d 1033, 1043 (NV 1997) (judge found guilty of publically endorsing a candidate for justice of the peace); See *Matter of Barrett*, 593 A. 2d 529, 537 (DE Jud. 1991) (judge's repeated attendance at political functions was part of the reason for her censure); See *Mississippi Judicial Performance Commission v. Peyton*, 555 So. 2d 1036, 1037, 1038 (MS 1990) (judge censured partly for remaining on the county executive committee of the Democratic party after taking position on bench).

Judges have jurisdiction to decide justiciable controversies, that is concrete disputes between individual litigants who can ordinarily be relied upon to assert their own legal rights. Thus, a judge in most circumstances is not to reach out to decide issues which the parties have not raised and argued to the court. Another requirement for jurisdiction is that a party must have standing, i.e., have suffered an actual injury in fact, in order to be able to assert the violation of a legal right. These requirements that a plaintiff have standing and that the parties assert their own legal rights assure that through proper advocacy all of the facets of a question will be presented to the court. If both sides of a question are zealously argued to the judge, it is more likely that the judge having heard all of the arguments on a particular issue will come to the right decision.

In applying the law to the facts of the case, the judge will ordinarily be bound by the legal arguments that the parties have actually raised. However, a judge is not simply a human computer mechanically determining whether the legal arguments raised by the parties are correct. To be sure, in deciding a case there is room for the court to apply its own analysis in order to reach a proper and just result. While a court cannot draw on its own personal knowledge of the facts to decide the case, its view of the law may very well be different from that of the attorneys. As a result, the judge may end up applying the law in a more refined or sophisticated fashion than was argued by either of the lawyers.

Occasionally when a litigant is *pro se* or counsel is inept, the court must go even further to protect the rights of the party. But the court should not cross the line where judging ends and advocacy on behalf of an individual litigant begins.

Needless to say, there is an entire body of procedural law dealing with the methods by which parties' substantive rights are enforced in court. Thus, there are rules as to what court has jurisdiction, which county is the proper venue, and how timely after the alleged injury must relief in court be sought. Also, there are procedures governing how much of a party's claim must be alleged in a pleading and how much evidence must be disclosed before trial. Most judges are reluctant to allow form to govern substance. However, the "law is the law" and a judge is obligated to enforce procedural niceties even if it may have a serious effect on a party's substantive rights. The general rule in civil litigation is that the parties are free to chart their own procedural course. Thus, the parties are ordinarily bound by the procedural choices which they make and the defaults which they incur. The reasons behind this rule are twofold: 1) to promote a more robust airing of issues, that the party whose rights are affected is most likely to assert the claims clearly and fully before the court, and 2) there must be an end to litigation. Cases would endure forever if a party were not bound by the procedural choices he/she had made. Thus, once a case has proceeded to judgment on the merits either in favor of one party or the other, and appellate remedies have run, the principle of *res judicata* bars further litigation on the particular cause of action.

Although the parties make their own procedural decisions, the court is not just a passive umpire ruling on questions of law. The court also has a responsibility to control the trial, to clarify ambiguous matters and, when necessary, to take an active role in the examination of witnesses. This is not only accurate in a trial by a judge where the court itself is the fact-finder, but is also true where a jury is deciding the facts and the court must be sure that the jury is not confused.

These rules represent the ethical precepts which guide judges in the performance of their judicial duties and the conduct of their personal affairs. Understandably, as judges are human, they are susceptible to human frailties. Nevertheless, judges are expected to engage in what is considered proper judicial behavior and to be completely fair in their deliberations.

Chapter 8

Noble Corruption– Police Perjury– What Should We Do?

Martin L. O'Connor, J.D.

Abstract

Police perjury is considered by some to be a serious criminal justice problem. This chapter critically reviews some proposals that have been made to address police perjury. These proposals range from sensitizing the police to police perjury, videotaping police actions, polygraphing police witnesses, changing the police organizational structure, flexifying probable cause and abolishing the exclusionary rule of evidence. Finally, the author offers some proposals to deal with police perjury which include research, changing the fundamental mission of police agencies, legislation, fixing responsibility for police perjury upon police administrators and holding municipalities and police supervisors accountable for failing to take action to address the police perjury problem.

In 1994, a notorious Los Angeles murder case captured the attention of the American public. The case involved a former football star, O.J. Simpson, who was charged with the murder of his ex-wife and her male companion. Although the verdict in the Simpson trial created substantial controversy, the case raised the issue of police perjury in regard to the testimony of some officers in the Los Angeles Police Department (LAPD). Police homicide detectives were criticized for their conduct and their testimony. The Simpson court judge found that one homicide detective demonstrated a "reckless disregard for the truth" in a search warrant application (Anon., 1994a). Serious credibility questions were also raised concerning why no less than four detectives appeared at Simpson's home shortly after the homicide. The four detectives testified that they went to the Simpson home early one morning not because O.J. Simpson was a murder suspect, but simply to notify Simpson of the murder of his ex-wife. Some found these statements incredible because four homicide detectives are usually not deployed for death notifications. Simpson's defense attorneys argued that the four detectives were actually searching for evidence to connect Simpson to the murders. Although the detectives' testimony raised the specter of police perjury, the court accepted the police version of the events (Anon., 1994b). Perhaps no member of the LAPD received more criticism than Detective Mark Fuhrman. Fuhrman swore that he would tell the whole truth and nothing but the truth, but he lied when he said he had not used certain racial epithets in the past ten years. His lies were disclosed when tape recordings were introduced into evidence demonstrating that Fuhrman frequently used racial epithets and engaged in other police misconduct. Fuhrman's credibility was seriously damaged and he subsequently pleaded guilty to an offense based upon his perjured testimony. It has been suggested that one of the benefits of the Simpson trial is that it may produce an increased awareness of the police perjury problem (Cloud, 1996).

Some believe that police perjury is ". . .recognized by the defense bar, winked at by the prosecution, ignored by the judiciary and unknown to the public. . ." (Sevilla, 1974, 839). Some criminal defense attorneys believe that police perjury takes place often (Kittel, 1986), and some have even said that perjury by the police is routine (Skolnik, 1982). In fact, it has been said that ". . .almost all officers lie. . .[and]. . .many prosecutors implicitly encourage police to lie about whether they violated the Constitution in order to convict the guilty. . .[and]. . .[a]ll. . . judges. . .and appellate judges are aware of [police perjury]. . ." (Dershowitz, 1983, Rule IV, VI, IX).

Yet others state that most police officers are honorable and honest, recognizing that police perjury occurs in some cases, and probably most frequently in cases of searches and seizures (Cloud, 1996). The highest court in New York State has stated that there is no proof that all police officers commit perjury and the police should not be singled out as suspect (*People v. Berrios*, 1971). Nevertheless, some police have developed their own name for police perjury "testilying" (Commission to Investigate Allegations of Police Corruption of the Police Dep't, City of New York, 1994).

The frequency of police perjury in criminal proceedings is difficult to measure, but there can be no question that it exists (Sevilla, 1974). Lying to convict the innocent is undoubtedly rejected by most police (Slobogin, 1996), but it is believed that police lie for the primary purpose of getting the "bad guys" (Sherman, 1982). Some police officers see themselves as noble individuals who represent a thin blue line of virtue positioned against the evil forces in society. This frame of mind has given rise to the term *noble cause corruption*, which ". . .suggests that illegal actions that violate a citizen's rights are morally right or excusable if a higher or greater purpose is accomplished. . .[and]. . .[t]he ends when they are noble. . .justify whatever means are necessary. . .and this moral justification encourages perjury. . ." (Bartollas and Hahn, 1999, 266). One of the problems associated with police perjury and getting the "bad guys" was best described by the late Judge Irving Younger in *People v. McMurty* (1970). Judge Younger, in his opinion, described the different versions of the same event offered by the arresting officer and the defendant at a suppression hearing. The arresting officer, Charles Frisana, testified as follows:

> At 8:30 p.m. on July 23, 1970, I was on duty driving a patrol car. While stopped at a light at West 3rd Street and Broadway, I observed two men in a doorway of a

building at 677 Broadway. One of these men—James McMurty, as I later learned—saw the patrol car and stepped out of the doorway. From his right hand he let drop a small plastic container. I got out of the patrol car and retrieved it. In my opinion, based upon a fair amount of experience, its contents were marijuana. I approached McMurty, who had begun to walk away, and asked him if the container was his. He said no. I said that I had seen him drop it and placed him under arrest.

Then defendant McMurty testified as follows:

On July 23, 1970, at 8:30 p.m., I was walking on Broadway near West 3rd Street when I saw Patrolman Frisina coming toward me. I knew that I had a container of marijuana in my pocket. I also knew, after twelve years of involvement with drugs and four or five prior convictions, that illegal search and seizure was my only defense. The last thing that I would do is drop the marijuana on the ground. I simply left it in my pocket. Frisina told me to get into the doorway. I obeyed, hoping that he would search me. He did just that and found the marijuana and arrested me.

The prosecutor stood on Police Officer Frisina's testimony. Since the marijuana was abandoned, he argued, the seizure was lawful. Defense counsel stood on defendant McMurty's testimony, arguing that the arrest occurred when McMurty was ordered into the doorway and since the officer did not have probable cause to arrest, the search which followed was unlawful.

Judge Younger offered the following cogent comments:

Were this the first time a policeman had testified that a defendant dropped a packet of drugs on the ground, the matter would be unremarkable. The extraordinary thing is that in our criminal courts policemen give such testimony in hundreds, perhaps thousands of cases—and that's in a nutshell, the problem of 'dropsy' testimony. . . Policemen see themselves fighting a two-front war—against criminals in the streets and against 'liberal' rules in court. All's fair in this war, including the use of perjury to subvert 'liberal' rules of law that might free those who ought to be jailed. . .Before Mapp, the policeman typically testified that he stopped the defendant for little or no reason, searched him and found the narcotics on his person. This had a ring of truth. It was an illegal search (not based on probable cause), but the evidence was admissible because Mapp had not yet been decided. Since it made no difference, the policeman testified truthfully. After the decision in Mapp, it made a great deal of difference. For the first few months, New York policemen continued to tell the truth about the circumstances of their searches, with the result that evidence was suppressed. Then the police made the great discovery that if the defendant drops the narcotics on the ground, after which the policeman arrests him, the search is reasonable and the evidence is admissible. Spend a few hours in the New York City criminal courts nowadays, and you will hear case after case in which a policeman testifies that a defendant dropped narcotics on the ground, whereupon the policeman arrested him. Usually the very language of the testimony is identical from one case to another. This is known now among defense lawyers and prosecutors as 'dropsy' testimony. . .Surely, though, not in every case was the defendant unlucky enough to drop his narcotics at the feet of a policeman. It follows that at least in some of these cases the police are lying.

Judge Younger ties the problem of "dropsy testimony" to police officers attempting to avoid the Mapp exclusionary rule. There are others who believe that the exclusionary rule of evidence has been crippled by police perjury (Sevilla, 1974). The problem of "dropsy testimony" is that some defendants do drop contraband on the ground so the police will not find this evidence upon them (*California v. Hodari D*, 1991). So, in some unknown number of cases the police may be lying or telling the truth.

PROFESSOR SLOBOGIN'S PROPOSALS FOR REDUCING POLICE PERJURY

Professor Christopher Slobogin in an article, *Testilying: Police Perjury And What To Do About It* (Slobogin, 1996), sets forth a range of measures he believes may assist in reducing police perjury. Some of Professor Slobogin's proposals have merit, some are impractical, and some propose draconian and troublesome changes with respect to the Fourth Amendment. His proposals include the following:

■ *Sensitize the police through training to the immorality and dangers of perjury.*

Sensitizing the police to the problem of police perjury has a great deal of merit. Although the police have been trained in search and seizure rules after *Mapp v. Ohio* (1961), there is little evidence that police departments have ever engaged in continual, systematic and comprehensive training of officers with respect to the problem of police perjury. Police academy training often does not include the role of the police in a free society, due process, and other ethical issues dealing with investigation and enforcement (Pollock and Becker, 1995). Therefore, this proposal makes a great deal of sense and if it is fully accepted and implemented by all police agencies it would be helpful in addressing the problem of police perjury.

■ *The prosecution should provide the defense with information about police perjury when it comes to their attention.*

It is difficult for anyone to disagree with this proposal since it appears that the constitution (*Brady v. Maryland*, 1963), and various federal and state rules of discovery require such disclosure. Although some state that there is a prosecutorial hesitation to address police perjury, some former prosecutors say that perjury is not condoned or ignored (Chin and Wells, 1998). The real problem with this proposal is that prosecutors will argue that although they may sometimes be skeptical of an officer's testimony, rarely do they have sufficient information about police perjury to bring such information to the attention of the defense. Therefore, although this proposal has merit, its value in addressing police perjury is minimal.

■ *The structure of police departments should be changed and police departments should be reconstructed like the European model which is "less adversarial in nature."*

Reconstructing police departments like the so-called European model is a "pie in the sky" proposal. First, there is no one European model of policing. Second, Europeans have different legal and political systems which significantly affect the operation of their police agencies. Third, there is no evidence that policing in Europe is "less adversarial" than in the United States. Fourth, policing in America is balkanized and there are more than 17,000 law enforcement agencies (Reaves, 1993). Hence, attempting to change the organizational structure of each of these agencies would be a formidable, if not impossible, task. Fifth, there is no evidence that there is a nexus between police perjury and organizational structure. Sixth, this proposal presupposes that the European criminal justice systems do not suffer from problems of noble corruption that is believed to exist in the United States (Delattre, 1995). Finally, the problem of police perjury stems not from organizational structure, but rather from a police culture that supports "catching the bad guys" at any cost, including police perjury.

■ *The warrant requirement should be expanded to all "non exigent searches and seizures" and the exigent warrant exception should be defined narrowly.*

At first blush, this proposal may seem to have merit because it would require greater judicial oversight of police conduct. Although some expansion of the warrant requirement may be reasonable, the problem is that the police are involved in many searches and seizures without warrants because of the practical necessities of police work. It is unrealistic to require warrants for routine arrests (*United States v. Robinson*, 1988), vehicle searches (*Carroll v. United States*, 1925), inventory searches (*South Dakota v. Opperman*, 1976), consent searches (*Schneckloth v. Bustamonte*, 1973), searches of abandoned property (*Abel v. United States*, 1960), stop and frisk confrontations (*Terry v. Ohio*, 1968), and a host of other cases. Moreover, this proposal, if implemented, would require that judges and other court personnel be available twenty-four hours a day, seven days a week. Although Professor Slobogin believes that this proposal will only inhibit police perjury "minimally," he endorses this proposal, recognizing that the warrant requirement ". . .can be eviscerated in several ways by police who have no qualms about lying. . ." (Slobogin, 1996, 1050). In short, this proposal is impractical and would unduly burden an overburdened criminal justice system. Moreover, there is no reason to believe that this proposal would have any impact upon police perjury.

■ *The police should be required to produce their informants in front of an issuing magistrate.*

Professor Slobogin argues that this proposal is designed to stymie the practice of inventing snitches. However, he recognizes that ". . .police who have no scruples about lying can wink at this rule. . ." (Slobogin, 1996, 1050). Well, if police who lie are going to perjure themselves anyway, how can this proposal reduce police perjury? A requirement that all informants be produced before the issuing magistrate will significantly burden and lengthen the warrant application process and discourage people who want to bring forth information because they will no longer be permitted to remain anonymous. In addition, this proposal will seriously undermine the telephonic warrant application system that is available in many jurisdictions. More important, how often the police "invent snitches" is unknown. Other than anecdotal information and speculation, there is little information to suggest that "inventing snitches" by the police is a frequent problem. Hence, the benefits and burdens of requiring informants in all cases to appear before the issuing magistrate is extremely burdensome and may have little or no impact upon the problem of police perjury.

- *Lay persons should be required to accompany the police when the police search a house so that there would be a neutral source of information about such search.*

It is proposed that police officers who conduct a search of houses should be accompanied by a lay person who will be a ". . .neutral source of information about the search of the house. . .[and]. . .who would confront lying officers with eyewitnesses who, unlike defendants, are not tainted by criminal charges. . ." (Slobogin, 1996, 1051). This proposal is impractical, costly, potentially dangerous, and provides little or no assurance that police perjury will be reduced. First, police searches of homes are accorded significant constitutional protection and searches are limited to searches by warrants, consent or exigent circumstances (*Payton v. New York*, 1980). By necessity, this proposal would require a volunteer citizen to be present in every police car in America because the search of a home can take place at any time. Would a sufficient number of lay persons be attracted to this activity? Would lay persons attracted to this kind of activity be police "buffs" who would quickly bond with the police and not be neutral sources of information? If not, could such lay person effectively function as a neutral person while being in daily, close, routine contact with the police? In addition, there is the issue of liability. If such lay person were injured while accompanying the police, who would assume the costs of such injuries? If the municipality assumed the costs, budgets would increase and if a lay person assumed the risk and costs of injuries, there would be very few hearty souls who would volunteer to become neutral warrant observers. Finally, who would assure that the citizen would not invade the privacy of the person being searched, tamper with evidence, or otherwise remove valuables from the home of the person being searched? Would the police officer overseeing the police search be responsible for overseeing the citizen observer who is overseeing the police officer? Would the police be permitted to reject a volunteer believed to be "too neutral" or partial to a potential defendant? It should be noted that approximately eighty percent of a police officer's time is spent dealing with non-criminal activity such as auto accidents, traffic conditions, sick or injured calls, etc., (Bayley, 1994). However, this proposal would require a lay person to be available at a moment's notice when officers may have to quickly search a home. In short, the benefits of this approach are illusory and the burdens significant.

- *Subject police witnesses to lie detection.*

Here Professor Slobogin half-heartedly endorses a proposal that would subject police witnesses at the end of a suppression hearing to a polygraph examination if the court determines that the outcome depends upon the credibility of the police. In such cases it is believed that the court should be authorized to request that the parties supplement the record with a polygraph examination. The judge would not be bound by the polygraph examination, but in an appropriate case would be authorized to give the polygraph dispositive weight. It is proposed that the threat of a polygraph examination will make the police tell the truth or tell straighter stories. This proposal assumes two important facts:

1. The polygraph is a useful device in determining when a person is telling the truth or lying.
2. In a close case involving the credibility of police witnesses, the police witness should not be trusted.

Polygraph evidence is still not admissible in most courts in America because scientific studies cast doubt upon its reliability and the last expression of the United States Supreme Court regarding polygraph is that ". . .there is simply no consensus that polygraph evidence is reliable. . ." (*United States v. Scheffer*, 1998, 1265).

More than thirty years ago, a then future Justice of the United States Supreme Court, Warren Burger, said, ". . .it would be a dismal reflection on society that when the guardians of its security are called upon to testify in court under oath, their testimony must be viewed with suspicion. . ." (Bush v. United States, 1967). This proposal regarding polygraphing police officers who testify at suppression hearings goes a long way toward fulfilling Warren Burger's grim prophecy. In fact, Professor Slobogin recognizes this fact when he says that ". . .[h]ooking police men and women up to machines undermines. . .trust; it tells the public that the credibility of officers of the law needs to be tested like that of criminal suspects, suspected traitors and job applicants. . ." (Slobogin, 1996, 1054). Aside from the issues of the reliability and admissibility of polygraph evidence which are significant, it would truly be a sad day if this proposal became reality and we relied upon machines for truth finding in our courts. No court should subject any person's credibility to such a dubious device and we should not abandon trust in all police officers who testify in "close cases" at suppression hearings.

- *Require that all police actions be videotaped.*

Today, videotaping has become quite commonplace in our society and videotaping police interrogations and other police actions should be considered whenever practical. Videotaping by a civilian bystander presented the American public with the ugly truth of the LAPD brutality in the Rodney King case. The problem of police videotaping is that it is impractical to tape *all* police actions and videotaping involves increased expense, sacrificing privacy interests, and moving further down the road toward an Orwellian society. In addition, there is no guarantee that videotaping will not be subject to tampering by dishonest police officers. Furthermore, what impact videotaping by the police will have upon the problem of police perjury is speculative at best.

■ *Under rewards and punishment it is argued by Professor Slobogin that police officers who perjure themselves should be convicted of perjury and fired. Officers who corroborate their actions via videotape or other means should be promoted for their efforts. Officers who expose police perjury should be given favorable treatment.*

Professor Slobogin states that ". . .criminals themselves lie all the time. . ." and the police ". . .impetus to lie is. . .great. . ." (Slobogin, 1996, 1054), so he proposes certain rewards and punishments. First, he suggests that police who lie should be subjected to perjury conviction and dismissal from the force. Who could disagree with a proposal to convict and fire police officers who commit perjury? The real problem is how can we find sufficient evidence to do what is proposed. When LAPD Detective Mark Fuhrman lied under oath he was prosecuted. Clearly, we should punish officers who violate their oath and commit perjury and we should reward officers who perform in an exceptional manner. The real problem with this proposal is twofold:

1. How do we prevent police officers from committing perjury?
2. How do we distinguish between police officers who are telling the truth and police officers who are lying under oath?

Prosecutors and defense attorneys may have a hunch or notion that a police witness may be less than truthful and prosecutors may not be as zealous as they should be in weeding out police perjury, but there is no persuasive evidence that prosecutors are systematically ignoring evidence of police perjury. In regard to rewarding good police officers, it is understandable that one would want to encourage and support officers who provide corroboration for their testimony, but this proposal is clearly flawed. Corroboration of cases involves good basic police work that should be performed whenever possible. Police promotions should be granted to officers who have demonstrated that they have the knowledge, skills, ability, and experience to perform at a higher rank. Officers should not be promoted simply because they corroborate their cases or do what they should be doing. This proposal misperceives the role of a promotion in a police organization. With regard to officers who expose perjury, they should be treated as favorably as possible because the goal of each police administrator should be, as Frank Serpico has stated, to "create a climate whereby the bad cops will fear the good cops and not the other way around."

■ *There should be a "flexifying of probable cause" and the exclusionary rule of evidence should be abolished.*

The most troubling and draconian of Professor Slobogin's proposals to reduce police perjury are his proposals to "flexify probable cause" and abolish the exclusionary rule of evidence. In flexifying probable cause he argues, in effect, that the traditional probable cause standard is "unwieldy" and should be relaxed or diluted. He believes that if the police possess reliable information that a person sold drugs five months earlier, when combined with recent police observation of people routinely leaving his house with small packages, this constitutes probable cause to search the house. This position was rejected in *United States v. Leon* (1984). It seems to me that the restraint that Professor Slobogin finds so unwieldy represents the essence of Fourth Amendment protections. Professor Slobogin begins his argument to flexify probable cause by stating that ". . .[p]olice lying is not always a calculated assault on the Fourth, Fifth and Sixth Amendments. . ." (Slobogin, 1996, 1055). He then asks the reader to consider an example of a cop who saw a person on a public street. The officer observed a person who the:

> ". . .cop knew to be an addict turn away from him with his left fist closed. . .[t]he officer felt that he had enough evidence to search the man's hand. . .but. . .that he did not have probable cause. . .[so]. . .in such a situation, elaboration of the facts, perhaps adding that the person tried to run away, or that the drug was in plain view, is a natural reaction on the part of the officer. . .[and that has been referred to]. . .as an 'instrumental adjustment', [a] slight alteration in the facts to accommodate an unwieldy constitutional restraint. . ." (Slobogin, 1996, 1056)

There is an old cliché that one cannot be a "little bit pregnant." By parity of reasoning, one cannot be involved in a little bit of police perjury. No matter what euphemism is used, "elaboration of the facts," "instrumental adjustments," "testilying," or "noble cause corruption," police lying under oath is police perjury. I do not understand how Professor Slobogin can decide what the "natural reaction" of all or most officers would be to these circumstances. However, if we assume that the "natural reaction" of all or most officers to these circumstances is to make an illegal search and then commit perjury by an "instrumental adjustment" of the facts, then the problem is not an unwieldy probable cause standard. Rather, the problem is threefold:

1. The individual officer does not understand his or her role in a free society and the importance of Fourth Amendment values.
2. The ethics of the individual officer who would willfully violate his or her oath and commit perjury.
3. The organizational culture of the police agency that encourages, condones or permits an illegal search and perjury to be the "natural reaction" when officers do not have probable cause.

Officers who perjure themselves in this way should be charged with perjury and, if convicted, dismissed from the police department. If an officer does not have reasonable suspicion that he or she can articulate (*Terry v. Ohio*, 1968), or probable cause, (*Draper v. United States*, 1959), the officer should not interfere with the Fourth Amendment rights of any citizen. If police perjury (elaboration of the facts, instrumental adjustments, testilying) is not an assault on the Fourth Amendment—what is? Perjury is a serious felony and when it occurs it represents a malignancy in the criminal justice system. In no case is an officer justified in engaging in perjury, no matter how noble he or she perceives the goal of catching the bad guys. In a free society, the ends cannot justify the means.

A colleague of Professor Slobogin's advises that he not only supports the concept of flexifying probable cause but believes that the ". . .probable cause. . .should be diluted. . .much more than Professor Slobogin suggests. . ." (Reitz, 1996, 1068). I disagree. It is sheer sophistry to think that we should dilute the protections of the Fourth Amendment so that the police will obey the Fourth Amendment. Diluting constitutional standards is not a remedy for police perjury. Probable cause is part of the bedrock of our Fourth Amendment values and to dilute this standard would ". . .leave law-abiding citizens at the mercy of [an] officer's whim or caprice. . ." (*Brinegar v. United States*, 1949). Probable cause is not an unwieldy constitutional restraint. Rather, it is a vital constitutional standard. If police officers are not complying with the constitutional standard of probable cause and are perjuring themselves with respect to their actions, that is not a justification for lowering constitutional standards. Rather, it is a justification for demanding that police officers obey the Constitution and swiftly punish those officers who violate constitutional rights. When a person assumes a position of public trust as a police officer, such person takes on new obligations and if such a police officer is unwilling or unable to live up to these obligations, he or she is free to decline the job (Delattre, 1989). It is also proposed that we should ". . .ask police departments around the country what kind of Fourth Amendment law they would like to have. . ." (Reitz, 1996, 1068). It seems to me that this question was answered more than two hundred years ago by the framers of the Constitution. They decided that freedom from unreasonable searches and seizures is a vital constitutional right and that probable cause is an important Fourth Amendment value. Hence, rather than diluting Fourth Amendment values, police officers should be told that they live in a society that treasures individual freedom and constitutional rights and its citizens expect and demand that their Fourth Amendment rights be protected and police officers should not engage in police perjury.

Professor Slobogin's proposal to abolish the exclusionary rule and rely upon damage remedy as a method of reducing police perjury is unrealistic. The purpose of the exclusionary rule is to deter police misconduct. Before *Mapp v. Ohio* (1961), the police didn't respect constitutional rights (Bouza, 1990). Although the exclusionary rule has been harshly criticized (Burger dissenting, *Bivens v. Six Unknown Named Agents of the Federal Bureau of Narcotics*, 1971), ". . .[i]t is fanciful to believe that abolishing the exclusionary rule and replacing it with a civil remedy would [be] an effective deterrent against police misconduct. . ." (Sevilla, 1974, 849). We should remember the eloquent words of Justice Brandeis who said:

> ". . .[o]ur government is the potent, the omnipresent teacher. For good or for ill, it teaches the whole people by its example. . .If the government becomes a lawbreaker, it breeds contempt for law; it invites every man to become a law unto himself; it invites anarchy. . ." (*Olmstead v. United States*, 1928)

Abolishing the exclusionary rule to lessen police perjury is an illusory and ill advised remedy that would create anarchy in our criminal justice system.

In summary, there are numerous problems with many of Professor Slobogin's proposals, but the major problem in regard to creating almost any remedy for police perjury is that most of the evidence of police perjury is composed of anecdotal information, visceral feelings, and limited studies. The fact is that we know very little about the extent and nature of police perjury across the more than 17,000 police agencies in the United States. There may be some similar problems of police perjury

". . .in some communities, especially in congested areas of large cities [where the police]. . .place a higher priority on maintaining order than operating legally. . ." (Goldstein, 1977, p. 13). However, it has been noted that some of the studies regarding police perjury are "primitive," "methodologically suspect," "undocumented opinions," "studies lacking in rigor," and "impressionistic and anecdotal accounts of police behavior, heavily weighted by the shoutings of defense lawyers who are usually the first to discern police fraud. . ." (Reitz, 1996, 1062, 1063).

POLICE PERJURY—WHAT WE SHOULD DO!

1. *Police perjury should be called police perjury.*

First, we should cease calling police perjury "testilying," "instrumental adjustments" or "elaboration of the facts" or even "noble corruption." Police perjury is lying under oath and is a serious felony that undermines the criminal justice system. Euphemisms tend to mask the problem of police perjury and should not be used to describe this serious problem.

2. *Research should be conducted regarding the frequency, extent, and nature of police perjury.*

We simply do not have enough information about police perjury to engage in most of the reform strategies that have been suggested. We should get the facts before we act. Hence, research should be conducted in a wide variety of police agencies across the United States so that we can better understand the frequency, extent, and nature of the police perjury problem and what police departments themselves can do to assure that officers testify truthfully.

3. (a) *The fundamental mission of all police departments should be the "protection of constitutional rights," and legislation should be enacted to provide that "protection of constitutional rights" is the fundamental mission of all police departments.*
(b) *Police administrators and police supervisors must be held accountable for assuring that officers within their agency obey the Constitution and that all reasonable actions are taken to weed out police perjury.*

Even though there is much that we do not know about police perjury, some action can be taken to address the police perjury issue. First, police supervisors and administrators can take action to raise the consciousness level of the police to the problem of police perjury. Second, police departments can continually reaffirm the duty of every officer to obey the Constitution and testify truthfully. Third, management systems can be put in place to monitor the actions and testimony of police officers. Fourth, compliance with the Constitution can be made the yardstick for measuring the actions of all police officers. Toward this end, it should be noted that police departments are powerfully influenced by their values (Wasserman and Moore, 1998), and police frequently put the apprehension and conviction of criminals as their foremost value (Crank, 1998). The fundamental mission of police departments has traditionally been to prevent crime, protect life and property, preserve the peace, and detect and arrest offenders (Wilson and McLaren, 1963). These are all worthy goals, but they must be pursued in light of the values that are embodied in our Constitution. Therefore, all actions of the police should be value driven and fundamentally grounded in the protection of constitutional rights. A prominent former chief of police in presenting an argument for a police code of ethics has stated that the values in the Constitution ". . .contain everything we need to know. . .so long as we do not blink at the implications of its provisions, [and] so long as we are willing to apply its tenets fully and equally to all. . ." (Williams, 1992, 100). It is important that all police officers know, understand, and cherish the fundamental value that no matter what the nature of a criminal case, in a free society the ends do not justify the means. Hence, fundamental values and a code of ethics for police agencies must be developed and implemented. Historically, even where police departments have engaged in some formal training regarding ethics and values, the training has been directed at new employees and the mission of such programs ". . .has been simple and direct: provide a one time inoculation of 'ethics' in the basic academy with the naive expectation that this brief rub down will endure an entire police career. . ." (Carlson, 1998, 3). Training with respect to constitutional values must go well beyond exposing police recruits to a few hours of police academy platitudes that will have little or no impact upon their operational decision making. All police officers in all ranks must be continually trained and committed to the protection of constitutional rights. After the protection of constitutional rights is established as the fundamental mission of a police agency, a support structure must be developed consisting of directives, training, and supervision to assure that the lofty mission statement is more than a piece of paper that occupies space in a police rule book. If a police department constantly measures a police officer's performance in light of the officer's strict adherence to the Constitution, police perjury should be significantly reduced. This will require continual monitoring of suppression hearings, warrant applications, court appearances, affidavits and the seeking of feedback regarding a police officer's actions and testimony from members of the judiciary, prosecutors, defense bar, and citizen groups.

Since there are more than 17,000 law enforcement agencies in America, it is wise for each state to consider legislation mandating that a commitment to constitutional values be the fundamental mission of all police agencies within the state. Upon entry to a police agency, sworn officers typically take an oath of office and swear allegiance to the Constitution of the United States. A mission statement reiterating one's oath of office and providing continual direction, training, and supervision regarding the implications of one's commitment to the Constitution is vital to assure that police officers know and protect constitutional rights. State legislation mandating this commitment will accomplish the following:

1. It can identify the fundamental values that each state believes should be the operating ethos of all police officers and police departments within the state.

2. It can fix accountability upon police administrators and supervisors for appropriately implementing a commitment to constitutional values within their department.
3. It can mandate that police administrators and supervisors engage in continuous training and supervision to assure that police officers are complying with the Constitution and are not perjuring themselves with respect to their actions.
4. It can provide for sanctions against any municipality that fails to commit its police agency to respecting the Constitution and individual liberties.
5. It can provide a tort remedy against police supervisors, police administrators, and municipalities who willfully, recklessly or negligently fail to train and supervise officers regarding their commitment to the values embodied in the Constitution.
6. This legislation can grant a license to all police supervisors and administrators when these individuals are appointed or promoted to supervisory or administrative ranks in a police agency.

More importantly, this legislation can mandate that an appropriate state agency suspend or revoke the license of any police supervisor or police administrator who willfully, recklessly or negligently fails to commit himself or herself and the officers under his or her supervision to the protection of constitutional values. It is vital that police supervisors and administrators be held accountable for assuring that police officers within their agencies obey the Constitution and that these supervisors and administrators take all reasonable actions to recognize and weed out police perjury within their agency. "...The worst problem in policing is not bad police; it is bad police departments..." (Braunstein, 1998, 124). Police administrators and police supervisors who fail to provide leadership and institute management systems and values that create an environment for a commitment to constitutional values share the responsibility for constitutional violations and police perjury. The *see no evil defense* of police supervisors and administrators with respect to constitutional violations and police perjury occurring within their agency should be abolished. This proposal is consistent with the procedures and practices that are in effect for licensing numerous professionals such as doctors, lawyers, and engineers. No professional who engages in egregious malfeasance, misfeasance, or nonfeasance should be licensed to practice his or her craft in any municipality. These actions will surely raise the consciousness level of the public and the members of all police agencies with respect to the problem of police perjury.

Finally, there are those who say that prosecutors and judges are the villains with respect to police perjury and they can do more about police perjury than anyone else (Dershowitz, 1983). Certainly, prosecutors and judges have a role to play, but the primary control agents for police perjury are police administrators and supervisors who can address the organizational culture that permits police perjury to flourish. The highest court in New York State endorsed the concept of police departments themselves addressing the police perjury problem (*People v. Berrios*, 1971). It is well known that police departments are resistant to change (Goldstein, 1990), and when change in American police departments takes place it is usually forced by the demands of the external environment (Zhao, 1996). For change to occur there must be a stimulus for change, administrative commitment and accountability, and change must be grounded in logical and defensible criteria (Radlet and Carter, 1994). For example, police agencies have undergone major changes with respect to their response to spouse abuse victims and this change has been forced by external social and legal forces (O'Connor, 1998). If external social and legal forces demand that the police testify truthfully and respect constitutional values, and these forces set in place appropriate controls for administrative and supervisor accountability, the police perjury problem will be dramatically reduced or eliminated. Police are what they value and the police administrators and supervisors can significantly influence the values of their police departments.

REFERENCES

Anonymous. (1994a). Noble, Kenneth. *Ruling aids prosecution of Simpson.* New York Times, September 20, 1994, A16.

Anonymous. (1994b). Noble, Kenneth. *Simpson move to suppress evidence turned down.* New York Times, September 20, 1994, A14.

Alderson, John. (1998). *Principled policing protecting the public with integrity.* Winchester, England: Waterside Press.

Bartollas, Clemens, and Hahn, Larry D. (1999). *Policing in America.* Needham Heights, MA: Allyn and Bacon, 254–278.

Bayley, David H. (1994). *Police for the future.* New York: Oxford University Press, Chapter 2.

Bouza, Anthony. (1990). *The police mystique: An insider's look at cops, crime and the criminal justice system.* New York: Plenum Press, 162.

Braunstein, Susan. (1998). Are ethical problems in policing a function of poor organizational communications? *Controversial issues in policing,* 124.

Carlson, Dan. (1998). Handling the tough questions. *The ethics roll call,* 5 (1), 3.

Chin, Gabriel J., and Wells, Scott C. (1998). *The "blue wall of silence" as evidence of bias and motive to lie: A new approach to police perjury.* 59 U. Pitt. L. Rev. 261.

Cloud, Morgan. (1996). Judges testifying and the Constitution. *Southern California Law Review, 69,* 1341–1387.

Commission To Investigate Allegations of Police Corruption and Anti-Corruption Procedures of the Police Dep't, City of New York, Commission Report, 36–43.

Crank, John P. (1998). Understanding police culture. Cincinnati, Ohio: Andersen Publishing Company, 238.

Delattre, Edwin J. (1995, April 21). *Address to police executive research forum annual meeting,* Orlando Florida.

Delattre, Edwin J. (1989). Ethics in public service: Higher standards and double standards. *Criminal Justice Ethics, 8, (2),* 79–83.

Dershowitz, Alan M. (1983). *The best defense.* Rule IV, VI, IX. New York: Vantage Books.

Dershowitz, Alan M. (1992). *Contrary to popular opinion.* New York: Pharos Books.

Goldstein, Herman. (1977). *Policing a free society.* Cambridge, MA: Ballinger Publishing Company, 13.

Goldstein, Herman. (1990). *Problem oriented policing.* New York: McGraw-Hill Publishing Company, 29.

Kittel, N.G. (1986). Police perjury: Criminal defense attorney's perspective. *American Journal of Criminal Justice XI, 1,* 11–22.

O'Connor, Martin L. (1998). From arrest avoidance to mandatory arrest: Some historic, social and legal forces that have shaped police spouse abuse policies in the United States. Roslyn Muraskin, Editor. *Women and justice development of international policy.* Gordon and Breach Publishers, 165–185.

Pollock, Joycelyn M. and Becker, Ronald F. (1995). Law enforcement ethics: Using officers' dilemmas as a teaching tool. *Journal of criminal justice education, 6, (1),* 1–19. The Netherlands.

Radelet, Louis A. and Carter, David L. (1994). *The police and the community,* New York, NY: Macmillan, 98, 216.

Reitz, Kevin R. (1996). Testilying as a problem of crime control: A reply to professor Christopher Slobogin. *University of Colorado Law Review, 67,* 1061–1073.

Reaves, Brian A. (1993). *Census of state and local law enforcement agencies, 1992. Bureau of Justice Statistics,* 1–2.

Sevilla, Charles M. (1974). The exclusionary rule and police perjury. *San Diego Law Review, 11,* 839–857.

Skolnik, Jerome H. (1982). Deception by police. *Criminal justice ethics, Summer/Fall,* 40, 42.

Slobogin, Christopher. (1996). Testilying: Police perjury and what to do about it. *University of Colorado Law Review, 67,* 1037–1060.

Sherman, L. (1982). Learning police ethics. *Criminal justice ethics 1, (1),* 10–19.

Wasserman, Robert and Moore, Mark H. (1988). Values in policing. *U.S. Department of Justice Office of Justice Programs Perspectives on Policing No. 8:* 1–7.

Williams, Hubert. (1992). Why we should establish a police code of ethics. *Criminal Justice Ethics, 11, (2),* 100.

Wilson, O.W. and McLaren, Roy Clinton. (1963). *Police administration,* 3rd ed. New York: McGraw-Hill Book Company, 5.

Zhao, Jihong. (1996). *Why police organizations change: A study of community oriented policing.* Washington, DC: Police Executive Research Forum.

Cases Cited:

Abel v. United States, 362 U.S. 217 (1960).

Bivens v. Six Unknown Named Agents of the Federal Bureau of Narcotics, 403 U.S. 388 (1971).

Brady v. Maryland, 373 U.S. 83 (1963).

Brinegar v. United States, 338 U.S. 160 (1949).

Bush v. United States, 375 F2d 602, 604 (1967).

Carroll v. United States, 267 U.S. 132 (1925).

California v. Hodari, D., 499 U.S. 621 (1991).

Draper v. United States, 358 U.S. 307 (1959).

Mapp v. Ohio, 367 U.S. 643 (1961).

Olmstead v. United States, 277 U.S. 438 (1928).

People v. Berrios, 270 N.E.2d 709 (1971).

People v. McMurty, 314 N.Y.S. 2d 194 (1970).

Payton v. New York, 445 U.S. 573 (1980).

Schneckloth v. Bustamonte, 412 U.S. 218 (1973).

South Dakota v. Opperman, 428 U.S. 364 (1976).

Terry v. Ohio, 392 U.S. 1 (1968).

United States v. Robinson, 414 U.S. 218 (1973).

United States v. Scheffer, 118 S.Ct. 1261 (1998).

United States v. Leon, 468 U.S. 897 (1984).

Chapter **9**

VICTIMS—
PRIVATE VENGEANCE

Meredith George Eichenberg

Abstract

In a civilized society, crime victims and their families are expected to delegate revenge for criminal wrongs to a system of legal, rather than personal, justice. Using recent cases, and literature on the social contract, social control, and punishment, this paper will explore the ethical arguments for and against personal revenge, and why, when such acts occur, they often do so with relative impunity. It will conclude with an ethical analysis of participative retribution, the concept of permitting victims and families to participate in the justice process through such means as victim impact statements, addressing the convicted in open court, and witnessing executions of the murderers of family members.

INTRODUCTION

Personal acts of revenge occur in a variety of forms in our society. We "get even" with those whom we perceive as having wronged us by such diverse means as making obscene gestures, covertly damaging property, physical assaults, and anonymous reports to the IRS. The methodology of vengeance is dependent on the nature of the original act, the circumstances of the precipitating act as well as of the individuals involved, and the personality of the avenger.

Physically violent retaliation is probably what most people think of when they hear the phrase "personal vengeance." Most acts of vengeance, however, are far subtler than direct, violent confrontation. We generally obtain revenge through humiliating our antagonist by way of gossip, public or private criticism, or through besting them in some type of competition. Additionally, many supposedly "random" and "senseless" acts of vandalism are doubtless motivated by the urge to avenge some personal wrong. And of course, there may be those who follow the exhortation of the late Frank Sinatra that, "Living well is the best revenge."

For purposes of this essay, we shall, as much as possible, limit our discussion of vengeance to personal actions that in some manner relate to a formal system of justice. The ethical issues in personal vengeance, however, remain the same whether the act invokes a response on the part of a formal justice system or not. The reader should, therefore, remain mindful of the previously mentioned diversity of vengeful acts.

REVENGE IN AN ETHICAL-HISTORIC CONTEXT

Revenge exists because it fulfills a need. It is rational, therefore, in that it serves a purpose. The intent of vengeful acts is to restore balance to an imbalanced relationship (Marongiu and Newman, 1987). You have wronged me, therefore I wrong you, and this returns us to our social starting point. Most every child old enough to play with other children seems to intuitively understand the idea of personal vengeance and its application to interpersonal relations. The concept has certainly existed for as long as humankind and was probably understood by the Neanderthals. Additionally, at least in Western Civilization, we have identified the concept of personal vengeance with the more complex concept called "justice" for several thousand years (Marongiu and Newman, 1987; Foucault, 1995). Personal vengeance as justice forms the plot of many ancient myths (see for example the classic book of mythology, *The Golden Bough*) as well as several Shakespearean tragedies and numerous recent movies.

It would be logical, therefore, to conclude the desire for revenge is inborn and thus falls under the concept of natural law. Hobbes (1949), for example, took this view, presenting revenge as an innate human need. He believed that, at least partially, this need for vengeance governed our relationships with one another both within and without organized society and, to the same degree, created the need for a well ordered state.

The psychologist Eric Fromm (1983), on the other hand, while admitting that vengeance was a universal reaction to victimization, denied that it was a natural one. He argued that since vengeance was not an act of self-defense or self-preservation, it could not be instinctual. Additionally, he concluded, the nature of vengeful acts being inherently self-destructive argued against them being natural. Fromm, however, defined self-preservation rather narrowly as the confrontation of immediate threats only. Retaliation, however, may be seen as a means of deterring future threats, thus ensuring self-preservation in the long term.

The rationality of self-preservation aside, most human beings, throughout history, seem to have intuitively accepted revenge as a natural human urge (Marongiu and Newman, 1987). As such, some societies, recognizing its potential destructiveness have roundly condemned it as sinful and/or illegal, the ancient Israelites being one example (Johnson, 1988). Other societies, perhaps recognizing its deterrence potential have raised personal revenge to cult-like status, nineteenth century Sicilian society being an example (Marongiu and Newman, 1987). Some have done both. The American "Old South" is perhaps a classic example of this (Wyatt-Brown, 1986; Cash, 1991).

Mixed societal attitudes toward revenge exist because, while revenge at the personal level does seem to be an innate human need and while it does possess some deterrence value, it is also potentially very destructive to a society (Hobbes, 1949). The potential destructiveness of private vengeance exists because the balance we seek to restore is rarely if ever attainable. After all, how does one commit an act of vengeance of the same magnitude as that of the original act? Such exactitude simply is not possible within the realm of human action. If the vengeful act falls short of restoring the balance between the participants, the aggrieved party must continue in the quest to restore the balance. If the vengeful act exceeds the level necessary to restore the balance, the original party may retaliate, thus upsetting the balance again. Or, the original party may simply retaliate anyway. The result is a cycle of violence, almost certain to spiral out of control, eventually having a negative impact on a far greater number of persons than the original participants who began the cycle.

In its most virulent form, this cycle of vengeance results in the so-called "blood feud" where one murder leads to another, each side honor bound to even the score through the taking of one more human life. Such occurrences are not relics of the past nor relegated to novels about Sicilian godfathers. This writer once investigated a homicide that was the latest installment in a family quarrel begun 25 years earlier. At the time of the particular murder (the early 1980s) the body count in the feud had exceeded 20 with homicides having occurred in two U.S. states and Mexico. Similar action-reaction complexes may be seen on an almost daily basis in the gang warfare of many urban centers. The harmful effects of gang related vengeance on the rest of society may be documented simply by watching the evening news.

The innate human need to "even the score" and the potential destructiveness of private revenge creates a serious dilemma for organized societies. From an utilitarian viewpoint, this potential destructiveness makes personal revenge inherently unethical as it produces the exact opposite of the greatest good for the greatest number. An exploration of other ethical theory which is group centered, including but certainly not limited to Christian, Kantian, and Rawlsian ethics, leads to a similar conclusion, personal revenge is unethical. Kant taught that actions should be performed only if universally applicable and performed with "good will," that is, a righteous intent (Durant, 1993). Rawls (1971) extended the social contract to all persons, regardless of status, and defined justice as "fairness," that is, true equality. Kant and Rawls may thus be seen as antithetical to the concept of personal revenge.

Those ethical systems most concerned with individuals rather than societies, notably existentialism and Nietschien ethics, reach an opposite conclusion. We shall reject these individual-centered ethical systems as inherently destructive to the existence of a well ordered society. However, a well ordered society cannot totally ignore the needs of the individual. This leads to the question of how society may ethically deal with a concept acknowledged both for its universality and utility, and its destructiveness.

Private Vengeance to Public Justice

To solve the problem of permitting revenge, yet controlling its potential destructiveness, most organized societies have sought to obtain a monopoly on its practice. Society itself becomes the aggrieved party and is thus able to exact revenge in its own name. By doing so, revenge becomes public, organized, and may, therefore, be held within stated limits. Vengeful acts are seen to benefit the group rather than the individual and consequently possess utility. To complete the transformation from private to public vengeance, we rename revenge "punishment" and as such it restores the social balance disrupted by deviant actions. Additionally, it deters future wrongdoing and validates the reward system for the group itself.

The societal monopoly on vengeance has been obtained through various means. After all, it probably was not easy to get individuals to give up their "right" to revenge in response to greater societal needs. The ancient Hebrews, for example, gained a monopoly on vengeance by condemning personal revenge as sinful. Moses admonished them (and us) that "Vengeance is mine saith the Lord." In the Cain and Abel story in Genesis, God is seen to take revenge for the murder of Abel through the banishment of Cain. God, acting in Cain's behalf, thus becomes both victim and avenger.

But God was not always at hand to avenge earthly wrongs, so Israelite society as a whole was designated to take revenge in God's name, as carefully delineated in a formal, legal code. For example, in the famous, but much misunderstood passage from the book of Exodus, God commanded the people of Israel to take ". . .life for life, eye for eye, tooth for tooth. . ." (NIV, 1978). This was the most merciful code of justice for its time as it not only assured limits to, but equality of, punishment regardless of social status of victim and offender. It also firmly established vengeance as a societal rather than a private matter. That the Code was said to have come directly from God gave it additional force.

Other ancient Semitic peoples, those who believed their kings to be divine, saw the legal codes promulgated by their kings as divinely given. The Code or Hammurabi is perhaps the best known of these; lesser-known legal codes of the ancient era include the king as the lawgiver, whether regarded as divine or not, became the victim of all crimes and all crimes thus became his to avenge (Johnson, 1988).

The Ancient Greeks adopted ideas of vengeance similar to those of the Ancient Semites, granting the power of vengeance to the polis, the city-state, in the name of deity (Clark, 1969). The Romans, superceding the Greeks, shifted from Republic to Empire with the emperor as god, but still held vengeance to be a divinely sanctioned governmental enterprise. These governmental acts of revenge were regarded as ethical at the time simply because they were divinely sanctioned. Additionally, from a strictly utilitarian view, these actions may now be regarded as ethical because they satisfied the need for revenge yet preserved the sanctity of the community through limitations legally placed upon it.

The rise of Christianity, however, complicated the issue. Had not Jesus told his followers to "turn the other cheek" if someone struck them? Had he not also admonished them to forgive those who wronged them as much as "70 times seven times?" He had also commanded them to love their enemies as well as their friends. Even a cursory examination of the Gospels would suggest these as central tenets of Christianity. As to the notion of revenge, early church history as recorded in the New Testament speaks of God, not man, wreaking vengeance on sinners through divine rather than human acts (see especially the New Testament book of Acts).

From Divine Right to Constitutional Authority

From an individual's viewpoint, the early Christian conception of justice is quite simple and quite specific; God will act to avenge any wrongs done you. As long as Christianity remained a small, rather localized cult of Judaism, such requirements as turning the other cheek were not problematic (except perhaps for the individual whose cheek was in question). When Constantine, however, sought to run an empire based on the teachings of Jesus, the application of the "turn the other cheek" philosophy doubtless became very complex indeed.

As Hobbes intimated in *De Cive* (1949), an organized society cannot exist without the ability to use coercive force. While revenge is but one facet in the state's repertoire of force, it is an extremely important one. If the state does not avenge wrongdoing, many individuals will take vengeance upon themselves while others will violate the social contract with little fear of reprisal. This not only threatens the immediate security of the state, but also threatens the credibility of the state to act in society's name.

So how does a Christian state follow the precepts of Jesus and still justify vengeance and other uses of coercive force? Augustine (1957), searching the Bible for an answer to this question, resorted to the Mosaic concept of the people as emissaries of God. But, for Augustine, it was not the people, but rather certain people who were empowered to act in the name of God, that is, the developing Christian priesthood and church hierarchy. These people, delegated to act in God's name, delegated still others whom they empowered to use force, within stated limits, as a sacred trust.

Aquinas and other church philosophers took Augustine's concept still further by combining Aristotelian ideas of government and governmental use of force with the idea of Paul the Apostle (see Romans 13) of governments as God's earthly emissaries (Durant, 1933). The result was the concept that kings are God's personally appointed emissaries on earth. The king, therefore, rules by divine appointment or Divine Right.

It is not then, king or the state or any individual using force, but rather God, with men and women acting merely as tools. Governments are thus enabled to obey the teachings of Jesus by neatly sidestepping them, and are therefore able to keep a well-ordered state. The concept of divine right culminated with the transformation of the divine power of royalty into the constitutional or statutory power of the modern secular state. For us then, the state has assumed the position of both victim and avenger of crimes.

Thus, a key component of the last 4,000 years of Western Civilization may be seen through Hobbes' concept of a social contract designed to avoid the socially destructive nature of personal vengeance by transferring both victimhood and vengeance from the individual to the state. At the same time, the natural desire to avenge one's self is vicariously fulfilled through the state's actions.

This concept has worked for a number of reasons. One of which being, that, after all, one cannot logically seek vengeance for themselves or their families if they are not the "true" victims. If the king or the state is the true victim, it is the responsibility of the king or the state to balance the scales of justice themselves. The individual, now no longer the victim, may be called upon to assist in the process of revenge (justice), or may simply be told to mind her own business.

From the point of view of the social contract, this makes perfect sense; in fact, it may be said that this is the social contract. It also makes perfect sense from the point of view of the Utilitarians as it provides the greatest good for the greatest number: justice and deterrence within stated limits. Thus the scales of justice are balanced and the potential destructive effects of personal vengeance mitigated. For Kantians, such a system of state justice may be seen to raise vengeance to the level of a categorical imperative as it may be applied universally.

However, the concept of state as victim and avenger has not always made sense, perfect or otherwise, from the viewpoint of the individual. A person who has suffered at the hands of a criminal may be hard to convince that the state is the actual victim. And, while vengeance at the societal level is relatively easy to control and limit, it is also relatively easy to coerce or co-opt (Reiman, 1995). Particularly in modern America, vengeance via the criminal justice system is often viewed as a denial of the very concept. For example, plea-bargaining and early release programs seem to have few fans among the general public.

Victims are not having their innate need for vengeance fulfilled; which in turn has lead to widespread anger and bitterness toward the criminal justice system. The situation is not helped when politicians, perceiving the public mood, make the system a whipping boy and political toy.

Whether the public mood toward the justice system is justified or not is irrelevant. If the public perception of vengeance is not being carried out by the system, that perception is real in its effects. The effects of this loss of faith in the criminal justice system include the reluctance or refusal of victims and witnesses to cooperate with police and prosecutors, public accusations of system-wide racism and classism, and a widespread belief of corruption among practitioners.

Personal Vengeance and Modern America

It is clear that in modern civilized society, widespread personal vengeance is unworkable. Yet we tend to lionize those who break the social contract by evening the score themselves. While examples abound, this discussion will be limited to two nationally recognized cases: those of Gary Plauche and Bernard Goetz. Plauche publicly shot and killed the molester of his son in the mid-1980s (Marongiu and Newman, 1987). Found guilty of murder, he was sentenced to a year's probation, the light sentence due at least in part to widespread public approval for his act.

We may certainly understand his motive if not his actions. Indeed, under the circumstances, what parent would not at least contemplate such an act? However, what he did clearly violated the social contract, which grants the monopoly on revenge to the state. Additionally, it is difficult to see so personal an act as utilitarian, nor can it in any way be considered an act of justice, as many of us wish to understand the term.

Bentham, Kant, Rawls, the church and most other accepted ethical systems would condemn Plauche's act as morally wrong. We may understand his action, yet still condemn it as unethical.

Far more troubling is the case of Bernard Goetz, the so-called "subway vigilante" (Brooks, 1998). Goetz was hailed as a hero, a victim who stood up for himself. Approached in a subway car by four young African-American men whom he believed were intent on robbing him, he shot all four. Apparently his actions had been carefully planned long before the particular incident occurred. His act, rather than one of self-defense, appears to have been an act of vengeance for a past mugging committed by some other young black male. It was never entirely clear whether the outpouring of public approval following his actions was directed toward the defensive or the vengeful aspects of his motive.

From an ethical standpoint, the Goetz case is private vengeance at its worst. Innocent bystanders were put at risk in a manner not only breaching the social contract but also violating the utilitarian ethic. From a Rawlsian approach, since the young men upon whom he avenged himself for a past wrong were not the rightful recipients of his wrath, he denied their essential individuality, their full measure of humanity. As if that were not enough, at the bottom of the entire incident is the issue of race and the part it played in his motivation.

That Goetz received such widespread public approval for this act is quite unconscionable. And yet, in a time of widespread dissatisfaction with the justice system it is little wonder that Goetz became a hero for many. The wonder is that there are not more incidents such as the Goetz case. The public wants criminals to suffer. The public wants revenge and has been feeling cheated lately.

In response to the public mood, the state is building more prisons and incarcerating more people for longer periods of time. These demands for punitive retribution are self-defeating, however. Building more prisons and giving longer sentences merely increases the number of prison inmates. And at what costs? We are finding that we cannot build our way out of a prison population crisis. In many states, the expenditures for corrections have surpassed that of social services and education. While the public is currently willing to keep spending for the former, they appear less and less willing to spend for the latter. Building more prisons is hardly doing "the greatest good for the greatest number." Such an allocation of resources is a formula for a social disaster in the not so distant future. It begins to appear that granting the state the monopoly on vengeance also has a high potential to be self-defeating and destructive.

We would seem to have backed ourselves into a corner. If all vengeance is ultimately self-defeating and self-destructive how can it ever be ethical? If, however, vengeance is necessary as a deterrent to wrong doing and if vengeance fulfills some innate human need, how can civilization, as we know it survive without it?

PARTICIPATIVE RETRIBUTION

The base concept of vengeance is ethical, if from no other perspectives than those of the social contract and utilitarianism. Given human nature, an organized society cannot exist without the ever-present threat of coercive force. Vengeance is a necessary part of that coercive force. We have rejected personal vengeance due to its inherent incompatibility with organized society. Carried to the current extreme we are finding vengeance by the state to also be destructive to an organized society and therefore, at least in the current extreme, unethical.

This is no less a dilemma than that faced by the early church-state of Constantine. The question then was whether Christianity and the coercive force of vengeance needed to maintain an organized state were compatible. The question for us concerns the compatibility of the coercive force of vengeance and the ability to maintain a just, secular society. Perhaps the solution is in some sort of compromise between personal and private revenge.

In order for a compromise to be affected between private and governmental vengeance, American society must back away from the current overuse of coercive justice. To do this, government will need to abdicate some of its monopoly on vengeance. Is it moral for the government to do so? Indeed it is. For government to subsume more power than it can effectively wield violates the social contract and runs counter to the doctrine of utility on which democratic governments are based. Can certain responsibilities for vengeance ethically be returned to the individual? Yes, with qualifications. The government's sole ownership of the right to use coercive force cannot be surrendered to individuals. Realistically, it is simply too dangerous to do so, it is neither utilitarian nor just. What we can do is grant the individual victim the right to participate in the retributive process within guidelines set by the state. Such participative retribution falls within the parameters of utility, may logically be considered as a Kantian imperative, and, if carefully guided, should fulfill Rawls' requirements for a just society.

We are in the early stages of affecting participative retribution. We are as yet uncertain as how to proceed and efforts in this direction have been limited. Additionally, the effectiveness of these endeavors is unproven. Therefore, arguing that such techniques are ethical is complicated by insufficient information. Nevertheless, the ethical issues stemming from participative retribution should at least be identified.

Participative retribution most commonly takes the form of the use of victim impact statements for prosecutorial and administrative decision making. This would include sentencing, parole, and perhaps classification or assignment of inmates within the system. Less common, but becoming more frequent are permitting victims (or their families) to address the convicted offender either immediately prior to or after sentence is passed. Also within this category is the practice of allowing the families of murder victims to witness the execution of their loved one's murderer.

Victim Impact Statements

Victim impact statements are a relatively new addition to criminal justice practice. As usually characterized, victims, their families, friends, employers, and sometimes others are invited to write essays explaining the manner in which the criminal act has affected them and their life's prospects. These statements may run from one or two paragraphs to several pages and may express a full range of human emotions. Additionally, some victim impact statements may express the writer's view of appropriate punishment for the criminal.

These statements are generally collected by the prosecutor's office and are intended to play a part in the sentencing recommendations given to the court. Additionally, the documents are often turned over to the court as part of the presentence investigation packet to further aid, or influence, the sentencing decision of the judge or jury. In most states, prosecutors, judges, and juries are under no legal obligation to respond to or factor victim impact statements into the sentencing process.

Morally, however, the criminal justice system has an obligation both to listen to and in some way act upon victim impact statements. While the concept of state as victim of all crimes is important to the maintenance of the social contract, it makes it far too easy to forget the state's obligations to citizens under that contract. Courtrooms, for example, are sterile, controlled environments. When acting within the courtroom the chaos and pain wrought by criminal actions are easy to forget. It also becomes easy to concentrate on process and forget justice. Witnesses and victims, and by victims we must include the family and friends of those who were the actual, direct victims of the criminal act, rarely testify in open court to other than the facts of the act and not its aftereffects. In plea bargaining, victims rarely if ever testify at all.

To leave these people out of the process victimizes them a second time. The state has breached the social contract. As a result, society overall loses faith in the system, people refuse to participate in the justice process, and the process fails. A just society cannot endure under these terms; it will cease to be just and may soon cease to be civil. In other words, the state has an ethical obligation to both listen to and act upon the words and needs of victims of crime.

As long as the state is regarded as the victim and avenger of crimes it will be too easy to ignore the needs and wishes of the actual physical victims of crime. What may be necessary for the health of society is that we modify the view that the state is the sole victim and avenger of crime. Rather, under the social contract, the state should act as the champion for those who are the physical victims of criminal acts. That is, the state should act as avenger only, acting upon the wishes of the victim as far as may be possible within the legally mandated limits of a just society.

If we do not, or cannot, accept such a revision of the social contract, victim impact statements are still a moral necessity to the health of society and thus have great utility as Bentham defined the concept. Granting the opportunity to be heard by the criminal justice system may be all many people desire. Granting them a voice raises their status in society above that of mere victims. By expressing the damage done to their lives by the criminal they are returned a measure of the dignity and sense of self-determination that is often crushed by the perpetrator of the criminal act. The restoration of dignity, self-determination, and other such essentials to the health of the human spirit may be seen as a categorical imperative within the philosophy of Kant.

As victims regain their emotional health, they cease to become victims and thus are restored as more functional members of society, something that can only contribute to the well being of society as a whole. To at least be heard by those in authority will restore a measure of faith in the system by those directly involved in the particular crime as well as society more generally.

An Address to the Convicted

More problematic ethically than written victim impact statements is the practice, still apparently uncommon, of allowing the victim or certain family members to address the adjudicated criminal in open court. This usually takes place either immediately before or after sentencing. The most notable incident of this type occurred when the father of Polly Klaas, Marc Klaas (1998), was permitted to address her murderer. This case also may be viewed as an example of what can go wrong in such cases as the murderer used his statement before the judge passed sentence as an opportunity to respond to Mr. Klaas' remarks. The criminal's response can most tactfully be described as disgusting. It was certainly counterproductive.

The practice of allowing victims or families to address the convicted, at best, is ethically questionable. While berating the convicted may make the victim and the spectators in the courtroom feel good for the moment, the fact that it is done at the expense of the convicted person's dignity can only cheapen judicial proceedings in the long run.

The concept of natural law suggests that all people are entitled to receive a measure of dignity and self-respect regardless of their past actions. To deny any individual this modicum of status is to deny the inherence of human dignity itself. From another perspective, Kant would demand that this practice be adopted only if it were appropriate for every case, something clearly not possible. Finally, the principle of utility is not served by this practice, as it is highly questionable whether it brings about any true, lasting benefit for anyone, much less society as a whole. This practice is at best ethically questionable and should be abandoned.

Witness to the Execution

Early in 1998, Texas chose to execute Carla Faye Tucker, the first woman legally executed in that state since the Civil War. While a great deal of controversy arose over this case, very little of it concerned the fact that certain family members of her victims were allowed to witness her execution. Texas, Louisiana, and a few other states follow this practice (CNN, 1998). For some persons, perhaps, it brings a sense of closure, for others it may add to the trauma of an already damaged life. Victims' rights groups advocate the practice as positive, while anti-death penalty groups condemn it as barbarous. There is no empirical evidence as to what witnessing the execution of a family member's murderer actually does to or for a person (just as we have no definitive empirical evidence of what capital punishment itself does or fails to do for society as a whole).

Due to this lack of evidence, the utilitarian argument is inapplicable to either side of the debate. Nor does the Kantian hierarchy of imperatives seem totally relevant to the matter. Ethical systems as disparate as those of Rawls or Nietsche do not seem to reasonably apply either. Natural law thus seems our only recourse regarding the ethical nature of this issue.

Natural law teaches that all persons have a measure of inborn dignity by virtue of being human. Assuming belief in such a birthright is valid, whatever is done to another should be done to preserve as much of that dignity as possible under given circumstances. As part of this natural law concept of preserving human dignity, individual executions must be carried out with as much aplomb as possible. As the Tucker execution demonstrated, this is quite difficult. Aside from the "circus" which occurred outside the prison walls, the gravity of the events inside the death chamber were marred by the remarks of the former husband of one of the victims, "Here she comes baby, she's all yours now" (CNN, 1998).

Such conduct, most tactfully described as inappropriate, may be regarded as an isolated incident, the action of a single distraught individual. The state, however, has a moral obligation to protect the dignity of both the execution itself as well as all those involved in it. Other than banning family members of victims from the death chamber, it is impossible for the state to guard against such conduct as was displayed in the Tucker case. While the remarks made by the victim's husband in this case may be regarded as extraordinary, the danger of such comments, or worse, is present at every execution conducted with family members of victim present.

Assuming we could empirically establish that witnessing executions was beneficial for some individuals, we are left with the utilitarian trade-off of the emotional health of a few people versus the sanctity of the state and the dignity of its use of the ultimate act of coercion. The state's interests must be predominant for the social contract to be preserved. However, we have no such empirical evidence. Other than for speculative purposes, we must rely on the argument already posited. Allowing the aggrieved to witness the execution of their malefactor is, therefore, unethical and should be prohibited on ethical grounds.

SUMMARY AND CONCLUSION

In this discussion we have briefly traced the development of ethical thinking in regard to the issue of personal vengeance. While the desire for retribution seems to be a part of natural law, its long-term effects on the whole of society are extremely negative. From a functionalist/utilitarian viewpoint, personal acts of vengeance were regarded by organizing societies as destructive and thus violative of the social contract. Vengeance in some form, however, is necessary to preserve the peace of a well-ordered society.

On utilitarian grounds with religious justifications, early societies granted the power of vengeance to the sovereign who became both the victim and avenger of all crimes. This sovereignty was finally passed to the modern secular state. However, while this system of justice led to a more orderly society under a social contract, it led in modern times to dissatisfaction as the actual physical victims of crime became further and further removed from the retributive process.

In response to this isolation of victims, the criminal justice system has recently begun the use of victim impact statements in sentencing and other legal/administrative decisions. This practice is ethical under utilitarian, Kantian, and Rawlsian ideas of justice. Two other procedures, allowing victims/families to address the sentenced offender in open court or to witness executions is not ethical under the same concepts.

It is expected that we will continue to innovate in an attempt to reconcile the need for personal retribution with the need for an orderly society under the social contract. The set of programs known as "restorative justice" may be a more ethical if not more wholly satisfactory solution to this ancient dilemma. That, however, is another topic.

REFERENCES

Augustine. (1957). *The city of God against the pagans.* Cambridge: Harvard University Press.

Brooks, M. (1998). Stories and verdict: Bernard Goetz and New York in crisis. *College Literature, 25 (1),* 77–94.

Cash, W. (1991). *The mind of the South.* NY: Vintage Books.

Clark, K. (1969). *Civilization: A personal view.* NY: Harper & Row.

CNN, Cable News Network (1998). *Special report: The execution of Carla Faye Tucker.*

Durant, W. (1933). *The story of philosophy: The lives and opinions of the greater philosophers.* NY: Simon and Schuster.

Foucault, M. (1995). *Discipline and punish.* NY: Vintage Books.

Fromm, E. (1983). *The anatomy of human destructiveness.* NY: Holt Rinehart and Winston.

Hobbes, T. (1949). De cive *or the citizen.* NY: Appleton-Century-Crofts, Inc.

Johnson, P. (1988). *A history of the Jews.* NY: Harper Perennial.

Klaas, M. (1998). *Marc Klaas' trial journal* [on-line]. Available: http//www.klaaskids.org

Marongiu, P. and Newman, G. (1987). *Vengeance: The fight against injustice.* Totowa, NJ: Rowman and Littlefield.

NIV, New International Version of The Holy Bible (1978). Exodus 21:23, 24. Grand Rapids, MI: Zondervan Bible Publishers.

Rawls, J. (1971). *Theory of justice.* Cambridge, MA: Belknap Press of Harvard University Press.

Reiman, J.H. (1995). *The rich get richer and the poor get prison.* Boston: Allyn and Bacon.

Wyatt-Brown, B. (1986). *Honor and violence in the Old South.* NY: Oxford University Press.

Chapter 10

Probation and Parole Officers: Ethical Behavior

Roslyn Muraskin

Probation is a sentence that is given by the courts in lieu of a prison term, while parole is a form of a pardon meted out to those convicts deemed worthy of being released prior to the end of their sentence. This being the case it becomes necessary for probation and parole officers to have a plan of action. These officers are directed to lay out a set of objectives for the offenders under their direct supervision. To sit around and complain about the large caseloads and then to do nothing is deemed unethical practice. Probation and parole officers interact with the many criminal justice agencies thereby affecting a large spectrum of decisions involved in the judicial process. It is suggested that these two offices, probation and parole, are underfunded thereby resulting in lax supervision of serious felons. This results in large rates of recidivism, and the public's feeling of the inability of these offices to function properly.

PROBATION

Probation departments are most involved with the offender and his/her case. Frequently, the relationship commences at the time of arrest. It is the role of the probation officer to determine the eligibility of bail/release on recognizance (ROR) for detainees. It is their responsibility to prepare probation reports for the court to recommend that the detainee enter an alternative program and to report to the court if this individual has complied with the goals of this program. The probation officer prepares pre-sentence reports for the presiding judges in order to ascertain what kind of punishment/sentence should be meted out. It is the probation officer who will recommend for or against a prison sentence, as well as recommending the kind of facility (minimum, medium, maximum security) in which the defendant will be placed. Once the offender is sentenced and placed on probation, the probation officer's job is to supervise this individual and to make regular reports on his/her progress. There are more than 2,000 probation agencies throughout the United States, differing in terms of residing within the executive or judicial branches of government. There are differences in how they receive funding and whether they function under the Federal or local government.

The mission of probation is to help in the reduction of crimes committed by those on probation. Probation officers assist courts in making their decisions regarding sentencing. It is the role of probation to offer services and programs to the offender to bring him/her back into society. Probation officers and their office participate in those programs that use diversionary means of keeping offenders out of correctional institutions. All citizens have the right to be free from harm, therefore the use of probation is an added factor in making this determination. By the same token offenders have rights to be sure that they are treated fairly and justly under our criminal justice system. Included in this protection of rights are the victims, who continue to demand greater rights in order that they be treated in a humanitarian way as well. If we truly believe that individuals given extra help can change, then the role of the probation officer becomes more important. The current feeling is most offenders, as well as the community at large, are best served through community correctional programs.

Research on probation agencies shows that about 52 percent of the staff constitutes line officers; 48 percent are clerical and support staff, including management positions. Approximately 17 percent of these offices supervise adult felons, while the remaining line officers are involved with the supervision of juveniles. Estimating that there are about 50,000 probation employees, with approximately 23 percent supervising about 2.9 million adult probationers, and with a caseload of 258 probationers, it is not too difficult to see how some officers appear to be overwhelmed by their case load.

Not all offenders are supervised in the same manner, rather there are a variety of risk and needs classifications put into place. Basically, the funds to do the kind of job necessary are not available. Does probation really work? We are told that recidivism rates are fairly low for those on probation for misdemeanors, while high for felony probationers.

PAROLE

Parole is a process whereby inmates are released back into the community prior to the expiration of their confinement in a correctional facility. Parole officers need to maintain information on each of their cases; must supervise those who are released; must conduct investigations regarding parole violations; and assist their parolees in securing work positions, education, and/or vocational training.

Parole was developed in the late nineteenth century when it was felt that individuals serving time in correctional facilities should be entitled to early release under direct supervision where good behavior was evident. The whole purpose of parole is to "improve public safety by reducing the incidence and impact of crime committed by parolees." Parole is not leniency or clemency but a logical extension of the sentence to provide the opportunity to return offenders to society as productive and law-abiding citizens after a reasonable period of incarceration. The core services of parole are: to provide investigation and reports to the parole authority, to help offenders develop appropriate release plans, and to supervise those persons released on parole" (http://www.appa-net.org/position2.html).

The purpose of parole has always been premised on the following:

The majority of incarcerated offenders can benefit from a period of transition into the community prior to completion of their sentence.

Parole has been thought to be the transition from corrections to the outside community. The thought is that with the help of the parole officer, the offender can become reestablished into the community to lead a productive life. The protection of society has always been in the forefront of allowing someone to be released on parole. The feeling is that society will benefit if an offender succeeds outside of prison.

There is a serious concern in the general population that when weighing the rights of offenders, the rights and protection of victims must be given prime consideration. Victims have many interests, not all can be addressed by the probation and/or parole officers. There needs to be a balance between the welfare of the offender and the welfare of the victim. Both offices have as their goal the reduction of crime and the reduction of harm to future victims. The American Probation and Parole Association "supports the provision of effective community-based correctional intervention and supervision that are critical to reduce the risk of further victimization." It is their belief that "probation, parole, and other community-based correctional professionals should be acquainted with and sensitive to the needs of victims while performing their primary service responsibilities to the public and to offenders. This acquaintance and sensitivity must be reflected in agency programming, particularly as mandated by law" (http//www.appa-net.org/position9.html).

In order to do their job and accomplish the goals set forth by probation and parole offices, it has been suggested that the caseloads of the officers be reduced rather dramatically. In the 1960s it was suggested that a caseload of 50 should be established, this was modified later to a caseload of 35. It is evident that professionals working with the difficulties faced on a day by day basis should be limited to a specific number of cases per individual. However, this is easier to express than to practice. Because we live in a pluralistic society where there is decentralization of services, there is no one control over the offices of probation and parole, and therefore uniformity of standards is almost impossible to enforce. There is the feeling that not every offender needs the same type of supervision. Each offender needs a different amount of time meaning that the caseloads of officers can vary. There are those cases where the officer needs to have much contact with the offender, and others where little contact is acceptable. There is a balance to be made between workload and caseload. ". . .

if probation and parole agencies are adopting case management strategies that are based on differentiation of case supervision, then the method for assigning and accounting for those cases must accommodate that approach. It does not make sense to count every case as equal in assigning and accounting for total caseload if the basic supervision strategy is to purposely supervise cases differentially" (http://www.appa-net.org/position9.html).

Little has been done to insure consistency among the varying offices. The probation and parole offices vary in their agency policies on the following points:

- basis for classification (risk, needs, offense)
- contact standards (type and frequency)
- hours of work, leave policies
- collateral duties

To reach national standards is in the minds of the American Probation and Parole Association under certain constraints: To "(1) search for the single 'magic number' for the optimal caseload size is futile, and counterproductive. It runs contrary to the current knowledge and practice in the field, and sets forth an unrealistic expectation that such a standard can be set, be achieved, and produce desirable results. (2) The current (and foreseeable future) state of professional practice in probation and parole is such that national standards based on a workload model could not be achieved. There is too much diversity in practice to enable the basic research and development to be completed. It is not realistic (or desirable) to attempt to force a national model on agencies to facilitate compliance with a national standard. (3) The need for national standards is real and urgent. No group has spoken effectively to this dilemma. . ." (http://www.appa-net.org/position9.html). The recommendation is to have all agencies adopt workload models, and use terminology that is universally accepted. All of these factors impact on the work of the officer and his or her ethical behavior.

Probation and parole officers have been criticized for not doing their jobs. If the supervision is ineffective, if the workers are not doing their jobs and not living up to the ethical standard of doing the job they are paid to do, then there is reason for criticism. Probation and parole officers come out of a civil service system, a system that was "intended to protect employees from the graft-ridden spoils system of former machine politics," resulting in a system that "has created problems of organizational and individual inertia" (Whitehead, 1996, p. 245). John T. Whitehead, in his article, *Ethical Issues in Probation and Parole*, stated that "criminology has yet to set forth either an agreed upon theory of why individuals commit crimes or a proven technology to rehabilitate offenders" (p. 245). There are too many intervening factors within the methods used by probation and parole officers to accomplish their respective jobs. The basics are there: "set up case objectives, monitor offender compliance with court-ordered conditions of supervision, and inform the court when sentence conditions are not followed" (p. 245).

Historically, probation and parole were considered the stepchildren of American corrections. The emphasis had always been on incarceration of the defendant. Today, many convicted of crimes are placed on probation. Viewed from a correctional standard, probation is the most rational model, as it appears to be more humane, a better cost-effective means of tracking an offender, and is the more successful between corrections and probation, as it gives the offender an opportunity to re-do his/her life. "The philosophy of probation and parole is fairly basic: society is willing to take a chance on the offender who is willing to help himself; he would be allowed in the community, to have a job, to raise a family, and to earn a living, as long as he abandons crime" (Souryal, 1992, p. 348). Offenders are supposed to be supervised by officers who have a plan in mind established by both the court and the probation/parole expert.

Probation and parole when first started in this country, were less complicated than they are today. ". . .the initial purposes of probation and parole were as noble as they were motivated by goodness. Probationers and parolees were far less risky individuals than they are today, typically property offenders and first offenders" (Souryal, p. 348). We did not worry about offenders with mental and drug addiction problems as we do today.

The typical probation and parole officer came to this job because of his or her dedication, because of the feeling of being able to accomplish a social good, believing that he or she could change these offenders. These were individuals dedicated to a mission, dedicated to their work, at all times holding up to a good work ethic.

Probation and parole officers are considered professionals, perhaps more so than police officers, as they are required to be college graduates and have experience and/or knowledge of sociology, social work, and criminal justice. These are not typically individuals fresh out of school, but rather individuals who have had a working background in fields related to probation and parole. "Unlike the semi-military structure of police and correctional institutions in which emphasis is placed on discipline and obedience, the environment of probation and parole departments lends itself to more reasoning and greater reliance on self control. Focus is usually on learning the general philosophy, the goals and objectives of the profession, and the ways and means of effectively achieving such objectives. . . . probation and parole officers tend to take professional training much more seriously than police or corrections officials and eagerly absorb the new technologies offered by qualified in-house and outside instructors" (Souryal, p. 349). Probation and parole officers unlike police officers usually carry no weapons and do not have the concerns that police and correctional officers have regarding their personal safety.

Additionally, probation and parole officers identify themselves as professionals as they have more contact with "the centers of justice allocation—the courts" (Souryal, 350). Souryal sees the significant responsibility of the probation and parole officers as having a utilitarian obligation to both protect society and to protect the offenders' interests. He believes that "these two obligations represent the *ethical imperative* of probation and parole" (p. 350).

Any offender placed on either probation or parole can represent either the first-time criminal or the career criminal. The factors affecting probation and parole include the judicial climate, budgets, existing laws, the problem of prison overcrowding, and the community's attitude toward probation and parole. Each individual probationer or parolee brings to the front varying problems, be they psychological, drug addiction, ability to be employed, education or lack of education, and family ties. The officers "are expected to be 'all things' to all people" (Souryal, p. 351)—a feat that is almost impossible to accomplish. Like police and correctional officers, probation or parole officers are expected to do surveillance work, but unlike the former officers, they have to carry large caseloads, are immersed in report writing, and frequently meet resistance by the community.

There exists an ambivalent environment surrounding these officers. As indicated by Friel in Souryal's work, "this ambivalent environment forces devoted officers to 'trash out the definition of their profession and get hoodwinked into the shell game'" (p. 351).

Parole officers are considered unduly underpaid workers; they work in a system that is constantly being criticized (i.e., conservatives view the parole office as letting loose dangerous criminals, while liberals indict parole boards for making arbitrary release decisions that discriminate against or victimize minority group members); there is the impression that these offices are politicized, being compelled to please the politicians. Friel in *The Great American Shell Game* wrote:

> The policymaker says, Psst, parole guy, I don't know what you do, but they tell me you watch guys for 50 cents a day. Here is what I want you to do. Every time we need a bed in the prison, you get a guy out. Around midnight, you slip him out and keep him out. You take this huddled mass yearning to breathe free, drug dependent, mentally retarded, illiterate with no work ethic, psychopathic deviant, and you keep him out right? We will tell the public we are tough on crime and no taxes. OK?. . .Everybody agree? (Friel, 1990, p. 41)

It is no wonder that probation and parole officers resent this kind of borderless community in which they are said to reside. A community which is ambiguous and politically motivated is a hard one in which to accomplish one's job.

How then does one decide what the mission of probation and parole is? If we use community supervision as an example, the feeling is that it is "some combination of assistance and control, treatment and security, or service and surveillance" (Braswell et al., 1996, p. 246). The mission of probation and parole officers is to ensure that offenders are provided with proper services while protecting the streets. Arguments have been made to reorganize the way that probation and parole works. There has been suggested a risk control model, allowing the sentencing judge and the probation officer to focus more on the victim than on the offender. The probation officer, for example, would be more concerned with the victim being cared for than the offender. "Probation conditions should then be tailored to ensure minimal risk. Drunk drivers, for example, might be allowed to drive only to and from work and be ordered to attend both a driver education program and an alcohol counseling program" (p. 246). Presumably this would decrease risks to the community. To carry this further, rather than have an offender committed to a program and undergo treatment for a particular problem, the probation officer would need to determine the likelihood of the offender recidivating. We already have in place electronic monitoring, house arrests, and intensive supervision. There are calls for the abolition of parole, without consideration of what it would cost the typical taxpayer to house every single offender.

These concerns result more from the community's fear of crime than the reality of the situation. What society owes the offender becomes an ethical question. "The criminal has broken the law and he or she must pay his or her debt to society. This view is congruent with the current popularity of neoclassical theories of criminal behavior which emphasize free will and accountability. Offenders are seen as choosing crime and as responsible for their behavior. The only questions are the determination of the debt to society the offender must pay and the control of the offender so new crimes are prevented. Thus the focus is on retribution, deterrence, and incapacitation. None of these perspectives places primary emphasis on assistance to the offender" (Braswell et al., 1996, p. 247).

Crime according to the positivist school is not so simple. There are all kinds of theories that explain why people commit crimes: biologic, economic, psychologic, genetically influenced, and sociologic. Does society have an obligation to help the offender? "The ethical question is: Can society embrace a neoclassical perspective—assume offenders are totally free and responsible—and simply ignore any considerations of assistance to offenders? Or does society have some obligation to help offenders to some degree?" (Braswell, 1996, p. 247).

It is true that offenders and officers usually come from different social worlds. The state does have an obligation to provide probation and parole officers reasonable working conditions, in order for them to do their jobs well. However, with the use of house arrest, electronic monitoring of offenders, other kinds of intensive supervision available, and the call for the abolition of parole, is society ethically obliged to assist the offenders? If we have an environment in which there is more control over the offender, do we present a less than decent working environment for the officer, resulting in negative consequences?

There is also under discussion the possibility of charging the offenders a fee for being on probation and/or parole. This is an ethical concern. Would the collecting of such fees deflect from the job that the officer is obliged to accomplish? And, what if the offender is without funds?

Another ethical concern is the pre-sentence report prepared by the probation officer. The pre-sentence report is supposed to be an objective piece of work that delves into the background of the offender presenting to the judge materials needed to sentence the defendant. In the words of Rosecrance:

> [the pre-sentence report] allows defendants to feel that their case at least has received a considered decision. One judge admitted candidly that the 'real purpose' of the pre-sentence investigation was to convince defendants to feel that they were not getting the 'fast shuffle.' He observed further that if defendants were sentenced without such investigations, many would complain and would file 'endless appeals' over what seems to them a hasty sentencing decision (1988, p. 253 in Braswell, p. 250).

The ethical question here is, "is it appropriate for probation officers to delve into the lives of defendants for the alleged purpose of writing a pre-sentence investigation report when most of the information is not even used in arriving at the recommendation or in determining the sentence? Is it appropriate for officers to feign concern and rapport when they are gathering ammunition for harsh judicial sentences? If a plea bargain has already been reached and the sentence worked out or if a state's determinate sentencing law dictates the outcome, is it appropriate for a probation officer to pry into an offender's life for details which have no impact on the sentence? Is it ethical for a judge to hide behind a probation pre-sentence recommendation when it is actually the judge's responsibility for the sentence decision, no matter how unpopular?" (Braswell, 1996, p. 251).

There are those who argue that the pre-sentence investigation is only a ritual allowing the defendant to believe that something is happening, while at the same time allowing judges to hide behind such reports. On the other hand, we know that such delving into the background of the offender allows the probation officer to work with the offender, while at the same time providing necessary background information for the correctional facility. Such information provides background history regarding the offenders' health, educational and employment background, possible mental health problems, abusive use of alcohol and drugs, all of which tell the correctional facility whether the offender needs to be placed in a counseling program. Even in the case of a plea bargain, the report gives added weight to the kind of sentence to be agreed upon by all parties concerned. These reports should be taken seriously, but should not be used to allow a myth of justice being accomplished in the courtroom.

There is also the element of the whistleblower who makes complaints about his/her department. Probation and parole have always been immersed in the attitude of "cover your own ass," such a philosophy provides resistance to change. Administrators are faced with the ethical challenge of resisting taking the path of least resistance, and checking on the information that is brought to their attention.

Further ethical issues concern the role of the victim. In both probation and parole, we view the role of the victim. Many jurisdictions allow the victim to be heard during the pre-sentence investigation process. In many of the jurisdictions the officer is allowed, and will ask the victim for his/her opinion. The officer needs to check on the kind of damage done to a victim, but the officer need not/cannot simply listen to the victim. There is also the ethical concern about keeping the victim informed about the progress of the case. There is the question of who should inform the victim, if indeed, the victim has the right to know about sentencing, restitution, etc.

If there are questions of the amount of restitution, there is the ethical concern of how much is too much or too little. If it is a case of restitution for a car, how much is the car really worth? What is the market value of the car, how much has the car deteriorated, what are its make and model? The ethical question for the probation officer to consider, does he/she use "the depreciated value or the replacement value when determining suggested restitution figures for pre-sentence reports?" (Braswell, 1996, p. 254).

There is the interesting consideration of when to blame a victim. If your car was stolen because you left the keys in the car with the motor running, do you deserve less compensation than the individual whose car was broken into and stolen, without the use of the victim's keys?

How much influence should a victim have when the offender comes up for parole? How far should victim involvement go? Do victims have the right to talk against the offender when he/she is coming up for parole? Should the victim be informed when the offender is coming up for parole consideration? "Ideally, victim involvement is justified on the grounds that justice demands consideration for the one who has been harmed and that it can be cathartic to allow victims to participate. . . .Involvement often rests on 'two unverified assumptions: that a lot of criminals get off easy and that a lot of victims are interested in appearing and testifying at various stages in the criminal justice process" (Braswell, 1996, p. 255).

There is a disparity issue in that more middle and upper middle class persons participate in parole hearings than the lower classes, who do not have the capability of traveling to the hearing. Further, the system must consider whether there is undue emotion present at the parole hearings.

Probation and parole officers engage in varying work strategies. According to Abadinsky, the kinds of strategies that occur are:

1. *Detection.* This strategy involves identifying when a client is at risk or when the community is at risk. It serves three basic objectives: (a) identifying the individuals who are experiencing difficulty or who are in danger of becoming a risk to the community; (b) identifying conditions in the community that may be contributing to personal problems of the client (i.e., lack of jobs, lack of training, availability of drugs); and (c) determining whether the community is at risk from the probationer or parolee and taking steps to protect the community.

2. *Brokering.* This strategy seeks to steer clients to existing services that can be beneficial to them. The essential benefit of this strategy is the physical hookup of the client with the source of help. Examples include locating a job or a training facility where a client can be educated or retrained.

3. *Advocating.* This strategy attempts to fight for the rights and dignity of clients who need help. The key assumption in this strategy is that there will be instances in which practices, regulations, and general conditions prevent clients from receiving services or obtaining assistance. Advocacy aims at removing the obstacles that prevent clients from exercising their rights and receiving available resources. Examples include advocacy on the part of the Parole Officers Association in New York to change restrictions on parolees who need to operate a motor vehicle in order to pursue legitimate employment needs.

4. *Mediating.* This strategy seeks to mediate between clients and resource systems. The key assumption is that problems do not exist within people nor within resource systems, but rather in the interaction between people, resource systems and between systems. As opposed to the advocate role, the mediator's stance is one of neutrality.

5. *Enabling.* This strategy seeks to provide support and facilitate change in the client's behavior patterns, habits, and perceptions. The key assumption is that problems may be alleviated and crises may be prevented by modifying, adding, or extinguishing discrete bits of behavior by increasing insights or by changing the client's values and attitudes.

6. *Educating.* This strategy involves conveying and imparting information and knowledge as well as developing various skills. A great deal of what has been called social casework or therapy is simple instruction.

7. *Community Planning.* This strategy entails participating in and assisting neighborhood planning groups, agencies, community agents, or governments in the development of community programs to assure that client needs are represented and met to the greatest extent feasible.

8. *Enforcing.* This strategy requires the officer to use the authority of his or her office to revoke the probationer/parolee's standing due to changes in status quo which involves heightened community or client risk outside the control of the officer (Braswell, 1996, p. 364–365).

Reviewing these strategies, the ethical questions raised: how do professional probation and parole officers do their job? What is the population that they are serving? How is social harm minimized by the work of these officers? Do these officers disregard the welfare of the offenders? Is this practitioner, the officer, to become depersonalized in his/her work situations? Should the officer regard the probationer/parolee as a client in need of treatment and help? Should officers seek to provide adequate housing, training, employment, and psychological assistance, along with other needed services? Should the offenders be treated with a certain amount of dignity? Does the role of the officer preclude or include getting personally involved with the offender? How far does or should their relationship go? Should the officers have only minimal concern for the client as well as for the welfare of the community? Is the officer to be placed in a passive role, rather than an active role? Can the officers act with some moderation with regard to both the offenders they supervise and the community to which these offenders return? In the words of Abadinsky, "[t]heir (the officers') decisions are based on an intellectual view of the interests of 'community' as equal to the interests of 'corrections'" (Braswell, 1996, 368). To sum it up, the roles of the probation and parole officers are somewhat related to Solomon. Officers are thought to be rational, consistent, as well as practical. "When gifted with the virtues of goodness and morality, endowed with an application for social justice, and enveloped in good faith, such practitioners could be the most ethical yet. . ." (Braswell, 1996, 368).

The American Probation and Parole Association has adopted a Code of Ethics:

1. I will render professional services to the justice system and the community at large in affecting the social adjustment of the offender.
2. I will uphold the law with dignity, displaying an awareness of my responsibility to offenders while recognizing the right of the public to be safe-guarded from criminal activity.
3. I will strive to be objective in the performance of my duties, recognizing the inalienable right of all persons, appreciating the inherent worth of the individual, and respecting those confidences which can be reposed in me.
4. I will conduct my personal life with decorum, neither accepting nor granting favors in connection with my office.
5. I will cooperate with my co-workers and related agencies and will continually strive to improve my professional competence through the seeking and sharing of knowledge and understanding.
6. I will distinguish clearly, in public, between my statements and actions as an individual and as a representative of my profession.
7. I will encourage policy, procedures and personnel practices which will enable others to conduct themselves in accordance with the values, goals and objectives of the American Probation and Parole Association.
8. I will constantly strive to achieve these objectives and ideals, dedicating myself to my chosen profession (http://www.appa-net.org/ethics.html).

Probation and parole agencies fall somewhere between the therapeutic model, i.e., improving the welfare of the individual, and the intervention model, i.e., with a range of behavior modification of individuals to changing capitalist society as we know it, even if there is a contradiction to the conditions of the most popular interest of the community. The best ethical means is to serve both the client and the community. With the high number of offenders on probation and parole, the issue of proper ethical behavior is crucial.

References

Braswell, Michael, McCarthy, Belinda R., & McCarthy, Bernard J. (1996). *Justice, crime and ethics.* Cincinnati, OH: Anderson Publishing Co.

Souryal, Sam S. (1992). *Ethics in criminal justice: In search of the truth.* Cincinnati, OH: Anderson Publishing Co.

Whitehead, John T. (1996). Ethical issues in probation and parole. In M. Braswell, B. McCarthy & B. McCarthy (Eds.), *Justice, crime and ethics.* Cincinnati, OH: Anderson Publishing Co., 243–259.

Internet:

Parole APPA Position Statement, 1, http://www.appa-net.org/position2.html

Parole APPA Position Statement 1, http://www.appa-net.org/position9.html

Caseload Standards APPA Issues Papers, http://www.appa-net.org/issue1.html

Code of Ethics APPA, http://www.appa-net.org/ethics.html

Chapter **11**

THE ETHICS OF THE DEATH PENALTY[1]

Richard R.E. Kania

Abstract

Clearly among the criminal justice faculty teaching about the death penalty, many find the use of capital punishment highly objectionable, and some of them will use their classrooms to convey their arguments against it. At academic conferences vocal advocates have passed resolutions against the death penalty, and held panels to criticize its continued use. In the more important books on criminal justice ethics, it is customary to give the arguments both for and against capital punishment, but the full range of pro-execution arguments rarely appears, and the selected defenses often are the easiest "straw men" to bat down. Rarely are the social contract or religious bases adequately argued.

As a supporter of limited use of capital punishment, the author presents some pro-execution arguments either absent from, or seriously understated, in the prevailing literature. Support for executions as an ethical exercise of state power can be found in the moral and religious doctrines of the leading Western religions and in acceptance and interpretation of the social contract.

---

[1]This article was originally published in *The Justice Professional*, 12 (3), 145–157.

The author finds no necessity in showing that executions are deterrents for them to be ethical.

He shares the suspicion of many death penalty critics that executions are not economical in any utilitarian cost-benefit analysis approach. Yet he denies that they must therefore be viewed as narrowly retributive. In doing so, he finds executions defensible within established ethical frameworks. While not supposing to convince others of his views, the author does hope to provide his peers with knowledge of a wider range of pro-execution arguments, and thus open up their classrooms to a wider range of perspectives, pro and con, on the death penalty controversy.

In the contemporary academic community is an obvious moral revulsion to the use of the death penalty. Objections to it are grounded in enlightenment philosophies and more recent moral reason (Bedau, 1977, 1982; Bohm, 1991, 1992; Marshall, 1972; Peterson and Bailey, 1988; Reiman, 1993; Sellin, 1980; Stewart, Powell and Stevens, 1972). Most of the more progressive nations of the world have banned the death penalty, and criticize the United States soundly for not banning it (Amnesty International, 1987; Gray and Stanley, 1989). A condition of membership in the European Union is a death penalty prohibition.

Yet the defenders of the use of the death penalty seem unmoved by this intellectual and legal trend against using executions and hold to their views despite efforts by scholars to show that there is minimal deterrence value in executions and moral philosophers arguing for the ultimate sanctity of human life. Some continue to do battle on the deterrence issue, but their debate is not so much one of ethics as pragmatics: does it work? (Carrington, 1978; Ehrlich, 1975; Phillips, 1980). For other advocates of the death penalty though, different moral imperatives are operational. Frequently encountered are the retributional or "just desserts" arguments, often based on concepts of "natural law" (Berns, 1979; Green, 1969; Pollock, 1993; Sherman, 1982; Souryal, 1992; van den Haag, 1968, 1993), and sometimes more directly based on religious doctrine (Primoratz, 1992).

Among other pro-execution moral imperatives, religious ethics and social-contract-based moral reasoning are important, but frequently underrepresented in the debate. Both of these perspectives are firmly grounded in Western moral and ethical reasoning and ought to be recognized as equally valid ethical foundations for support of the death penalty.

THE MIXED MESSAGE OF WESTERN RELIGIONS

The death penalty has been with us far back into ancient history and mythology, but then so have less severe alternative punishments. A key source of this tradition is the Bible. The Torah and the Old Testament's first five books are not only the foundation for Jewish and Christian faiths, they were a main source for our Western European legal traditions. In the Old Testament we learn that Cain, on killing Abel, cried out "

'And I shall be a fugitive and a wanderer on the earth, and whoever finds me will kill me.' But the Lord said to him 'Not so! Whoever kills Cain shall be punished seven-fold.' Then the Lord gave Cain a token (the mark of Cain) so that no one finding him should kill him" (Genesis 4:14–15). The irony of God denying humankind the privilege of killing Cain, the first mythological murderer, and then threatening any potential executioner with punishment sevenfold, whatever that might mean, establishes both a Judeo-Christian precedent against the death penalty.

Yet the same God instructed that Moses put to death sinners against his holy place at Sinai: "Set limits for the people all around the mountain and tell them: 'Take care not to go up the mountain, or even touch its base. If anyone touches the mountain *he must be put to death*. No hand shall touch him; he must be stoned to death or killed with arrows. Such a one, man or beast, must not be allowed to live!' " (Exodus 19:12–15).

Exodus 20 (the Ten Commandments) and Exodus 21:12–17, "Whoever curses his father or mother shall be put to death." In Exodus 22:1, we are instructed that, "If a thief is caught in the act of house breaking and beaten to death, there is no blood-guilt involved." Exodus 22:17 admonishes, "You shall not let a sorceress live." In Exodus 22:18 is the warning that, "Anyone who lies with an animal shall be put to death."

Deuteronomy 13:7-10 says, "If [anyone] entices you secretly to serve other gods [. . .] do not yield to him or listen to him, nor look with pity upon him, to spare him or shield him, *but to kill him*" (italics added). Deuteronomy 16:18 adds, "You shall appoint judges and officials throughout your tribes to administer true justice for the people in all the communities which the Lord, your God, is giving you." Deuteronomy 17:4–5 cautions against idolatry, "And if, on being informed of it, you find by careful investigation that it is true [. . .] you shall bring the man or woman who has done the evil deed out to your city gates and *stone him to death*" (italics added). Deuteronomy 19:4–12 speaks of homicides with and without malice, and the role of cities of refuge, especially in 19:6, "the avenger of blood may in the heat of his anger pursue the homicide and overtake him and strike him dead. . . ." A murderer with malice who flees to a city of refuge must be turned over to the elders of the victim's city, who are to "hand him over to be slain by the avenger of blood."

The Old Testament is strict, dogmatic, morally righteous, and retributive in its approach to justice and punishment. The New Testament is less so with its shift of focus toward salvation, grace and forgiveness. Jesus, according to Matthew 5:21, says, "You have heard that it was said to the ancients, 'Thou shall not kill;' and that whoever shall kill shall be liable to judgment. But I say to you that everyone who is angry with his brother shall be liable to judgment." Continuing Matthew 5:38 says, "You have heard that it was said 'An eye for an eye, and a tooth for a tooth.' But I say to you not to resist the evildoer; on the contrary, if someone strike thee on the right cheek, turn to him the other also. . ." and Matthew 7:1 states, "Do not judge that you may not be judged. . . ."

However, these comments apply to the acts of individuals in seeking revenge and retribution. These same passages recognize the role of judges in settling human conflicts: "Come quickly to terms with the opponent. . .lest thy opponent deliver thee to the judge, and the judge to the officers and thou be cast in prison" (Matthew 5:25).

This apparent contradiction may arise because Jesus came, not to replace the old laws, but to advise men and women in the ways of true, spiritual justice: "Do not think that I have come to destroy the Law or the prophets. . .not one jot or tittle [a punctuation mark] shall be lost from the Law till all things have been accomplished" (Matthew 5:17).

Although post-dating the New Testament, and clearly aware of the teachings of Jesus, the Koran is no less demanding of death as punishment than the Old Testament is for crimes against its laws. In the Koran, Sara 33:60–70, says, "If the hypocrites and the men of tainted heart and the stirrers of sedition in Medina desist not, we surely will stir thee up against them. . . . Cursed wherever they are found; they shall be seized and slain with slaughter!"

Sara 9 continues, ". . .kill those who join other gods with God wherever ye shall find them. . ." Sara 10 adds, ". . .he who slayeth anyone, unless it be a person guilty of manslaughter, or of spreading disorders in the land, shall be as though he had slain all mankind. . .", and ". . .shall be that they be slain or crucified, or have their alternate hands and feet cut off. . . ."

"Verily, we have sent down the law [Towat] wherein are guidance and light. . . And therein we have enacted them; life for life, and eye for eye and nose for nose, and ear for ear and tooth for tooth, and for wounds retaliation. . .! And in the footsteps of the prophets caused we Jesus, the son of Mary, to follow, confirming the law which was before him: and we gave him the Evangel with its guidance and light, confirmatory of the preceding law [the biblical law of Exodus and Deuteronomy]. . . . And whose will not judge by what God hath sent down—such are the perverse".

Thus the prophets and lawgivers of the three great Western religions do concur in the use of death to punish and demand retaliation against the criminal—even though both Mohammed and Jesus spoke of the virtues of mercy—in preference to, not in place of the Law of Moses. So we cannot use religious prohibition against death penalties. The three great religious traditions of the West, Judaism, Christianity, and Islam, all advise both restraint against, and yet support the moral use of, the death penalty (Pollock, 1993, 178; Thiroux, 1980, 124). Clearly for a person turning to religious faith for moral and ethical guidance, support for the death penalty is there, equivocal, but undeniably there.

To the extent that Western political societies strive to remain secular and avoid being overly influenced by religious dogma, what the West's three great religious traditions hold may not matter in law and policy. But they do matter in teaching and analyzing ethical principals in the academic world. Many students and professors come into the discussion with religiously based ethical principles. It is to the discredit of the academic community to dismiss these as irrelevant to the discussion. So much of early European and subsequent Western legal tradition rises from the commandments and strictures of the Old Testament. Yet the trend in modern scholasticism seems to ignore these Biblical roots of jurisprudence. In Lawrence Sherman's otherwise admirable review of the ethical frameworks which may be brought to bear in criminal justice education, there is no mention of religious based principles (Sherman, 1982, 55–61). Kleinig and Smith (1997) similarly omit religious frameworks in their collection on *Teaching Criminal Justice Ethics*. John Rohr's *Ethics for Bureaucrats* mentions religion only in the context of the First Amendment (1978, 149–170). Sam Souryal's exhaustive text on the topic gives brief mention to the contradictions of religions (1992, 77, 81), reviews radical opinion on religion

(1992, 756), and quotes the Sermon on the Mount (1992, 79–80), but otherwise pays little heed to religious ethical principles in criminal justice education. He cautions, "The realm of faith is considered too personal to be subjected to scientific scrutiny" (Souryal, 1992, 74). Later he does return to the early Christian religious teachings of Saint Augustine and Saint Thomas Aquinas (Souryal, 1992, 129–140), but only modestly connects them into modern ethical issues in criminal justice. An exception to this trend is Joycelyn Pollock's text, *Ethics in Crime and Justice* (1993), which does give a balanced, if brief, recognition to the application of religious principles in ethical criminal justice decision making (1993, 14–18, 23, 31, 82–83, 106, 112, 119, 147, 159), including a balanced discussion of the death penalty issue (1993, 178).

More general studies of ethics are perhaps only a little better in examining the religious foundation of ethical decision making. George B. Wall (1974) devoted significant space to the discussion of religious principles in his *Introduction to Ethics*. He refers to Charles Hodge, Thomas Aquinas, Saint Paul, and Socrates in the discussion (1974, 19–40). Jacques Thiroux's *Ethics: Theory and Practice* also mentions religion, but largely to find reasons why not to rely upon it as a basis for ethical reasoning (1980, 8–10, 18–23). He does cite the Ten Commandments to lend support to some basic ethical principles (1980, 16, 124, 127–128). Thomas Mappes and Jane Zembaty's *Social Ethics* also incorporates some religious argumentation in a collection of articles on the death penalty (1992, 148–188), with some balance of viewpoint, but only one religion-based argument (Primoratz, 1992). Both William K. Frankena's popular *Ethics* primer (1973) and the frequently used *Social Philosophy* of Joel Feinburg (1973) give little attention to contemporary religious foundations of ethical thought, although the two small books are among the most widely used introduction to ethics and moral philosophy in undergraduate college courses.

THE SOCIAL CONTRACT

The social contract argument is based on the educated acceptance of the social benefits of living in the company of others and agreeing to follow their rules and thus taking the risks and disadvantages of living in such a society (Pollock, 1993, 75, 78–80; Souryal, 1992, 66–68). In a community, the social contract obliges each candidate resident to accept things such as the death penalty as part of the social package of options, or to move on.

In its simplest and most direct form, regarding life and death questions, each of us agrees not to kill others in exchange for the security that others will not kill us or those dear to us. As long as this trust is maintained, individuals can feel secure in the company of others. But if there are among us individuals who will not conform their behavior to this basic exchange principle, trust and security break down and the very fabric of cooperative society is at risk of unraveling, as events in Bosnia and Kosovo in the 1990s so painfully demonstrated. These homicidal persons, by their actions in killing us or those dear to us, are not abiding by the contract. Therefore their action nullifies our obligation to them (Thiroux, 1980, 162–163). Their lives may be forfeit, if that is the socially sanctioned response to their homicidal actions.

As in the preceding religious argument, the social contract does not require or compel a quid-pro-quo response. In this way it differs from some of the more direct retributionist arguments, which seem to require it. While the death penalty is not required in a social contract, if it is agreed upon, then society makes it as a term of our co-existence, "if you kill me or mine, you forfeit your life," then it is the just, ethical response to homicide.

This social contract argument protects juveniles and the mentally deficient from the risk of execution because they are judged to be immature or incapable of understanding the terms of the social contract. But for those with mature and sound minds the contract is binding. In terms of the modern applications of the death penalty, we are obliging ourselves not to kill others with malice and premeditation on the condition that they not kill us with malice and premeditation. If we fail to live up to our end of the bargain, then the rest of the community has no further obligation to preserve our lives; thus we risk forfeiting them.

We cannot reason, as did Cesare Beccaria incorrectly (trans. 1963, 45), that no human can contract away one's life: "Was there ever a man who can have wished to leave to other men the choice of killing him? Is it conceivable that the least sacrifice of each person's liberty should include sacrifice of the greatest goods, life?" Indeed it is possible. We do so frequently and willingly by our choices, especially when undertaking dangerous occupations and activities. We take our own lives far more often than we willfully kill strangers or family or friends. We are at greater risk of homicide from our hands than that of a homicidal enemy. While some do argue against the morality of suicide, still others defend the right as an expression of the principle of individual freedom (Thiroux, 1980, 149–152). In the latter view, we profess that our lives are truly our own to live and, therefore, to terminate when it suits us.

Some have reasoned that to die by our own hands is to deny our obligations to others; we leave unpaid debts to family, friends, associates, employers, and society at large. If we do so by our own hand, we are cheating on these obligations to others. Others do not feel that this is so. We are in a series of continuously mutual exchange relationships. We owe to others only so long as we draw from others. We cease to take, to give, to repay, to accrue obligations from others when we die. Our estate remains for the settlement of our debts. Our memory survives to comfort our next-of-kin, and what we have taught and shown others is their endowment.

Indeed, were we to reason that our unpaid debts are society's hold on us, would not that reasoning enslave us? Such an argument easily also could be used as a fearful rationale for society rejecting the company of those too old, too weak, too ignorant, or too unproductive to generate a balance between what they can give and what they must receive to survive. Modern legal tradition does not bind our next of kin with our debts, as it did in past ages. The laws of inheritance even protect a part of our estates from total debt collection to the benefit of our heirs. Thus in our laws we believe that our debts to society are settled at death, however imbalanced they may have been before.

So, many do believe we can—we have the moral, rational, and intellectual capacity—contract away our lives, or at least to place them at great risk. Indeed, many have done so, serving their countries in war, placing their lives at risk for the rewards of social life. As many others did, some have chosen Canada, or devised evasive strategies to avoid military service. The option was there—to serve and risk our lives—or to flee to safety or to evade the draft in various legal and devious ways. Those serving the community as police officers also accept a risk to life for the rewards of services; as do those who follow careers in fire-fighting, deepshaft mining, demolitions work, and many other hazardous professions and occupations. Such persons are aware that their career choices include acceptance of the real risk of increased danger of harm and death. Indeed, we offer our lives to every hazard we encounter. We drive the dangerous highways when staying in our homes would be so much safer; and prefer a flammable frame house over a safer, but damp and dark cave. Many engage in high risk sports such as sky diving, mountaineering, running with the bulls in Pampalona, in part because they are life-threatening.

Each activity we undertake has its risk, so why not indeed attach risk to extremes of criminality? It may be counter-argued that the death penalty is an artificial risk, one created by humankind; while other risks mentioned before are inherent to the activity. This is a compelling point. But it may be dismissed by pointing out that social occupations and industries are also human constructs, that other, safer means could be employed to achieve similar ends. Indeed, the occupational safety movement of modern times reflects this very thinking.

A second reasonable criticism of the social contract argument is that no one living today ever had a voice in framing the terms of the contract. In part this is true. We were not alive in 1787, much less delegates to the Constitutional Convention which framed the Constitution of the United States, but we do feel both bound and protected by its provisions. Yet we are aware that the social contract, be it a written constitution, or the body of social norms and mores into which we are thrust, can be changed. Only in a contract allowing no amendment and escape is there social tyranny.

So we do have the capacity to enter into a pre-existing arrangement which has risks associated with it—our social life—and our social contract. Does this mean each of us has agreed to all of the terms of this on-going social contract? The answer is a qualified "yes," so long as we retain the means to withdraw from that society or to participate in the amendment of the contract. We could go to another state or nation to live, finding for ourselves a society officially without the death penalty. Once there, we could obey or violate their laws without risk of the death penalty. Or we could stay in our own state or nation and lobby for abolition.

But what of the citizen of the former German Democratic Republic Hitler's Germany, or the Stalinist era U.S.S.R. and similar places that have closed their borders to their own emigres and denied them the choices we have had? They have not "voluntarily" agreed to anything. They were denied the opportunity to withdraw from that society and had no voice in bringing about social change within it. This is injustice in the reasoning of social contract theory; no social contract existed for these societies.

There is no injustice as long as there remains a recourse within our capacity to exercise. We exempt the mentally incompetent and the children from the penalties of our law because we know they cannot make reasoned choices. So too should we exempt the senile and those directly coerced to act against the law, including those living in totalitarian societies. The advocate of this model of the social contract does agree with Beccaria (trans. 1963) on the point that reason and will are necessary, and no will exists if no options are given.

Those among us possessed of mature reasoning powers and informed of the laws and penalties associated with them are free to choose to obey and avoid risk of penalty, disobey and accept the risk, obey while trying to amend the penalties, or flee to other social arrangements one might prefer. If we stay, we are doing so to accept both the benefits and the risks of our social lives in this company.

The contract argument is based on free will and the educated acceptance of the social benefits and risks of living in a society which has opted for the death penalty. Even if there is no educated acceptance on the part of an individual, the ethical aspect is present so long as such an individual retains the ability to raise objections and to act lawfully to change the law, the contract, on the death penalty and all major penalties. We accept the death penalty as one of the risks of living in this association and benefiting from it. We give control over our lives to it without loss of free will.

Thus there is no ethical disqualification in religious or social contract theory to justify abolition of the death penalty. However, while both permit it and provide for its ethical character when fairly administered, neither require it be used. In the religious creeds of both Christ's and Mohammed's teachings are appeals for mercy and forgiveness, accompanied by contrition. In the development of the contemporary social contract, it rests with the members of society to continue or to change the existing arrangements. The content of the contract is not the ethical element; it is adhering to what has been freely accepted that gives the contract its ethical character.

In this religious ethic, mercy, forgiveness, and contrition are linked together. So let us consider killers well-known to us via the mass media and literature, people such as Jack Abbott, the infamous author of *Belly of the Beast*. Where is his contrition? Examine Perry Smith in Truman Capote's *In Cold Blood*. Was there contrition? In Joseph Wambugh's *The Onion Fields*, Gregory Powell and Jimmy Lee Smith, the killers of a police officer they held as an unarmed hostage, knew how to be repentant at the right moments, only to shift to callous self-interest after it served their purpose. Perhaps Jimmy Smith was contrite. His partner Gregory Powell never was. He blamed anyone and everyone and anything: his broken home, latent homosexuality, institutionalization at an early age; always excuses, never contrition. Neither Jesus nor Mohammed argues for mercy when the offender shows no remorse.

In the unfortunate, highly publicized 1998 case of Karla Faye Tucker, the Texas woman put to death for her part in a double murder, her openly expressed and televised contrition was not considered by Governor George W. Bush of Texas. As a civil official he was not ethically bound to do so. Under the terms of the social contract expressed by the laws of Texas, it was his choice, and his decision was procedurally correct, and therefore unquestionably ethical.

The spiritual leaders who came to her defense were obliged to heed her contrition and to accept her among the congregation of the righteous. Their behavior in seeking her reprieve was moral and ethical; but then so was their behavior in standing aside and allowing the state to follow its less forgiving laws. Both their appeals to the governor and their acceptance of his decision were faithful to the teachings of Christianity.

Karla Faye Tucker had violated the most fundamental aspect of the social contract upon which a free society depends. She had taken two lives with malice and forethought, initially without contrition. Her actions had forfeited her fundamental right to live in society, and made her execution both lawful and ethical, even if tragic.

These two positions, religious guidance and the terms of the social contract are bound together in the teaching of the three great Western religious traditions, especially Christianity and Islam. While they do not require the death penalty absolutely, they oblige the religious to accept the judgment of the laws, including acceptance of the death penalty. The validity of this principle is most conspicuous in how Jesus himself accepted his own sentence of death, and earlier stayed the hands of his disciples who were prepared to resist his arrest.

SUMMARY AND CONCLUSIONS

In teaching students today about the principles of ethics, these religious underpinnings ought not be ignored. Nor should the essential notions of the social contract. The religious convictions of those who turn to their spiritual faith for ethical guidance are every bit as compelling as the analytic moral reasoning arguments of the enlightenment philosophers, contemporary rationalists, and moral relativist critics whose ideas are more popular among our academic colleagues.

Defenders of the death penalty continue to hold to their views despite efforts by scholars to show that there is minimal deterrence value in executions and moral philosophers arguing for the ultimate sanctity of human life. For some advocates of the death penalty the better known deterrence, retributional and "just desserts" arguments are sufficient. The social contract lends support to some advocates. For others, moral positions directly based on religious doctrine are compelling. Religious ethics and the social contract as foundations for moral reasoning are substantially underrepresented in the scholarly debate. Yet both of these moral perspectives are firmly grounded in Western thought and tradition and ought to be presented as valid ethical foundations for support of the death penalty. While neither requires the use of executions, both lend moral sustenance to its selective use. Those teaching about the death penalty owe it to their students to recognize these additional viewpoints and to introduce them to the moral discussion.

REFERENCES

Amnesty International. (1987). USA: *The death penalty*. London, U.K.: Amnesty International Publications.

Beccaria, Cesare. (1963). *On crimes and punishments*, (Henry Paolucci, Trans.) Indianapolis, IN: Bobbs-Merrill (original work published 1764).

Bedau, Hugo Adam. (1977). *The case against the death penalty*. American Civil Liberties Union (ACLU) pamphlet.

Bedau, Hugo Adam. (1982). *The death penalty in America*, 3rd ed. New York, NY: Oxford University Press.

Berns, Walter. (1979). *For capital punishment: Crime and the morality of the death penalty*. New York, NY: Basic Books.

Bible, New Catholic Edition. (1957). Confraternity-Douay Version. New York, NY: Catholic Book Publishing Company.

Bohm, Robert M. (Ed.). (1991). *The death penalty in America: Current research*. Cincinnati, OH: Anderson Publishing Co.

Bohm, Robert M. (1992). Retribution and capital punishment: Toward a better understanding of death penalty opinion, *Journal of criminal justice, 20 (3)*, 227–236.

Carrington, Frank. (1978). Death and deterrence. In *Death and deterrence* (pp. 82–101). New Rochelle, NY: Arlington House.

Ehrlich, Isaac. (1975). The deterrent effect of capital punishment: A question of life and death. *American economic review, 65 (3)*, 397–417.

Feinberg, Joel. (1973). S*ocial philosophy*. Englewood Cliffs. NJ: Prentice Hall, Inc.

Frankena, William K. (1973). Ethics (2nd Ed.). Englewood Cliffs, NJ: Prentice-Hall, Inc.

Gray, Ian and Stanley, Moira for Amnesty International USA. (1989). *A punishment in search of a crime: Americans speak out against the death penalty*. New York, NY: Avon Books.

Green, Arnold W. (1969). Capital punishment: Has it become cruel and unusual? *National Review, 21*.

Kleinig, John, and Smith, Margaret Leland (Eds.). (1997). *Teaching criminal justice ethics: Strategic issues*. Cincinnati, OH: Anderson Publishing Co.

Koran, translated from Arabic by J. M. Rodwell (1909). London, U.K.: J.M. Dent and Sons, and New York, NY: Dutton, Everyman's Library.

Mappes, Thomas A., and Zembaty, Jane S. (1992). *Social ethics: morality and social policy*, 4th ed. New York, NY: McGraw-Hill.

Marshall, Thurgood. (1992). Dissenting Opinion in Gregg v. Georgia. In Thomas Mappes and Jane S. Zembaty (Eds.) *Social ethics*, 4th Ed., 164–168.

Peterson, Ruth D. and Bailey, William C. (1988). Murder and capital punishment in the evolving context of the post-Furman era. *Social Forces, 66 (3)*, 774–807.

Phillips, David. (1980). The deterrent effect of capital punishment: New evidence on an old controversy. *American Journal of Sociology, 86 (1)*, 139–148.

Pollock, Joycelyn. (1993). *Ethics in crime and justice*, 2nd Ed. Belmont, CA: Wadsworth.

Primoratz, Igor. (1992). A life for a life. In Thomas Mappes and Jane S. Zembaty (Eds.) *Social ethics* 4th Ed., 168–175 [extract from *Justifying legal punishment* (1989). 85–94].

Reiman, Jeffrey H. (1992). Civilization, safety, and deterrence. In Thomas Mappes and Jane S. Zembaty (Eds.) *Social ethics*, 4th Ed. 184–187 [extract from "Justice, civilization, and the death penalty: Answering van den Haag *Philosophy and public affairs, 14* (Spring 1985), 141–147.

Rohr, John A. (1978). *Ethics for bureaucrats: An essay on law and values*. New York, NY: Marcel Dekker, Inc.

Sellin, Thorsten. (1980). *The death penalty*. Beverly Hills, CA: Sage Publications, Inc.

Sherman, Lawrence W. (1982). *Ethics in criminal justice education*. Hastings-on-Hudson, NY: The Hastings Center.

Souryal, Sam S. (1992). *Ethics in criminal justice*. Cincinnati, OH: Anderson Publishing Co.

Stewart, Potter, Powell Jr., Lewis F., & Stevens, John Paul. (1992). Opinion in Gregg v. Georgia. In Thomas Mappes and Jane S. Zembaty (Eds.) *Social ethics*, 4th Ed., 154–164.

Thiroux, Jacques P. (1980). *Ethics: Theory and practice*, 2nd Ed. Encino, CA: Glencoe Publishing Co., Inc.

van den Haag, Ernest. (1968). On deterrence and the death penalty. *Ethics, 78*, 280–288.

van den Haag, Ernest. (1993). Deterrence and uncertainty. In Thomas Mappes and Jane S. Zembaty (Eds.) *Social ethics*, 4th Ed., 182–184 [extract from *Journal of criminal law, criminology and police science, 60 (2)* (1969)].

Wall, George B. (1974). *Introduction to ethics*. Columbus, OH: Charles E. Merrill.

Chapter 12

CORRECTIONS/ PUNISHMENT/ CORRECTIONAL OFFICER

Roslyn Muraskin

The reason our system of justice exists as it does today is to take the place of private vengeance. Victims are not allowed to take revenge, rather the state metes out the punishment even to the extent of executing a criminal (Pollock, 1994, 166). After conviction, many defendants are given prison time. There are four rationales for corrections: retribution, prevention, incapacitation, and deterrence. How much punishment is enough? Over the years we have changed our views regarding the punishment of criminals. "Originally, criminals were viewed as sinners with no ability to change their behavior, and therefore punishment and incapacitation were seen as the only logical ways to respond to crime. Bentham (1748–1833) and Beccaria (1783–1794) viewed the criminal as rational and as having free will, and therefore saw the threat of punishment as a deterrent" (Pollock, 1994, p. 166).

The correctional system needs to be supported "by a caring ethic since it takes into account offender needs, and community corrections" (Pollock, p. 175). Correctional officers, similar to law enforcement personnel, wear uniforms that represent authority within their institutions. But the authority of the uniform is not what gets anything accomplished. Personal respect and proper use of authority is what gets the job of the correctional officer done. Those officers who abuse their powers, and the uniform, find themselves in abusive positions. Whereas "[P]robation and parole officers have a different type of authority and power over offenders," (Pollock, p. 179), than the correctional officers, their power lies in their ability to recommend release or revocation. "Yet the implicit power an officer has over the individuals on his or her caseload must be recognized as an important element of the role, not to be taken lightly or misused" (Pollock, p. 179).

Under the American Correctional Association Code of Ethics, there is noted "the importance of integrity, respect for and protection of individual rights, and service to the public. . ." (p. 181). What is described in this Code of Ethics (shown on the following pages) is the fact that there be respect for all individuals, concern for the welfare of all persons, cooperation between all agencies of criminal justice, no misuse of positions for personal gain, no conflict of interest, no discrimination, and a maintenance of integrity of private information. Where there is cause to believe that a member has acted in an unethical manner, such behavior must be reported.

The difficulty that the correctional officer has, similar to law enforcement officials, is that we look at the ideal, which is not necessarily reality. It has been said that there exists a subculture within the corrections system, that is, the enemy is the inmate, the use of force is acceptable/necessary, there is a disrespect for the supervisors, and the occasional use of deceit to cover up wrong doing is acceptable.

According to Kauffman's study (1988, p. 85–112) [taken from Pollock, p. 182–183], she found the following to be the norms of the correctional officer's subculture:

1. Always go to the aid of another officer. Similar to law enforcement, the necessity of interdependence ensures that this is a strong and pervasive norm in the correctional officer subculture.
2. Don't lug drugs. This prohibition is to ensure the safety of other officers, as is the stronger prohibition against bringing in weapons for inmates.
3. Don't rat. In similar ways to the law enforcement subcultural code and, ironically, the inmate code, correctional officers also hate those who inform on their peers.
4. Never make a fellow officer look bad in front of inmates. This applies regardless of what the officer did, since it jeopardizes the officer's effectiveness and undercuts the appearance of officer solidarity.
5. Always support an officer in a dispute with an inmate.
6. Always support officer sanctions against inmates. This includes the use of physical force as well as legal sanctions.
7. Don't be a white hat. This prohibition is directed at any behavior, attitude, or expressed opinion that could be interpreted as sympathetic toward inmates.
8. Maintain officer solidarity against all outside groups.
9. Show positive concern for fellow officers. Never leave another officer a problem, which means don't leave unfinished business at the end of your shift for the next officer to handle.

Such a subculture varies from system to system. Professional ethics or a conflict with professional ethics comes into play when the relationship between correctional officer and inmate becomes personal. The close proximity of officer and inmate over a period of time, as well as shared feelings about the facilities administrators, can at times bring the officer and inmate too close. When officers feel they have more in common with the inmates than with their administrators, the unethical conduct becomes noticeable. As officers can make inmates feel very comfortable, they also have the ability to make it very difficult for the inmates to exist, and this is behavior that is considered unethical.

AMERICAN CORRECTIONAL ASSOCIATION
CODE OF ETHICS

PREAMBLE

The American Correctional Association expects of its members unfailing honesty, respect for the dignity and individuality of human beings and a commitment to professional and compassionate service. To this end, we subscribe to the following principles.

Members shall respect and protect the civil and legal rights of all individuals.

Members shall treat every professional situation with concern for the welfare of the individuals involved and with no intent to personal gain.

Members shall maintain relationships with colleagues to promote mutual respect within the profession and improve the quality of service.

Members shall make public criticism of their colleagues or their agencies only when warranted, verifiable, and constructive.

Members shall respect the importance of all disciplines within the criminal justice system and work to improve cooperation with each segment.

Members shall honor the public's right to information and share information with the public to the extent permitted by law subject to individuals' right to privacy.

Members shall respect and protect the right of the public to be safeguarded from criminal activity.

Members shall refrain from using their positions to secure personal privileges or advantages.

Members shall refrain from allowing personal interest to impair objectivity in the performance of duty while acting in an official capacity.

Members shall refrain from entering into any formal or informal activity or agreement which presents a conflict of interest or is inconsistent with the conscientious performance of duties.

AMERICAN CORRECTIONAL ASSOCIATION
CODE OF ETHICS, CONTINUED

Members shall refrain from accepting any gifts, service, or favor that is or appears to be improper or implies an obligation inconsistent with the free and objective exercise of professional duties.

Members shall clearly differentiate between personal views/statements and views/statements/positions made on behalf of the agency or Association.

Members shall report to appropriate authorities any corrupt or unethical behaviors in which there is sufficient evidence to justify review.

Members shall refrain from discriminating against any individual because of race, gender, creed, national origin, religious affiliation, age, disability, or any other type of prohibited discrimination.

Members shall preserve the integrity of private information; they shall refrain from seeking information on individuals beyond that which is necessary to implement responsibilities and perform their duties; members shall refrain from revealing nonpublic information unless expressly authorized to do so.

Members shall make all appointments, promotions, and dismissals in accordance with established civil service rules, applicable contract agreements, and individual merit, rather than furtherance of personal interests.

Members shall respect, promote, and contribute to a work place that is safe, healthy, and free of harassment in any form.

ADOPTED AUGUST 1975 AT THE 105TH CONGRESS OF CORRECTION

REVISED AUGUST 1990 AT THE 120TH CONGRESS OF CORRECTION

REVISED AUGUST 1994 AT THE 124TH CONGRESS OF CORRECTION

Because prisoners are in a position of need, having to ask the officers for things as simple as permission to go to the bathroom, officers have the power to make inmates feel even more dependent than necessary and humiliated because of their dependency. The relative powerlessness of the officers in relation to their superiors, the administration, and society in general creates a situation where some take advantage of their only power—that over the inmate (Pollock, p. 184).

The good officer learns to live with the inmates on a daily basis, forming alliances, but maintaining their professional standing. Similar to the police officer, however, correctional officers are not necessarily in agreement with court decisions and administrative goals. In speaking to one correctional officer, he indicated, you hear what the supervisors say, but then you do what you want, as you are the one "locked up" with the inmates. The correctional officers feel insecure in their positions, as they feel the scorn of many. In the study by Kauffman, previously mentioned, she indicates that

Initially, many [officers] attempted to avoid engaging in behavior injurious to inmates by refusing (openly or surreptitiously) to carry out certain duties and by displacing their aggressions onto others outside the prison or themselves. As their involvement in the prison world grew, and their ability to abstain from morally questionable actions within the prison declined, they attempted to neutralize their own feelings of guilt by regarding prisons as separate moral realms with their own distinct set of moral standards or by viewing inmates as individuals outside the protection of moral laws. When such efforts failed, they shut their minds to what others were doing and to what they were doing themselves (Pollock, p. 187–188).

Correctional officers need a good ethical code that they adhere to. Maintaining such a work ethic is important in the officers' ability to do his/her job properly. "To maintain a sense of morality in an inherently coercive environment is no easy task, yet a strong set of individual ethics is probably the best defense against being changed by the negative environment of the prison" (Pollock, p. 188). Officers do not have free rein to punish inmates unmercifully as has been evident in reported cases of officers beating inmates. Officers need to adhere to the tenets laid out in the Ethical Code of Conduct established by the American Correctional Association.

Correctional staffs must understand how to "assess moral dilemmas and how to behave in an ethical fashion" (Braswell, McCarthy & McCarthy, 1996, p. 337). Correctional institutions have a high turnover, primarily because of the nature of the job. The "rookies," or correctional officers (many of whom are new to the job) must be able to confront a less than friendly population crowded into very close quarters. Frequently, the prisoners look to bribe the correctional officer in the hopes of getting favorable treatment. The inmates would like the officers to turn away from infractions while bringing drugs and weapons into the institutions. "Because these inmates may know as much about running the institution as some of the guards, it is often very easy for correctional officers to become dependent on inmates for assistance in doing their jobs. . . ." (Braswell, McCarthy & McCarthy, 1996, p. 337).

It was reported by Jessica Mitford in her study of prisons in 1973 that: The character and mentality of the keepers may be of more importance in understanding prisons than the character and mentality of the kept (Reid, 1981, p. 211).

There are corrupt practices that occur in the correctional facilities, negating the integrity of the work to be accomplished by correctional officers. Such corrupt practices can include simple acts of theft to large-scale conspiracies. Such corrupt activities undermine the respect that correctional offices should have for the system as well as the feelings of the inmates toward both the officers and the criminal justice system. "Corrupt practices may also lead to a breakdown in the control structure of the organization and to the demoralization of correctional workers" (McCarthy, 1996, p. 230).

Correctional officers must use discretion. Correctional officials are given what is termed as a broad mandate by law whereby they administer their agencies. They make the rules and write the procedures necessary to accomplish their jobs. The corruption occurs when there is a misuse of discretionary powers. For example, correctional officials are not to accept gratuities for special privileges or preferential treatment desired by the inmates. They are not to show preferential treatment to inmates in terms of better housing, while supplementing their own income. Officers are not to look the other way when inmates misbehave and/or violate the rules of the institution. The opportunities are always present, the officer needs to uphold his/her own ethical/moral values. The officer cannot look the other way when fellow officers are acting in a less than professional manner.

Sykes has referred to the fact that inmates suffer from the pains of imprisonment. ". . .the deprivation of liberty, goods and services, heterosexual relations, autonomy, and security" (McCarthy, p. 235). The incentives for corruption of morals is always there. There are defects in the organization of the prison's structures. Coercive power is an important element in the correctional facility. "In order to successfully do their job, coercive power must be supplemented with informal exchange relations with inmates" (McCarthy, p. 236).

Sykes pointed out more than thirty years ago that:

> The custodians (guards) . . . are under strong pressure to compromise with their captives for it is a paradox that they can insure their dominance only by allowing it to be corrupted. Only by tolerating violations of minor rules and regulations can the guard secure compliance in the major areas of the custodial regime (McCarthy, p. 237).

The reasons for undermining the formal control as put forth by Sykes are "friendships with inmates, reciprocal relationships, and defaults" (McCarthy, p. 237). There is corruption because of friendships with the inmates, corruption through the factor of "you do for me and I will do for you." Corruption also occurs in the correctional facilities when staff members start to rely on inmates to do their jobs (i.e., that of the correctional officer). Problems arise when the correctional staff begins to provide the inmates with goods and services forbidden by the rules.

Cloward provided an example of an inmates way of getting to the officer:

> You go to make arrangements with the mess sergeant. He gets the ingredients and when we're in business . . . It's one of those you do this for me and I'll do this

for you sort of thing. . . .The sergeant has to feed 1,500 men. It don't look good if he goofs. He wants the job done right. Now we're the ones who do the work, the cooking and all of that. So the sergeant, he says, okay, you can make a little drink. But see to it that you get that food on the lines or the deal's off (McCarthy, p. 237).

Part of the problem also lies in the quality of officers chosen for the job. The quality is often uneven and, due to substandard conditions in many facilities, much discretionary authority is turned over to individuals who lack proper education, training, and/or ability to handle the job. The chances of corruption occurring are high when the quality is low. It is the primary fault of management when they fail to take the proper steps to insure that the opportunities of corruption are lessened. Working conditions need to be improved upon so that the actions of the correctional officers are not questionable. Accountability, protection of the employees, a freedom from political pressures are all factors in a good working relationship for anyone, but in particular for the correctional officers who are indeed "locked up."

If no basic set of moral rules exists in our society, it is up to the professional organizations to endeavor to regulate members' behavior. They need to do so by enumerating what behavior is acceptable, and what behavior is not. ". . .[C]odes of ethics embody moral ideals that are basic and uncontroversial from the perspective of the members of the profession" (Close & Meier, 1995, p. 18). There exists no attempt in any code of ethics to present a rational justification for their grounds. Therefore, in "some professional codes, . . .the rules may be viewed as justified only insofar as they tend to protect the profession from external review and regulation" (Close & Meier, p. 18). If there is no so called "super rule" to explain how to resolve conflicts, then there is a difficulty that is hard to overcome with regard to enforcing the rules. It happens that most codes of ethics fail to make contact with reality. The codes of ethics are designed to direct the correctional officer or for that matter any officer to act in the proper direction. But like a compass, it can point you to the right direction, "but it is not by itself a means of getting you to the destination" (Close & Meier, 19).

The example is given that in the "International Chiefs of Police Canons of Police Ethics," what is demanded is that the decision of the officers never be influenced by personal feelings. This does not take into consideration the discretionary powers that officers have. There are considerations to be taken into account other than simply relying on written codes.

All criminal justice practitioners should follow departmental policies as written. However, as all officers have discretionary powers, this seems to be an unreasonable expectation of behavior. Where discretion is encouraged, there is a breakdown of the behavior that is expected of the professionals. Many of the law enforcement agencies function as military-type operations. If everything has to go by the book, the system starts to fall apart.

A checklist of sorts has been developed:

- Does the action violate another person's constitutional rights, including the right to due process of law?
- Does the action involve treating another person only as a means to an end?

- Is the action under consideration illegal?
- Do you predict that your action will produce more bad than good for all persons affected?
- Does the action violate department procedure or a professional ethical canon? (Close & Meier, p. 130).

According to the tenets of Aristotle, both experience and intellectual study leads us to act ethically, but to be ethical is not easy. This challenge is very difficult in a system such as the high-pressure world of criminal justice. Here we have "not only personal pressures, but also victims, the media, supervisors, and many others [who] exert powerful influences" (Close and Meier, p. 134). In the words of Aristotle, "[A]nyone can get angry...that is easy...or give or spend money; but to do this to the right person, to the right extent, at the right time, with the right aim, and in the right way, that is not for everyone, nor is it easy; that is why goodness is both rare, honorable, and noble" (Close and Meier, p. 135). What stands out from all of this is that you are to tell the truth when asked or all else is a sham. If you are asked to testify, you tell the truth. You cannot allow the criminal justice system to become a system that relies on lies. If you serve the public and you are a public servant, lying is forbidden.

Justice Brandeis commented in the case of *Olmstead v. United States* (1928), "Our government is the potent, omnipresent teacher. For good or for ill, it teaches the whole people by its example. If the government becomes a lawbreaker, it breeds contempt for law; it invites every man to become a law unto himself; it invites anarchy" (277 U.S. 438, 479). The acceptable credo is that you cannot make everyone happy, including the prison administrators. Playing it straight is the correct way. It was Aristotle who said that you treat all humans as humans, regardless of the fact that all humans may not act human. Ethical conduct is expected in all instances.

VICTIMIZING THE PRISONERS

Throughout the literature there is much evidence that correctional officers victimize the prisoners they are paid to watch over. The evidence demonstrates primarily what goes on in male facilities, and while there is victimization in the female facilities, not much evidence is brought forward. One of the problems faced by supervising personnel is what constitutes appropriate behavior in instances when brutality occurs. Excessive victimization is easy to identify, but borderline cases are not. Traditionally there are known to be "goon squads." These "are groups of physically powerful correctional officers who 'enjoy a good fight' and who are called upon to rush to any area of the prison where it is felt that muscle power will restore the status quo" (Bowker, 1995, 380). When a correctional officer notes that there is a disturbance in the cell, such as a prisoner ripping up the cell, this goon squad can be called, resulting in correctional officers quieting the prisoner with force, possibly by administering blows to his body. How does one draw the line between the absolute necessary use of force as measured against the misuse of power? There is a handbook given to all correctional officers indicating appropriate and inappropriate behavior. There is a line drawn, often times in the sand. "When they implement a policy or regulation that is victimizing or potentially victimizing, [the wards and top-level correctional officers] must take responsibility for having created a definition of the situation within which correctional officers may carry out what amounts to victimizing behavior as they perform their duties in conformance with institutional regulations. . . .[T]hese administrators balance one evil against another, and decide to implement a potentially victimizing regulation because they feel that this regulation will solve more problems than it creates" (Bowker, p. 381).

Not having a clear and definitive definition of what constitutes victimization, and not listing extenuating circumstances frequently leads to the breakdown of what should be deemed proper ethical behavior.

As bad as prisons may be today, Bowker points out in her work that at one time, "it was common for correctional officers to assault prisoners with clubs and their fists, but by the late 1930s, . . .the frequency of these attacks had declined to the point at which they occurred 'only rarely'" (Bowker, p. 381).

Demonstrating the mistreatment of prisoners, one needs to review the works of *Killing Time, Life in the Arkansas Penitentiary* by Bruce Jackson as well as *Inside Prison U.S.A.* by Tom Murton and Joe Hyams. "The latter includes a description of the infamous 'Tucker telephone,' as well as blow-by-blow accounts of beatings. In the Tucker telephone incident, a naked prisoner was strapped to a table and electrodes were attached to his big toe and his penis. Electrical charges were then sent through his body which, in 'long distance calls,' were timed to cease just before the prisoner became unconscious" (Bowker, p. 380–381). In many cases the prisoners were literally driven out of their minds by such treatment.

There is much discussion as to how far correctional officers should go. There is demonstrated a subcultural norm that favors violence against prisoners, much as there is a subcultural norm favoring police brutality. Most correctional officers do not engage in acts of brutality; however, there are a sufficient number of officers who favor the use of brutality and apply force beyond that which is deemed necessary. "If an officer who favors the brutalization of prisoners is careful, he or she can limit the application of excessive force to incidents that fit the prison's definition of the appropriate use of force to maintain prison discipline or prevent escapes" (Bowker, p. 383).

A prison is characterized as a totalitarian state. "The six basic features of a totalitarian regime [consists of a] totalitarian ideology, a single party typically led by one person, a terroristic police, a communications monopoly, a weapons monopoly and a centrally directed economy. . ." (Bowker, p. 391). Evidence of brutality, blackmail, bribery, and favoritism will be evident in such a state. Those correctional officers who become integrated totally into the system will tend to be more brutal that those living on the periphery.

At one time correctional officers were referred to as "guards." The slang terms used to describe the officers are *hack, screw,* and *turnkey.* Such terms still exist. There is evidence of increasing professionalism on the part of the officers today, but, because of the place that they work, i.e., the prison, the thought is more often that of negativity associated with punishment. Correctional officers, like police officers, wear uniforms. The uniform represents authority and power. There are some who are uncomfortable with such authority and power and do not handle it well.

According to Kauffman, (1988, p. 50) as reported in a work by Pollock,

> [Some officers] don't understand what authority is and what bounds you have within that authority. . . . I think everyone interprets it to meet their own image of themselves. 'I'm a corrections officer [slams table]. You sit here! [Slam!] You sit there!' Rather than 'I'm a person who has limited authority. So, you know, I'm sorry gentlemen, but you can't sit there. You are going to have to sit over there. That's just the rules,' and explaining or something like that the reason why (p. 179).

There are officers who believe themselves to lack power and therefore society reacts to this perceived powerlessness as the officer misusing his power. There is also the phenomenon of discretion. Certainly the police use discretion in making arrests, stopping suspects, etc. Correctional officers also have available to them a certain amount of discretion. They write disciplinary tickets, they will give strong verbal instructions to an inmate, they make decisions or recommend that an inmate receive punishment for some infraction, and all this depends on the officer and his ability to make decisions.

What correctional officers should not do is to have personal relationships with those they are guarding. The officer who identifies with the inmate is someone not to be trusted. "Just as officers may act in unethical ways when they like an inmate, officers have the power to make life difficult for the inmate they do not like. These extralegal harassments and punishments may include 'forgetting' to send an inmate to an appointment, making an inmate stay in keeplock longer than necessary, or pretending not to hear someone locked in a cell asking for toilet paper or other necessary items" (Pollock, 184). Correctional officers work on a daily basis with men and women who simply do not like them. There is a strong potential for injury and attack, therefore, officers are always on their guard that at any minute they may become the victim. That is not to say that there are no inmates who are cooperative and nice. But the credo of the correctional officers is that "you can be friendly with inmates, but you can never trust them" (Pollock, p. 184).

While this writer was working in the holding pens of the detention facilities in New York City, I found that the correctional officers were decent human beings, but at times were provoked by the yelling and bad behavior of the detainee, and I was witness to many beatings and the use of force to keep a particular individual quiet as well as to show by example the power of the officer. The officer never hit the detainee in the head, only in the side and/or groin area. It has been noted that ". . .in prison the violence inmates perpetrate against each other desensitizes officers to violence in general, and specifically to the violence used by officers against inmates. After witnessing scores of stabbings, beatings, and mutilations, some corrections officers may view such beatings as utilitarian in that they serve as warnings to all inmates that they can expect similar treatment" (Pollock, p. 185).

The difference between the correction officer and the police officer, is that the correction officer deals with the same individuals on a daily basis. Police officers also move about much more freely than the correction officer who is truly "locked up" for his/her work day. Because the officers rely on each other for back up, many offenses are not reported. A code of silence exists.

Correction officers hold power over the very basic needs of inmates. But though there are cases of abuse of power, this is not to suggest that the majority of correction officers do not act in an ethical manner.

REFERENCES

Bowker, Lee H. (1995). The victimization of prisoners by staff members. In Daryl Close & Nicholas Meier (Eds.). *Morality in criminal justice: An introduction to ethics.* Belmont, CA: Wadsworth Publishing Company.

Braswell, Michael C., McCarthy, Belinda R., & McCarthy, Bernard J. (1996). *Justice, crime and ethics* (2d Ed.). Cincinnati, OH: Anderson Publishing Co.

Kauffman, Kelsey. (1988). *Prison officers and their world.* Cambridge, MA: Harvard University Press.

Pollock, Joycelyn M. (1994). *Ethics in crime and justice: dilemmas and decisions* (2d Ed.). Belmont, CA: Wadsworth Publishing Company.

Cases Cited:

Olmstead v. United States, 277 U.S. 438 (1928).

Chapter 13

CONCLUSIONS

Roslyn Muraskin

A major problem in relationship to professional ethics is not enforcement, but the assumption that the actors ought to live up to them. For some reason professionals have convinced the public that what they do is so special, so important, so vital and/or unique that they are exempt from ordinary morality.

But the duty not to cause harm overrides the duty to honor one's promises. At the core of any ethical system, are the duties and obligations basic to moral norms. Professional ethics is not a subspecies that should have special moral force, nor can it be used to exempt or immunize professionals against their actions and behaviors.

The American Bar Association's Code of Professional Responsibility dictates that lawyers "pursue the interests of their clients as vigorously as possible within the limits of the law." Lawyers are expected to act at all times in an ethical manner, while affording maximum protection for the accused, while doing their very best to see that justice is served, and preventing them from imposing their own personal judgment and views into the system.

> There are many competing frameworks that can be applied to criminal justice ethics. Some of them are widely rejected, such as the theory that might makes right. But others are widely accepted, and the means for choosing among them are unclear. Mill's utilitarian framework and Rawls' deontological framework may produce very different conclusions, but. . . [there is a need] to be very clear about the reasoning principle on which they differ (Sherman, 1982, p. 3).

151

As pointed out by Murphy:

There is no area, perhaps, in which ethical dilemmas are more prominently seen and their mishandling more forcefully placed before the public eye than the criminal justice system. Morally enigmatic choices continually challenge the personnel on all operational and managerial levels of the system's three major branches: the police, the courts, and corrections (1983, p. 1).

In the words of the Honorable Ruth Bader Ginsburg:

For judges to do the heavy work our society constantly entrusts or punts to them, courts must be checked by lawyers whose training fosters independence. To check against bad apples and behavior unbecoming to the fair administration of justice, courts have the contempt power and many other controls, including award, reduction, and forfeiture of counsel fees, disqualification for conflict of interest, and injunctions against disclosure of a client's confidence (1996, p. 3).

Ethics/morality generally represents good behavior. To sum all this up, with regard to legal ethics in the case of attorneys, we understand that there are three questions to be asked. "Is it proper to cross examine for the purpose of discrediting the reliability or credibility of an adverse witness whom you know to be telling the truth? Is it proper to put a witness, including the defendant, on the stand when you know he will commit perjury? And is it proper to give your client legal advice when you have reason to believe that that knowledge you give him will tempt him to commit perjury?" (Dershowitz, 1996, p. 16). In addition to these questions, what do we do when a prosecutor puts on the stand an individual who is knowingly committing perjury, particularly a police witness?

How do we define the good cop? "A good cop is defined as a policeman who would not plant evidence, though he might stretch the truth of a search and seizure to fit an exception to the exclusionary rule, a rule which in their view disserves ultimate truth" (Dershowitz, p. 18).

"Justice, justice shalt thou pursue," is a quote from the Bible. The question is asked, why is the word justice mentioned twice. As indicated in the Bible, ". . .the reason that justice is mentioned twice is that it was intended to refer to the two kinds of justice—the means of justice and the ends of justice." The question posed is, do we focus too much on the ends rather than the means?

Nebraska lawyer, Robert Kutak, described in so many ways how rules are needed to preserve the order: It may be a dog-eat-dog world, but one dog may eat another only according to the rules" (1983, p. 175).

References

Dershowitz, A. (1996). Is legal ethics asking the right questions? *The Institute for the Study of Legal Ethics, 1.*

Ginsburg, R.B. The Honorable. (1996). Supreme court pronouncements on the conduct of lawyers. *The Institute for the Study of Legal Ethics, 1.*

Kutak, R.J. (1983). The adversary system and the practice of law. In David Luban (Ed.). *The good lawyer.*

Murphy, P.E. (April, 1983). The teaching of applied and professional ethics. Paper presented at the annual meeting of the Criminal Justice Educators Association,

Sherman, L.R. (1982). *Ethics in criminal justice education.* New York: The Hastings Center.

INDEX